T0305223

Global Outsourcing Strategies

Global Outsourcing Strategies

The Internationalisation of the Electronics Industry

Lucio Cassia

Professor of Strategic Management and Entrepreneurship
University of Bergamo, Italy

Edward Elgar
Cheltenham, UK • Northampton, MA, USA

Published by
Edward Elgar Publishing Limited
The Lypiatts
15 Lansdown Road
Cheltenham
Glos GL50 2JA
UK

Edward Elgar Publishing, Inc.
William Pratt House
9 Dewey Court
Northampton
Massachusetts 01060
USA

A catalogue record for this book
is available from the British Library

Library of Congress Control Number: 2009941285

ISBN 978 1 84980 151 5

Printed and bound by MPG Books Group, UK

Contents

Figures

Tables

Dedication

To my mother and father, for everything they have done for me and everything they mean to me.

To my wife, Marisa, and our children Laura, Luca and Matteo. During my career they have endured the absence of a husband and a father with patience and love.

1. Introduction

Among the economic macro trends that have marked the beginning of the new millennium, the opening of markets and economic globalization are the forces which have worked more than others to promote a radical rethink of the world's economic, political and social relationships. As in the past some of the most important changes in the relations between economies have benefited from technological innovations, such as the art of navigation in the 16th century, the railways in the 19th century and the growth of air transportation in the 20th century, so too it is a shared opinion that the most recent globalization phenomena would not have been possible without the involvement of today's pervasive, fast and low-cost digital electronic technologies.

The economic globalization and the diffusion of information technologies are mutually supporting phenomena which have contributed to an increased transparency in the global markets, a reduction in the uncertainty of transactions and information asymmetries, a higher speed in exchanges and an increase in the competition level in all economic sectors. Thanks to electronic and telecommunication technologies, the market today is more similar to the 'perfect market' described in treatises on the economy, compared to what it was at the end of last century. The reductions of companies' and consumers' costs are visible and have not yet been run.

Similar to the information technology and communication sectors, the electronics industry is ubiquitous in the economic context because of the pervasiveness of its own applications, not only in manufacturing, through its support to automation and industry, but also in consumer fields, where everyday life is affected.

Electronic technologies have also contributed to the cultural and social changes which have led to the so-called 'information society', where the exchange and the processing of multimedia information contents take place in an ever cheaper, faster and geographically extended way. The information society is characterized by the spreading of information technology; changes are catalyzed by the diffusion of computers and new communication media, whose peculiarity is the ability to connect everyone, instantly, at low cost, at any time and everywhere. In this stage of development of global markets, electronic technologies have fostered a kind of space–time compression, where both distance and time have been reduced to the point of transforming the world into a global village, full of economic interdependences never experienced so intensively by earlier generations.

The use of terms like e-commerce, e-business, e-mail and e-government or words containing the adjective 'electronic' (electronic control, electronic guide, electronic passport, electronic sheet, electronic ticket, electronic book) has become so widespread that they have entered the common vocabulary, showing how electronics is being applied to all sectors: from the car industry to telephony, from computer science to industry automation, from safety to biomedical life support systems. Sometimes, the word 'electronic' identifies objects with superior performances or even a certain degree of 'intelligence' (intelligent washing machines, intelligent traffic lights, intelligent devices, intelligent instrumentation), referring to the fact that the device has a seed of intellectual ability based on an operational decision-making logic and is thus somewhat self-governing. Unlike most technologies, electronics represents not only the expression of human intelligence, but it also simulates its behavior. The development of electronics technology involves not only an improvement in performance and efficiency in comparison with the past, it also means doing more and in an absolutely different way.

The relationship between the availability of electronic technologies, which are becoming increasingly powerful and pervasive, and market globalization is not unidirectional. Not only has been the opening of the markets initially fostered by new media, but the subsequent diffusion of electronic applications has been, in turn, supported by the availability of newly industrializing global markets. Through a mutual support mechanism, new electronic technologies have facilitated the globalization, which in turn has made available new low-cost manufacturing resources and new markets for electronics. Again, the increased competition has sustained the development of new technologies and widened the worldwide availability of communication tools.

The mutually supportive virtuous relationship does not yet seem to have come to an end. In particular, the wide and diversified development of the electronic industry applications would not have been possible without recourse to a strategy of globalization in the electronics industry. One of the most important elements has been the growth of electronics outsourcing, that is, the contracting out of electronic technologies and a world-based value chain.

A global strategy of outsourcing is one of the catalysts of the impressive growth in the electronics sector and in its applications. Businesses that rely on external companies for the electronic technologies crucial to their products include in their business model some competitive advantages in structure flexibility: they do not need to invest in specific production plants, providing financial resources for materials and semi-finished products, nor maintain a workforce skilled in electronics. Electronic products are subject to a high-speed evolution, directed towards higher technological levels and growing constructive complexity, requiring production and organizational processes that are more and more sophisticated. Therefore, those companies that incorporate electronic technologies in their products encounter serious problems in maintaining adequate technological competence that is not inherent to their distinctive skills. Electronics outsourcing thus appears to be a natural solution and it has generated a new industrial domain whose dimension is so wide that it includes companies that are among the largest in the world in terms of turnover and number of employees.

Outsourcing is constantly evolving across different fields, industrial and service, and shows a trend towards the undertaking of complex activities and products with a higher level of intelligence. For instance, regarding the outsourcing of services related to information technology, if in the beginning they include standard and simple activities, such as the management of information systems or client profiling (Business Process Outsourcing), scholars now agree that more and more complex activities will be outsourced in the future, such as product profitability analyses and company merger studies (Knowledge Process Outsourcing).

In particular, the outsourcing of electronic technologies, both in activities with a high content of intelligence, such as design and engineering, and in processes for the construction of components and electronic systems, is increasingly looked at as a strategic solution for the improvement of companies' competitive positioning, at the same time maintaining the flexibility required of enterprises in the new millennium. Considering the growing and pervasive presence of electronics in most industrial fields, it is not surprising that the trend related to outsourcing has led to the creation and development of a new sector, which includes companies that supply services for the design, engineering and production of electronic devices.

This book aims to provide a strategic interpretation of the global outsourcing phenomenon in relation to the internationalization of the electronics industry, covering the origin and the availability of the new technologies over recent decades, to the changes that have occurred in the competitive positioning of businesses. It is meant for those academics and scholars who observe and analyze patterns of global growth and the interactions of companies with the technological innovation. It is also intended for entrepreneurs and professionals who are involved in the enterprises' decision-making processes aimed at outlining competitive strategies within globalization processes.

This book is comprised of three parts. Firstly, it starts with a description of the electronics industry, focusing on the related supply chain and on the relationship among the main players of economic transactions. It examines in depth the correlation between strategic paths and outsourcing processes, highlighting determinants and criticalities, considering above all the economic globalization phenomena which, starting from the last decade (the 2000s), have been redefining the relationship between the world economies. Therefore, special emphasis has been paid to global outsourcing and to the relations between Western countries and Asian economies, which are increasingly in charge of the manufacturing segment of the supply chain.

In the second part special attention is given to electronics outsourcing; the definition of the peculiarities of its value chain is carried out through an analysis of the electronics supply chain and through a description of the role of the individual actors, to which specific chapters of the book are dedicated. A detailed quantitative analysis of the economic-financial aspects assigns a dimension to the economic and strategic positioning of the companies operating in this field.

The dynamics of the growth of electronics outsourcing has strongly benefited over the last decade from the pervasive strategy of business aggregations between companies with different kinds of specialization. In the third part of the book we highlight the merger and acquisition (M&A) operations, their determinants and the subsequent criticalities. The facts represented here derive from a specific database that has collected all of the information related to operations in this sector over the last decade. The economic profile of the phenomenon as well as a consideration of strategic facts are explained in order to set some indications to define the paths of growth of the companies. The next chapter deals with business models and competitive scenarios, and it also defines the present position of this sector within the theory of the corporate life cycle. Despite the normal and expected slowdown of the growth of this sector after the start-up phase, there is a continuous trend of the economic system towards an increasing use of outsourcing, thanks to the non-stop rise of electronic components, in both industrial and consumer appliances, and to the technological innovation processes.

Discussion of sector trends and some hypotheses about the evolution of strategic models are described hereafter. The market ranges from mega-firms, which show a turnover of tens of billions of US dollars, to small companies with sales of not more than a few million dollars each. There is a need for strategic positioning to acquire clients who, due to their different size, sector, geographic area, intellectual property and organization, can benefit from a choice of levels of electronics outsourcing.

This book is structured on a quantitative basis and developed from a wide range of information and data. The aim is to build a useful scenario of one of the leading sectors of the world economy, the electronics industry, in relation to the global outsourcing strategic trends along a worldwide value chain. The considerations of business strategies, the evaluations of the growing paths and the macroeconomic analyses were therefore inspired from and found their starting point in empirical analysis.

PART ONE

Global Outsourcing in the Electronics Industry

2.   Electronics Industry

The birth of the electronics industry can be traced back to the invention of the first thermo-electronic device in 1904, the vacuum diode, by John Ambrose Fleming (1849–1945), thus taking shape as a business category that followed sectors born from the first industrial revolution (textile industry, metallurgy, steam engines) and the second industrial revolution (mechanical, chemical, electrical).

Sometimes we hear of a third industrial revolution, making reference to the growth of the electronics sector, which since the second half of the 20th century has allowed the development of ICT (information and communication technology) and has contributed to the rapid global economic growth of the second half of the 1990s. Many important economic phenomena, such as the opening and globalization of the markets, would not have been possible without the availability of new low-cost digital-communication electronic technologies.

From an economic standpoint, the electronics industry is ubiquitous thanks to the pervasiveness of its usability, in consumer applications as well as industrial and service sectors. The most dynamic elements of our society take shape around electronic technologies, in terms of computer systems as well as telecommunications, production and control. Furthermore, electronics is a pervasive key element for innovation in many other industries that deal in hi-tech sectors such as telecommunications, information technology, aerospace, robotics, air and rail transport, biomedical equipment, fine chemicals, agribusiness. Even technologically mature sectors, such as automotive and tool machinery, derive benefits through the use of microelectronics devices, so that they are experiencing a new expansion.

Until the early 1990s, the verticalization strategy was the rule for the majority of firms who incorporated electronic technologies in their products; electronic components and systems were manufactured within the firms themselves. The global market for electronics had an estimated value of 100 billion dollars at that time, only 5 per cent of which was being outsourced. However, the following decade brought a substantial increase in technological outsourcing, which has progressively acquired an extremely important position due to a very rapid technological evolution, increasing structural complexity, and ever more sophisticated manufacturing and organizational processes.

Those companies that incorporate electronic technologies in their products encounter serious problems in maintaining satisfactory technological competence that is not inherent in their distinctive skills; electronics outsourcing thus appears to be a natural outcome. Following the growing diffusion of electronics across most industrial sectors, it is not surprising that the trend associated with outsourcing has favored the emergence and the development of a new sector that includes companies who supply services such as project design, product engineering and manufacturing of electronics equipment on behalf of other companies that incorporate them in their own products.

Electronics outsourcing companies are continuously growing because they are able to supply cheaper products while maintaining an adequate profit margin for themselves. They apply, for instance, electronic systems re-engineering techniques using less expensive components and more efficient production processes as well as high speed automated plants, which reduce manufacturing costs while allowing satisfactory quality standards to be achieved. The outsourcing trend allows growth and continuous improvement in the industrial domain thanks to the 'cross-fertilization' feature of this activity. Having the opportunity to be involved in different market segments (industrial, telecommunications, personal computers, automotive, and so on), companies that supply electronic technology outsourcing can extend the know-how they acquire in a specific field to other sectors.

For example, the need for immunity from environmental conditions and vibrations for ABS system control devices developed by the car industry fosters skills that can be transferred to other industrial contexts, such as the electronics controlling machine tools. Similarly, the solutions to reduce components to ever smaller dimensions for mobile phones can be extended to personal computers for the development of the latest ultra-compact notebooks.

Being active in different fields is therefore a constant in electronics outsourcing and one of its strong points. This inter-field activity is valuable for clients, who can benefit from the specific know-how that their suppliers have acquired in other sectors, and for suppliers as well, who can thus moderate the unpredictability of sales to a specific customer, thanks to their presence in multiple fields.

Electronics outsourcing was historically born in Western countries around the 1980s with the emergence of small and medium electronics firms, considered by big businesses to be a resource providing an alternative to internal production in periods of intense market demand. In those years, the suppliers were mostly organized as small firms serving a single customer.

Later, some big customers started to contract the complete construction of their products, not just the parts exceeding their productive capacity, thus propelling rapid growth of suppliers in both size and technology.

More recently, electronics outsourcing firms have acquired a remarkable skill in handling materials, a high level of technological construction ability, and a good control of testing processes. The most efficient firms have even acquired added value facilities for the design and industrialization of their products.

SUPPLY CHAIN CONFIGURATION

The relationships between firms that operate within the electronic supply chain are described in Figure 2.1, which highlights the specificities of this sector and the main players involved.

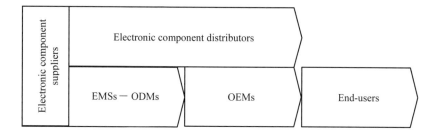

Figure 2.1   Electronics supply chain

- Electronic component suppliers
- Electronic component distributors
- Companies which are active in electronics outsourcing: electronics manufacturing services (EMSs) and original device manufacturers (ODMs)
- Client firms: original equipment manufacturers (OEMs)
- End-users

Either directly or through distribution channels, manufacturers of electronic components provide the supply chain with the electronic devices used by manufacturing firms. These manufacturers (EMSs and ODMs) perform the industrial production of electronic boards and equipment for their customers (OEMs), who finally deliver their products to end-users (Table 2.1).

Table 2.1   Electronics supply chain and products

Supplier	Product progress stage	Client
Silicon wafer supplier	Silicon wafers	Electronic component supplier
Electronic component supplier	Electronic components	Electronic component distributor, EMS, ODM, OEM
Electronic component distributor	Electronic components	EMS, ODM, OEM
EMS	Electronic boards, electronic sub-systems, end products	OEM
ODM	End products	OEM
OEM	End products	End-user
End-user		

Through different levels of design and assembly operations, the supply chain handles the transformation of basic electronic components into increasingly complex devices such as electronic boards, sub-systems and complex final systems.

Starting from integrated circuits, resistors, capacitors, connectors, printed circuit boards and still more devices, the plants assemble the equipment that pervades our daily life, from notebook computers to microwave ovens, from car automatic gearboxes to digital watches, from the management of a power plant to the playing of a song on CD player, from the control panel of an elevator to mobile phone, and so on.

Every actor along the chain adds some intellectual and industrial value. For instance, the difference between EMSs and ODMs lies in the different levels of intellectual property that each brings to the production process. The added value, mainly technological, allows the supply chain to work properly, from the production of single electronic components to the complex transformation of many hi-tech components into high-cost valued equipment. The large amount of intellectual property content in semiconductor chips and in electronic boards allows the supply chain to generate economic value for the actors involved.

ELECTRONIC COMPONENT SUPPLIERS

The producers of electronic components are the suppliers of devices used in the electronics industry. These are mainly 'active' (silicon based) solid state components, such as microprocessors, memory units, power supplies, signal amplifiers and programmable logic devices. Although the active components are the most valuable and are associated with a higher added value, there are also key 'passive' components, such as resistors, capacitors, inductors, connectors, printed circuits, and other kinds of devices included in electronic systems.

The industry of active semiconductor devices owes its origins to the 1948 invention of the transistor which has gone through a major expansion over the years. In 1965 Gordon Moore, founder of Intel, hazarded a guess that the number of transistors to be integrated on a single chip was going to double every 18–24 months without any increase in price. Although the guess had no scientific basis it is known as 'Moore's Law' and has demonstrated its predictive accuracy over more than four decades, from 1965 to 2009 (Figure 2.2).

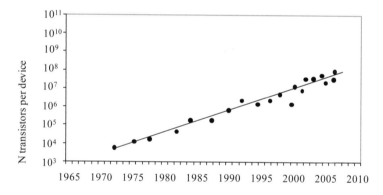

Source: GP Bullhound.

Figure 2.2   *'Moore's Law'*

Technological innovation is one of the most important competitive forces in this industry. Since the early 1990s, the growth rate of expenses related to research and development on electronic devices has increased more rapidly than market sales; in fact, R&D expenses have increased by a 12.7 per cent CAGR (compound annual growth rate) between 1990 and 2007, against a growth of 9.9 per cent in the market of semiconductors over the same period.

Table 2.2 lists the most important electronic component suppliers, having revenues in excess of 5 000 M$.[1]

Table 2.2   Main electronic component suppliers

	Sales 2007 ($M)	EBIT (%) 2007	Employees 2007	Headquarters	Stock Market
Intel	38 334	24.0	94 000	California (USA)	NASDAQ
Samsung	19 951	10.1	84 721	South Korea	Seoul SE
Texas Instruments	13 309	26.7	30 175	Texas (USA)	NYSE
Toshiba	11 850	4.6	190 706	Japan	Tokyo SE
STM	9 966	−4.2	52 180	Netherlands	Milan SE
TSMC	9 813	9.0	2 749	Taiwan	NYSE
Hynix	9 614	n.a.	15 200	South Korea	Seoul SE
Sony	8 040	n.a.	n.a.	Japan	NYSE
Renesas Technology	8 001	n.a.	25 000	Japan	Not Listed
NXP	6 026	n.a	30 000	Netherlands	Not Listed
AMD	6 013	−46.6	16 420	California (USA)	NYSE
Infineon Technolog	5 772	−2.4	43 079	Germany	NYSE
Qualcomm	5 619	41.0	12 800	California (USA)	Nasdaq
NEC Electronics	5 593	−5.0	23 982	Japan	Tokyo SE

Source: IC Insight, Datastream.

It is not surprising that Intel is in the first position, supported by the huge development of information technology over the two previous decades and by the Wintel platform on the greatest number of personal computers. Above all, manufacturers show a strong bargaining power where semiconductors are concerned, in accordance with their high technological content. An aggregation process has led to the creation of large global American, European, Japanese and South-Korean companies (Intel, ST Microelectronics, Toshiba and Samsung, respectively).

Figure 2.3 shows the cumulated turnover in the year 2007 of the ten biggest electronic component suppliers, in relation to the overall turnover of this sector. There is a high concentration in the first five companies which represent a cumulative total share of 33 per cent. This oligopolistic market frame is not surprising; a critical mass is required for financial resources for both R&D activities and the construction of production plants whose complexity and cost increase exponentially as the dimensions of the electronic devices decrease. The investment needed for a high integration semiconductors diffusion plant can be as high as several billion dollars.

The level of concentration and the content of technological intellectual property give substantial bargaining power to those suppliers who have been involved in an aggregation process.

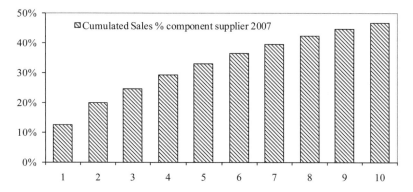

Source: iSuppli, Gartner, Thomson One Banker.

Figure 2.3   Cumulated sales of electronic component suppliers

DISTRIBUTION CHANNELS

Within the electronics supply chain, electronic component distributors play a particularly active role within the value chain over the middle stage between component suppliers and clients. The electronic distribution acts as a liaison element between the electronic component suppliers and the tens of thousands of EMS, ODM and OEM users who employ hundreds of thousands of different components in their products. In a broader sense, the distribution channels also supply sectors, such as the information technology sector, which in turn depend on the use of electronic components.

The component distribution aggregates the demand from OEMs, EMSs and ODMs and directs it towards the offerings of many component manufacturers. The main role of component distributors is to preserve this kind of many-to-many connection.

Table 2.3 shows the composition of the distribution sectors given by world market shares and highlights the strong market concentration made by the two American companies Arrow Electronics and Avnet.

Table 2.3   *Main electronic component distributors*

	Sales 2007 ($M)	Market share 2007	EBIT (%) 2007	Employees 2007	Headquarters	Stock Market
Arrow Electronics	15 985	25.5	4.3	13 300	USA	NYSE
Avnet	15 681	25.1	4.3	12 600	USA	NYSE
WPG Holding	4 670	7.5	3.0	2 700	Taiwan	Taiwan SE
Future Electronics	4 416	7.1	n.a.	n.a.	USA	Not Listed
Bell Microproducts	4 050	6.5	n.a.	n.a.	Canada	Not Listed
Others	17 797	28.3				
Total	62 600	100				

Source: Datamonitor.

The existence of dominant positions on one hand allows Arrow Electronics and Avnet to establish long-lasting and profitable relationships with the manufacturers of semiconductors, but on the other hand limits the competition level because the entry of new players is made virtually impossible. There has been negligible growth of the most important ten independent distributors within the US market over the period 2002–2006.

ELECTRONICS MANUFACTURING SERVICES

Electronics manufacturing services (EMS) are companies that carry out outsourcing activities in the electronics industry, in design services, product engineering, production and after-sale services for electronic equipment and systems.

EMS companies do not normally operate directly with their own brand to end-users and therefore, despite their remarkable size in terms of turnover and number of employees, are mostly unknown to them. The electronic control of a robotized Ferrari gearbox might not be manufactured by the prestigious carmaker, just as the control system of an automatic drink dispenser might not be built by N&W Vending, and the electronic power control system of an elevator may have not been manufactured in a factory belonging to Kone. Ferrari, N&W Vending and Kone are leading companies in the sport automotive, vending machines and elevators sectors, respectively, and make major investments in innovations, mainly in the technologies where their core competences are unquestioned. In terms of the electronics supply chain, they act as OEMs (original equipment manufacturers), that is as customers who assign the manufacturing of electronic parts to EMS suppliers, whose brands are generally not known to the drivers of an F430, or to those who sip coffee from an automatic dispenser, nor to those who move floor to floor in the Almas Tower in Dubai using a Kone elevator.

OEMs and EMSs are bound by contracts and by job production relationships. OEMs often provide EMSs with the project or the ideas for an electronic device (a component, a semi-finished product or even an end-product) necessary for the working of their products (gearboxes, drink dispensers, elevators). EMS firms use their own skills and resources in the design, labor, materials, tools and plants that are necessary to manufacture the requested device. Therefore, their relationships lie within the wide domain of technological outsourcing and have become the standard in many industrial fields, like the automotive, aerospace, energy management, electro medical and diagnostics, and mechanics sectors.

Electronic contract manufacturing activities were initially limited to sub-contracting, but since then they have been transformed into the broadest function of EMSs and have grown remarkably due to the outsourcing of production. The consolidation of this production typology, based on a network company model, is related to changes in the value chain and to the growth of companies in key segments of information technology and electronics, which often lack their own production plants. For example, in the area of electronic semiconductors, the fabless model has spread: this model refers to a manufacturer of integrated circuits that does not have a production plant for the diffusion of silicon wafers, but that is the owner of the know-how and the design of the devices. Fabless companies (Analog Devices, Qualcomm, Xilinx) have developed a strategic business model based on their resources in R&D and microelectronic technologies; they assign the production process to specialized factories owned by other firms (silicon-foundry), usually located in Asia, but have their R&D and technologies inside the company.

An electronic contract manufacturer is an independent company that assembles electronic equipment at the customers' request. The mechanical design and engineering of products can be listed among the services that contract manufacturers have gradually been able to provide, though they started with simple assembly operations. Their extension to added value

activities, such as the engineering of electronic boards, the setting up of
production processes, supply, logistics, distribution and after-sale repair
services, and sometimes even onsite installation, has gradually transformed
contract manufacturing into EMSs.

Table 2.4   Main electronics manufacturing services

	Sales 2007 ($M)	EBIT (%) 2007	Employees 2007	Headquarters	Stock Market
Foxconn	52 495	6.3	550 000	Taiwan	Taiwan SE
Flextronics	29 336	0.6	162 000	Singapore	NASDAQ
Jabil Circuit	12 291	1.5	61 000	Florida (USA)	NYSE
Sanmina–SCI	10 384	−9.2	45 610	California (USA)	NASDAQ
Celestica	8 684	0.9	42 000	Canada	Toronto SE
Elcoteq	5 911	−2.6	24 222	Finland	Helsinki SE
Benchmark	2 916	3.6	10 522	Texas (USA)	NYSE
Venture Manufacturing	2 690	8.0	n.a.	Singapore	Singapore SE
USI	2 008	3.8	12 905	Taiwan	Taiwan SE
Plexus	1 546	5.7	7 900	Wisconsin (USA)	NASDAQ
SIIX	1 445	3.9	6 504	Japan	Tokyo SE
TT Electronics	1 085	7.0	7 546	United Kingdom	London SE
Technitrol	1 027	7.3	12 000	Pennsylvania (USA)	NYSE

Source: Thomson One Banker.

In the early 2000s, market concentration led to the consolidation of some
world-class EMSs (among them Flextronics, Foxconn, Jabil Circuit,
Sanmina–SCI and Solectron). This strengthening was characterized by
intense acquisition activity that was the main tool for the growth of the leader
companies.

Despite the remarkable size that many firms in this field have reached (the
total 2007 turnovers of the first four companies exceeded 100 B$, see Table
2.4), the names of EMS businesses are unknown to most people because they
normally do not apply their brand on the end products. This sector is

generally identified with the terms 'stealth manufacturing' or 'ghost manufacturing'.

The 1990s marketing campaign of Intel ('Intel Inside') tried to make the brand value visible; until then Intel was unknown to the public because it was hidden inside personal computers manufactured by the market leaders of the time (Compaq, Dell, Hewlett-Packard, IBM).

The sector is very concentrated; the three largest companies represent more than 50 per cent of the sector and the contribution of the companies beyond tenth position is marginal (Figure 2.4).

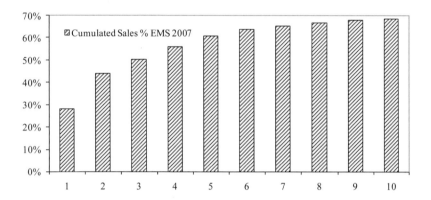

Source: Thomson One Banker, iSuppli.

Figure 2.4   Cumulated sales of EMSs

ORIGINAL DESIGN MANUFACTURERS

When the EMS activity further expands the added value by designing its own products it is designated as an original design manufacturer; the products are brought to the market through the distribution network and the brand of one of their OEM clients.

ODMs do not manufacture subcontracted products, but are the owners of the intellectual property; the relationship with the OEM no longer refers to the sale of products but rather to labor production. After having designed, developed and manufactured the product, ODMs sell it to large OEM firms, which test its quality and its compliance to standards; they sell it to end-users with their brand. This is what happens, for instance, in the portable notebook and mobile phone domains: many products are designed and manufactured by ODM companies, most of them based in Asia, although the final product trademark often belongs to Western companies.

Within the general growth of outsourcing, some EMSs have even acquired the basic skills to provide design and engineering services based on the client's specifications, cooperating in the design of sub-systems and end products. EMSs carry out this activity essentially rewarded with a fixed compensation, while OEMs hold and acquire the intellectual property rights on any innovation. However, in later years, those OEMs working in the mass markets (computers, telecommunications, consumer devices, automotive) gave rise to the new ODM model, often through spin-off operations, in which the suppliers' responsibilities were extended from the product specifications, through the design and engineering processes, to the final supply. As a result ODMs are the holders of the specific technological know-how of a product line and take full responsibility for end products to be sold to different OEMs, who will resell them with their own brand name.

Notwithstanding that ODMs' activities are partly similar to those carried out by EMSs, the two business models are different. Opposite to EMSs, ODMs invest to achieve the required know-how for market knowledge and for the design of end products. Moreover, unlike EMSs, they hold the intellectual property rights.

In exchange for intangible investments, whose costs are then included in the sales price applied to OEMs who buy the products and resell them with their own brand, ODMs seize a higher share of the margin in the supply chain. ODMs gain a higher profitability with respect to EMSs because they take a higher entrepreneurial risk. The counterpart in the relationship with OEMs is a lower level of customer loyalty, because ODMs can sell the same products, or a similar one, to more customers. This situation, however, does not normally occur in a trusted EMS–OEM relationship, as the firms often enter into confidentiality and exclusivity agreements.

The ODM business model is expanding and the sector is also growing along with the economic globalization. The spreading of productive localization in low-cost countries such as China and India has led to the birth and growth of many local firms which can be defined as ODMs, able to use economies of scale to provide Western companies with lower-price products. The size of the most important ODMs in terms of turnover has rapidly become remarkable, as highlighted in Table 2.5.

A 2006 study showed how more than 80 percent of portable computers sold worldwide by the main IT brands are actually manufactured by only a few factories based in Asian countries, that design and manufacture for the global market. This is not surprising if we think about the low labor costs, the reduced shipping costs, and the proximity to the semiconductor factories. ODMs take care not only of the original project of a portable PC but also manage the design process, which includes the analysis of the materials to be used and the functions to be offered. They also take care of testing, packaging and addressing environmental impact issues. Only the marketing and sales actions are actually left to the customers.

Table 2.5   Main original design manufacturers

	Sales 2007 ($M)	EBIT (%) 2007	Employees 2007	Headquarters	Stock Market
Quanta Computer	23 969	3.4	67 291	Taiwan	Taiwan SE
Asustek Computer	23 289	5.2	8 885	Taiwan	Taiwan SE
Compal Electronics	15 362	4.1	38 656	Taiwan	Taiwan SE
Wistron	8 841	3.1	31 682	Taiwan	Taiwan SE
TPV Technology	8 459	3.0	27 320	Hong Kong	Hong Kong SE
Inventec	8 087	2.6	26 447	Taiwan	Taiwan SE
Lite-on Technology	8 074	5.3	68 127	Taiwan	Taiwan SE
Tatung	7 060	7.6	39 140	Taiwan	Taiwan SE
Innolux Display	4 846	11.6	29 300	Taiwan	Taiwan SE
High Tech Computer	3 645	27.3	7 179	Taiwan	Taiwan SE
Elitegroup Computer	2 912	1.1	15 493	Taiwan	Taiwan SE
Inventec Appliances	2 857	4.1	18 566	Taiwan	Taiwan SE
Cal Comp Electronics	2 785	3.7	12 677	Thailand	Bangkok SE
Mitac International	2 782	8.0	12 878	Taiwan	Taiwan SE

Source: Thomson One Banker.

Initially, the ODM model was applied to simple products characterized by a low technological content. The following trend, however, has been oriented towards technologically complex products. In some ways, the ODM business is close to the EMS one, but with a higher margin because of the larger content of intellectual property and its greater growth opportunities. This consideration has ignited a significant interest on some EMS firms towards the ODM sector, whose activities sometimes blend into one another causing a convergence of the two sectors.[2] It is likely that pressure from some large EMS firms to enter the ODM sector, could lead to an increase of competition, a reduction of profit margins and the further aggregation of large ODMs.

Figure 2.5 shows the cumulated turnover of the top ten ODMs, in terms of 2007 sales. The very high degree of concentration that characterizes this sector is clear. The top ten players, most of them based in Taiwan, hold more than 90 per cent of the market.

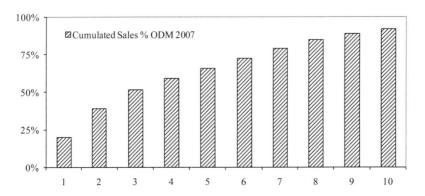

Source: Thomson One Banker, iSuppli.

Figure 2.5   Cumulated sales of ODMs

ORIGINAL EQUIPMENT MANUFACTURERS

The electronics industry sector has developed some words which identify the single players within the global supply chain. Expressions and acronyms are sometimes very helpful in clarifying the concept. Sometimes, however, they can be misleading due to different, even contradictory, interpretations that a word has taken on over the years. One of these expressions is 'OEM'.

In the context of the electronics industry supply chain, the expression 'original equipment manufacturer' (OEM) describes the companies that buy electronic sub-systems to be incorporated in their own products. They are therefore the client companies of outsourcing service suppliers; every company that uses external services to design and manufacture electronic parts within a complex system and wants to enter the market with its own brand is, in this sense, an OEM.

Originally, the meaning was different (and contradictory with respect to its modern use) and referred to the supplier of parts incorporated into a complex system. The name was coined in the 1970s by IBM and identified the original manufacturer (hence the use of this adjective in its name) of a product which was incorporated into the customer's system.

The IBM PC presented to the market in 1981 incorporated a two-floppy driver manufactured by Tandon; in this case, Tandon was called an OEM, since it was the original manufacturer of the element incorporated into the PC.

Over the years, however, this meaning has changed, and today the acronym OEM refers to a company that buys a product whose design and manufacture are completely, or in part, under the responsibility of another specialized company, in order to insert into an own system offered to the marketplace with the company's own branding.

Sometimes an OEM outsources both the design and production of the complete system according to its own specifications, identifying and guaranteeing the product with its own brand. This is, in effect, the meaning which is currently accepted especially in the information technology domain:

> This confusing term [OEM] has two meanings:
>
> 1) Originally, an OEM (original equipment manufacturer) was a company that supplied equipment to other companies to resell or incorporate into another product using the reseller's brand name. For example, a maker of refrigerators like Frigidaire might sell its refrigerators to a retailer like Sears to resell under a brand name owned by Sears. A number of companies, both equipment suppliers and equipment resellers, still use this meaning.
>
> 2) More recently, OEM has been used to refer to the company that acquires a product or component and reuses or incorporates it into a new product with its own brand name.
>
> *Source*: Searchitchannel.

In technical publications as well, we find references to the double meaning of the term OEM:

> OEM is an organization that sells products made by other companies. The term is confusing because the OEM is really not the 'original' manufacturer, but the vendor of the equipment to the end-user. However, the OEM is often the designer of the equipment, and 'original equipment designer' or 'original concept designer' would be more fitting terms.
>
> *Source*: Infoworld.

In order to avoid any potential confusion generated by the semantic evolution of the acronym OEM as a consequence of globalization and outsourcing, it will be used in a specific modern meaning, being a company that within its supply chain outsources a part of the specific design, product engineering, manufacture and testing after-sale services to third companies, while keeping the system design activity as well as the marketing and sales to itself.

Table 2.6 shows the ten largest OEMs with respect to the purchasing of electronic active components; they take up approximately one third of the total production value.

Table 2.6   Main original equipment manufacturers

	Purchase of electronic active components 2007 (M$)
HP	15 000
Nokia	13 000
Dell	11 000
Samsung	10 000
Sony	9 000
Motorola	9 000
LG	6 000
Siemens	6 000
Apple	6 000
Matsushita	6 000
Total	91 000

Source: Gartner.

OEM companies, although using the same raw materials, are differentiated where their end markets are concerned; in fact, companies like Nokia, HP and Dell are focused on mobile phones and computers, respectively, while Sony and Samsung have a highly diversified product portfolio.

It seems evident that the sectors that lead in the purchasing of semiconductors by the large OEMs are related to mass market products and to the consumer market (mobile phones, music players, notebook computers, television sets and digital equipment). The industrial, medical and instrument sectors, although based on the use of electronic technology, include OEMs that are more specialized but smaller in terms of sales and purchases.

Along the electronic sector value chain, the role of the OEM has changed following the expansion of economic globalization. While in the past, the OEM firms were placed between the semiconductor manufacturers and the end market, the growing need for flexibility has brought them to a higher level of intermediation, while maintaining control over the end customer.

NOTES

1. Excluding Intel, STM, Hynix, Renesas Technology, NXP, AMD, Infinenon Technologies and Freescale, the values related to the EBIT margin and to the number of employees refer to the overall activity of the single firm and not to the specific semiconductor division.
2. In 2006, Flextronics employed approximately 6000 technical designers to support the ODM business.

3. Outsourcing Strategy and Processes

out·source [out-sawrs, -sohrs] verb, -sourced, -sourc·ing
–verb (used with object)
1. (of a company or organization) to purchase (goods) or subcontract (services) from an outside supplier or source.
2. to contract out (jobs, services, etc.): a small business that outsources bookkeeping to an accounting firm.
-verb (used without object)
3. to obtain goods or services from an outside source: U.S. companies who outsource from China.
[Origin: 1975–80]
—Related forms
outsourcing, noun
Based on the Random House Unabridged Dictionary, © Random House, 2006

Outsourcing is a word that identifies the process of relying on external services and suppliers to whom a company delegates some activities considered non-strategic; activities that until then had been carried out internally.

In order to align to the fast and complex structural changes occurring in the global economy, companies are adopting business models which allow a faster reactivity to the worldwide market requests, a reduction of the risk due to the fixed assets and an easier achievement of the breakeven point. The use of outsourcing as a strategic tool available for management emerges naturally. The guideline is summed up in the idea that the company should focus on distinctive activities, increasing flexibility and, at the same time, reducing costs. The companies can concentrate their resources in the core competences, through which they reach a competitive advantage position, and strategically outsource all of the activities in which they do not have any particular technical or managerial skills.

Although it is commonly thought that outsourcing is a recent practice dating to the 1980s, in economic history there have been several assignments of non-strategic activities to third parties. During the Renaissance, the economic activities of the textile industry were organized by entrepreneur traders who bought raw materials and dyes from different countries of the world and entrusted the dyeing operations to specialized craftsmen. In the 17th and 18th centuries, sugar production was carried out through a range of stages that were under the entrepreneur's control but not necessarily owned by him. In 19th century England, where the first industrial revolution had already taken place, companies often set up a worldwide network of outsourced activities. In modern terms, outsourcing started to appear more clearly after World War II, accomplishing its maximum development in the 1980s. Since then, it has shown a sizeable growth in the economy of Western countries. It has been estimated that in 1946 more than 20 percent of the activities of North American firms were already being outsourced; this estimate was tripled over the next 50 years.

The modern use of outsourcing was born in the car industry and established on a larger scale in the large Western and Japanese manufacturing industries. It is now diffused in many industrial domains, such as that of machine tools, where quite often the design and the construction of electronic control systems are assigned to external companies with specific know-how in industrial electronics. The service sector too is often engaged in the outsourcing phenomenon, such as through the outsourcing of the information system.

Several studies have investigated outsourcing and provided important contributions to the field. Definitions of outsourcing have adapted over time to the competitive situation, incorporating new aspects and characteristics of the process. Loh and Venkatraman (1992) have given a definition of outsourcing which is focused on information technology due to the outsourcing of IT processes during the early 1990s. Lei and Hitt (1995), instead, supported the idea that outsourcing is not limited to the low-added-value support activities but is, on the contrary, a common fact also used in complex productions. Linder (2004) highlighted the typical characteristic of outsourcing, which is the giving out of some activities that were previously carried out within a company. According to Kotabe and Mol (2004), outsourcing is the process of acquiring goods and services from external suppliers as opposed to vertical integration and the process of insourcing. The following summarises the definitions of these authors.

- The important contribution by external vendors in the physical and/or human resources associated with the entire or specific components of the IT infrastructure in the user organization (Loh and Venkatraman, 1992).
- The reliance on external sources for the manufacturing of components and other value-adding activities (Lei and Hitt, 1995).

- Purchasing ongoing services from an outside company that a company currently provides, or most organizations normally provide, for themselves (Linder, 2004).
- The procurement of goods and services from external suppliers. The counterpart of outsourcing is vertical integration. A range of actions within a clearly identifiable timeframe that lead to the transfer to outside suppliers of activities, possibly involving the transfer of assets including people as well, that were previously performed in-house or procured from other units within a corporate system. The counterpart of the outsourcing process is the insourcing process (Kotabe and Mol, 2004).

Other researchers have also developed an organic and comprehensive definition of the outsourcing trend. Some common traits have emerged:

- A set of activities entrusted to an external supplier
- Strategic decisions related to the transfer of activities from the company to an external supplier
- A set of activities which were previously carried out within the company

FROM TAYLORISM TO OUTSOURCING

Innovation in industry, meaning the skill to generate new technological and production-related knowledge, is a driving force in economic evolution and finds its real expression in creating new business models. Actually, many scholars agree that economic development can be reached through the fundamental contribution of technological, institutional and organizational innovations.

Outsourcing can be considered as a significant change in the business model with reference to a different competitive strategy that distinguishes the evolution of the industrial system. In fact, over almost the whole of the 20th century a widespread organizational model was the Taylorist one, adopted in the first instance by the car industry where the company, strongly verticalized, had full control over every activity and every productive asset. The development of this 'one best way' approach was encouraged by a growing mass market, so that organization techniques were focused on reaching economies of scale, with the consequent reduction of the unit cost of each product.

The advantage of possessing the complete know-how, however, was offset by the need to manage large and not flexible organizational structures. The Taylorist model criticalities became clear in the mid 1970s, related to the 1973 oil crisis, when the beginning of a recessionary period was marked by slow growth and reduction of mass demand. To face the new market conditions, companies moved towards a deep change in their business model in search of flexibility. In order to recover competitiveness and performance, many big firms developed new strategies focusing on distinctive activities, which were controlled internally as they were considered to be the real source of the competitive advantage and of the following profitability. Conversely they decided to outsource some non-strategic functions.

The scientific identification of outsourcing as a business strategy dates back to the 1980s, and was initially carried out through simple patterns, in non-strategic areas and in low value activities. With the increasing competitive pressures due to globalization and the new technologies, companies started to include other secondary processes among the outsourced activities, such as, for instance, information technology and logistics. Nowadays outsourcing has acquired a strategic position, being a tool for the optimization of the organizational structure, able to make it more flexible and agile. The development of technologies has recently been applied to further levels of outsourcing, also involving technologically specific activities whose in-house development would be extremely costly and time consuming.

From a microeconomic perspective, the problem can be traced back to studies on transaction costs and, in particular, to those by Ronald Coase on the nature of the firm (Coase, 1937), in which the Nobel Prize economist investigated the reasons for the existence of firms, where a wide segment of production activities are not coordinated through market exchanges, but take place inside the firms themselves. What are the firm's limits within which transactions take place not as true market exchanges, but as a result of the entrepreneur's or management's authority? Based on what factors is the decision to manufacture internally or to rely on the market made? The question goes back to the 'make or buy' issue, which acquires importance not only in economic issues, that is in the evaluation of whether the costs of a certain part of a process are higher when carried out internally or when outsourced, but also in strategic terms. The decisions concerning the level of outsourcing depend on the level of integration of the activities, upstream or downstream along the supply chain; then, the cost structure, the organization and the market positioning are defined. The make (or hierarchy) option, besides preserving the intellectual property, ensures direct control over the overall know-how, the manufacturing process, provisions and product quality. The 'buy' option (or market) allows an evolution which is consistent with the growing flexibility inherent in a market that is no longer limited to national boundaries, next to the financial aspects involved, connected to the reduction of working capital and fixed costs (Carlsson, 1989; Sanchez, 1995). The modern paradigm which assigns a competitive advantage not so much to dimensional factors, that is to the size of firms, but to time factors such as the time-to-market, is supported by the outsourcing option (Dean et al., 1998). It is interesting here to quote John Chambers, Chairman and CEO of Cisco Systems:

> The competition will be between the fast and the slow, and not between the big and the small. There is no place for laggards here.

The growing use of the market, not only for manufacturing activities but also for the implementation of production services (information technology, human resources, and so on), qualifies the strategy that companies have been following since the 1990s.

The level of outsourcing has changed over the years: it started with simple sub-contracting operations, which implied the transfer to external suppliers of some processes with no intellectual property added value (Van Mieghem, 1999), and evolved to include the outsourcing of crucial parts of the business process (for example, the whole production segment or after-sale service). In the latter case, we always find the transfer of intellectual property, and the company which is outsourcing the process gives up its capability to carry out the activity internally.

The firm that entrusts part of its production process to external organizations, however, maintains the responsibility for the outsourced activities and liaises with the suppliers about functional characteristics, technical specifications, quality standards, and any other characteristics of the outsourced product or process (Domberger, 1998). In any case, the use of outsourcing involves stability in the collaboration and a partnership between the firm and the suppliers (Lin and Tsai, 2005). Firms that use outsourcing also benefit from greater flexibility and ability to respond to market needs.

Table 3.1 shows what is being outsourced according to a survey from the Outsourcing Institute. It shows the pervasiveness of outsourcing in all that concerns the management of processes throughout the business world, namely information systems, accounting and personnel administration as well as more critical areas such as finance and marketing, though perhaps to a lesser extent.

Outsourcing is a global economic trend (Grossman and Helpman, 2005), and in Western countries no longer limited to activities that are connected to production factors; outsourcing also involves more non-material activities, such as specialized design, purchase operations and data analysis, which are assigned to external partners performing more efficiently thanks to their specialization and economies of scale. The use of outsourcing allows the firm to focus on its core business, and above all on R&D, marketing and sales management. Outsourcing, together with the consequent reduction of the

firm's average size, is part of the trend that replaces the massive industrial
monoliths, dropping their size and creating new medium-sized enterprises,
highly specialized and tightly connected with one another, not necessarily
through ownership relations, but as company networks (Figure 3.1).

Table 3.1   What is being outsourced

Position	Involvement in outsourcing (%)
Information Technology	58
Administration Accounting	50
Human Resources	24
Distribution & Logistics	23
Real Estate | Facility Management	23
Manufacturing	20
Contact | Call Centers	19
Finance	17
Sales | Marketing	11
Transportation	10

Source: Survey 7th Annual Outsourcing Index, Outsourcing Institute.

The Taylorist model, which is marked by large dimensions and by a
functional-type organization model, is increasingly being replaced by a
network company model where, to attain higher flexibility, companies reduce
their size and contract out their non-core activities.

- *Traditional outsourcing (subcontracting)*
  Traditional outsourcing refers to the outsourcing of activities with a low
  level of managerial complexity, among them, for instance, human
  resources administration. The implementation process is similar to that
  of sub-contracts, where there is no need for a high level of interaction
  between the players involved. Sometimes, this is referred to as contract
  manufacturing.
- *Operational outsourcing*
  Operational outsourcing has a higher level of managerial complexity, as
  happens in the case of outsourcing of IT systems. The firm–supplier
  relationship is more cooperation-oriented.

• *Strategic outsourcing*

Outsourcing has evolved beyond being viewed as a purely tactical exercise to reduce costs and increase operational efficiencies. Strategic outsourcing represents a more evolved form of the outsourcing process, but at the same time it shows a remarkable implementation effort. In fact, the outsourcing does not involve single activities, but complete processes defined by highly complex management. The outsourcing of functions such as production, marketing, or after-sales service implies a long-term client–supplier relationship, based on cooperation and goal-sharing.

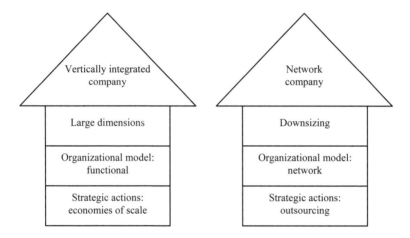

Figure 3.1   Vertical integrated and network companies

From the contract point of view, some different typologies of outsourcing relationships can be established, depending on the degree of innovation of the outsourced activity and on the extent of the client's control over the supplier.

• *Cost-plus*

The price paid by the client is set by the costs incurred by the supplier (labor, facilities depreciation, materials and services), known to and shared with the client, plus the margins agreed upon during the negotiation. Companies that choose this type of agreement want to set a high degree of control over their suppliers and, in general, they expect from them nothing but a very limited level of product/process innovation.

- *Fixed-price*

  A fixed-price contract is a contract where the amount of payment does not depend on the amount of resources or time expended. This kind of contract is defined by a target cost that should be reached. The ways to accomplish the target are entirely left to the supplier; production parameters and transaction prices are defined jointly. This is an incentive to the suppliers towards a non-stop research of process and product innovations to reduce the costs and, more in general, increase the overall efficiency.

- *Gain-shared*

  This is an intermediate solution between the cost-plus and fixed-price typologies. On the one hand, the supplier is given a certain degree of freedom in terms of innovation; on the other hand the client maintains significant control over the outsourced activity, finding an agreement on costs. If the costs are lower than estimated, the client and the supplier share the economic advantages.

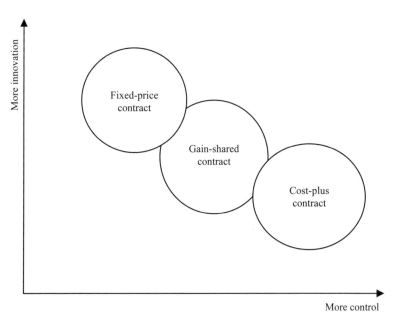

Figure 3.2   Outsourcing contracts

Cost-plus contracts are preferred when the outsourced activity is clearly defined and the supplier is not required to create a high degree of innovation. Conversely, where the strategic decision of whether the firm should use outsourcing or not is the result of the search for a constant improvement in the product/process, fixed-price contracts are more common. The management takes the risk connected with a lower degree of control against a substantial innovative role of the supplier.

Although the word 'outsourcing' is commonly used for any contract involving outsourced activities, it is the strategic side that raises the greatest interest within the study of the economic system transformations; globalization, strategic outsourcing and delocalization have a strong influence on one another. Management complexity, uncertainty, strategic relevance and long-term client–supplier relationship are common traits in strategic outsourcing cases such as the partnership between carmaker Fiat and TNT.

In the early 1990s, Fiat decided to assign the management of the spare parts department to TNT Automotive Logistics. This strategic decision could be attributed to the high criticality of the stock management and the poor in-house skills. Therefore, the search for a partner was directed not only by the need to reduce costs, but also to improve the process and to find specific know-how. An agreement was then signed by Fiat Auto for the transfer of Italian logistics activities and of European branches. The Turin industry maintained instead all of the commercial activities related to spare parts, the service activities, and the selection of suppliers. The outsourcing practice continued and, in 1998, TNT Production Logistics was created. Fiat assigned the management of the entire industrial logistics process including collection of goods at the supplier's facilities, transportation and, of course, material management and stock control. This partnership with the Fiat group represented one of the biggest logistics outsourcing operations of those years.

DETERMINANTS OF OUTSOURCING

The reasons for outsourcing are strategic as well as operational regarding flexibility and performance.

- *Strategic focusing and specialization*
  Outsourcing of minor activities allows a company to focus on strategies and to allocate resources to the core competences. The increase in the specialization level of the company's own activities leads to improvements in operational performance.
- *Reduction of operational costs*
  Firms that rely on outsourcing get not only an improvement in the efficiency associated with product specialization, but they can also reduce their costs by outsourcing to more specifically skilled

organizations whose production takes place in a global context and in lower-cost labor countries.

In January 2002, NEC and Celestica entered into a five-year manufacturing outsourcing relationship, covering a broad range of products and supply chain services. Under the agreement, Celestica assumed supply chain management, sub-assembly, final assembly, integration, and testing for a broad range of NEC's optical backbone and broadband access equipment–all areas previously owned by NEC. This arrangement provided NEC with a flexible and lower-cost solution than they otherwise would have been able to accomplish on their own, leveraging the capabilities and economies of scale provided by a tier 1 EMS provider.
Source: Celestica (2002).

- *Access to technology*
  The access to specific technologies that do not belong to the company's own supply chain can be an expensive option, both in economic and time-to-market. In this sense, technological outsourcing has found a specific position within the electronic technologies industry.
- *Better quality standards*
  The use of the specific competences and know-how owned by external companies allows the outsourcer to reach higher quality standards, also through access to world-class competences.
- *More operational flexibility*
  The firm has a higher ability to fit its production parameters to the market needs (for example quantity and technical characteristics). Furthermore, the firm exchanges a proportion of fixed costs with variable costs, so that it can respond better to increasing variability in the global market demand.
- *Time-to-market reduction*
  Access to external specialized capabilities usually enables a time reduction from the idea of a product to its availability to the end-user. It also enables a decrease in the time required for the re-engineering of a product in pursuit of technological evolution and cost reduction. From a strategic point of view, it increases the ability and the pace to adjust to structural changes in the competitive environment, which reshape the boundaries of the industrial fields faster than in the past.

OEMs also have used outsourcing to help quickly and cost effectively enter a new market. One of the best examples is Microsoft. Microsoft's software business model traditionally has been based on licensing its intellectual property-operating system and applications software. But in 2000, in a strategic shift,

Microsoft added game consoles to its product mix with the Xbox. To avoid the need to build fabrication facilities and repair capabilities, neither of which was available in-house at the time, Microsoft hired Flextronics to introduce the product and ramp up manufacturing to meet global demand. Ultimately, the Microsoft Xbox product was built in Flextronics's existing manufacturing facilities around the world. In this way, Microsoft gained world-class, global manufacturing capabilities without investing in new plants.
Source: *Time Magazine* (2001).

- *Decrease financial requirements*
  Many fixed costs become variable through a reduction in investments for manufacturing plants, with a following decrease in debt-financing. The purchase of intermediate goods has a positive impact due to the drop of the stock. In the sector of electronics outsourcing, the firm sometimes agrees to transfer its productive assets that are taken over by the outsourcing company, thus releasing further financial resources.

In January 2002, IBM outsourced manufacturing of its NetVista desktop computers to Sanmina–SCI as part of a broader strategy to reduce both fixed and variable costs. Under the $5 billion arrangement, Sanmina–SCI assumed manufacturing responsibility for some IBM desktop computers in the US and Europe and agreed to acquire two IBM buildings (along with capital equipment) in Research Triangle Park, NC, where the IBM computers are manufactured. Sanmina–SCI also agreed to hire 900 former IBM employees there, along with the 100 employees at IBM's smaller Greenock, Scotland, facility that manages European production of the NetVista computers. This agreement supported IBM's strategy of keeping PCs as an important element of their e-business infrastructure offerings, while making this business even more cost-competitive in the marketplace. It also leveraged EMS industry skills and scale to improve cost performance, allowing IBM to focus more of their own investments on areas that deliver the highest value to their customers.
Source: Reuters (2003).

A survey carried out by the Outsourcing Institute (Table 3.2) on the determinants of externalization highlights the trend towards focusing (53 per cent) and cost reduction (52 per cent). The opportunity of releasing resources that can be reallocated to other activities (33 per cent) and the creation of agreements with leader companies giving access to world-class capabilities (33 per cent) are important facts in the decision to outsource.

As 44% of the respondents throughout the survey results were from companies with fewer than 500 employees. The second most represented group was made by buyers from corporations with more than 10 000 employees (23%).

Table 3.2   Determinants of outsourcing

Factor	Important item for outsourcing (%)
Improve focus	53
Reduce/control costs	52
Gain access to world-class capabilities	33
Free up resources for other purposes	33
Resources not available internally	25
Accelerate re-engineering benefits	20
Reduce time-to-market	19
Share risks	18
Take advantage of offshore	15
Difficult function to manage	10

Source: Survey 7th Annual Outsourcing Index, Outsourcing Institute.

The outsourcing relationship must be strategically framed, with a medium–long-term view. Several factors contribute to making it long-lasting and profitable for both players involved in the transaction, such as good management of the relationship, updated and adjusted in the context of changing conditions, and contractual precision in terms of costs and performances. There must be a complete and shared understanding of the objectives, because any misunderstandings in expectations can cause an outsourcing operation to fail.

Table 3.3 lists the main cost determinants in the outsourcing decision-making process, that is in the decision to choose in-house production (insourcing) or to rely on the market (outsourcing). A company must compare the costs related to the internal production process and the supporting structure (accounting, technical, and logistic) with the costs of the external supplies of goods or services and the expenses associated with the management of the outsourcing process.

Through a deep comparison between the strategies of 'make or buy', a company can choose the appropriate level of outsourcing.

Table 3.3   *Cost determinants of outsourcing*

Insourcing	Outsourcing
Human resources costs	Feasibility costs (evaluation of opportunities, costs of the search for suppliers)
Materials costs	Costs to set up the outsourcing process (contracts, agreements, procedures)
Accounting costs	Costs of the process implementation (organizational changes, coordination and monitoring)
Logistics costs (provisions, stock, space)	Switching costs (to find new suppliers)
Technical costs (machinery, plants)	Costs caused by returning to insourcing (in case of failure of the outsourcing process)
Know-how costs (technologies, training, patents)	

CRITICALITIES IN OUTSOURCING PROCESSES

The strategic importance of outsourcing is due not only to increased competitiveness in terms of costs, but also to a wider aspect of competition. The use of outsourcing with the aim of reducing costs, but without taking into account the company positioning, a deeper focus on the core business and a different allocation of the resources released, can hamper achievement of the strategic target.

Furthermore, the use of outsourcing techniques must be subject to applicability tests within the background of the company's activity and internal dynamics, which, if not correctly understood, can cause the outsourcing option to fail.

Firstly, it is useful to highlight some of the basic conditions for a company to choose outsourcing. One exogenous condition lies behind the presence in the marketplace of subjects who are able to carry out the outsourced activity efficiently and correctly. Another condition is endogenous and is related to the managers and to their fear of losing control over the outsourced function, with the resulting downsizing of their power within the company.

Secondly, the outsourcing option often meets internal resistance, especially in the lower levels of the organization. On the one hand the top management can hold the advantages of outsourcing regarding variable costs and increased flexibility; on the other hand trade unions are often critical towards outsourcing and delocalization because of the subsequent cut in the local labor.[1]

The following classification scheme can summarize the risks that may arise with outsourcing.

- *Operational risk*
  This is related to the definition of new internal operational modes and to the proper coordination between the outsourced activity and the closest in-house activities.
- *Organizational risk*
  This is related to problems associated with the organizational change caused by outsourcing. For instance, the reallocation of the resources released by outsourcing can be complex and expensive.
- *Strategic risk*
  This is related to the loss of control over the outsourced activity. In some cases, when the outsourced activity has a high technological content and is therefore subject to a high degree of innovation, outsourcing can imply a loss of knowledge and know-how, which may affect the company's core business.

Table 3.4 shows how the effects of the outsourcing option may show criticalities. It is evident, for instance, that outsourcing has a generally positive impact on the finance area, allowing the variabilization of costs. Meanwhile in the HR area it could cause an internal reduction in company cohesion.

Sometimes, there may be a cost–benefit trade-off as in the case of logistics. For example, the advantages resulting from the reduction of stock may be counterbalanced by the increased complexity in management due to the greater number of companies involved.

In the specific area of electronics outsourcing, the criticality of subcontracting has been highlighted by some events which have characterized the client–supplier relationship since the 1990s, associated with the extension of the functions delegated outside the firm. A well-known case was the litigation between Motorola and BenQ. Motorola had delegated the design and production of millions of cell phones; according to Motorola, the necessary transfer of know-how between the two companies allowed BenQ to produce and sell new cell phones with its own brand in China in open competition.

A limited outsourcing can reduce potential criticalities by giving out only a few of the development steps to EMS/ODM firms, never sharing their entire know-how.

Table 3.4   *Effects of outsourcing*

Area	Effects of outsourcing
Marketing	Outsourcing can modify consumers' preferences. The product price decreases, as does the uniqueness of the product itself.
Purchasing	Outsourcing favors growth in this area, increasing the number of relations with suppliers and new contracts. The main task of this department is the management of outsourcing operations.
Operations	Outsourcing might reduce the quality of the work, but in some cases it might also increase it. With outsourcing, the need to coordinate operations between more business organizations increases.
Finance	In terms of financial benefits, fixed costs decrease to the advantage of variable costs.
Information system	A more complex information system is needed which integrates all the information coming from a range of suppliers.
Human resources	Potential reduction in organization solidity. It might be more difficult to create a corporate philosophy shared by the employees and by the outsourcing suppliers.
Logistics	Outsourcing makes the logistics tasks more complicated because it increases the number of the organizations involved but, at the same time, reduces the stock.

Source: Mol (2007).

A different criticality is the risk of finding indistinguishable products in the marketplace with complete deletion of the value linked to differentiation. For example, in the market of personal computers two products were available in 1999 that were identical in their performance and design, although with a different brand name. The problem was caused by the outsourcing to the same supplier. The key model for proper management of the outsourcing process lies in keeping the distinctive capabilities and in tracing the boundary line of know-how. The core competences above that line must remain internal, while the commodity competence can be disclosed and delegated. Companies are thus requested to consider strategically how much of the intellectual property should be kept inside and how much be delegated to the market.

It is evident that the total outsourcing of an innovation, although it brings an immediate benefit in terms of the profit and loss account thanks to the reduction in R&D investments, causes a structural impoverishment of the company.

GLOBAL OUTSOURCING

Growth in outsourcing processes is extremely fast also because of some macro-trends that are particularly favorable to the spread of this phenomenon. One noteworthy macro-trend is the worldwide growth in trade liberalization.[2] Together with the increased availability of communication and transportation infrastructures, the relationship with suppliers from all over the world has thus become extremely easy and less expensive. Geographical proximity to the client used to be considered a competitive advantage and sometimes a position advantage, but takes a less important role relative to a world-scale partnership where the client companies look for the best supplier in both economic and technological terms.

Labor and material costs are driving factors for the purposes of the geographical selection of the country where to outsource; other factors associated with specific country risks can also affect selection of geographic location.

- *Geopolitical risk*
  Government measures, such as nationalization acts, can affect the economic environment and cause patrimony losses for investors. Political stability, safety levels and any ethical problems in business management are important variables in the decision making process.
- *Macro-economic risk*
  The characteristics of a country's economic system are crucial for the investment decisions; the exchange rate of the local currency, the country's trends and its future growth scenario can affect a company's earnings.
- *Infrastructure risk*
  The status of a country's infrastructure – transportation as well as communications – and the future investments in this sector are central for an accurate assessment of the return on economic investment.
- *Legal risk*
  This refers to the law system in general, with special attention being given to protection of intellectual property. A lower degree of guarantees concerning the respect of patents causes a lower degree of delocalization of products with a high content of intelligence.
- *Human capital risk*
  This refers to risk factors related to human capital and takes into account variables such as the quality of the educational system, the availability of skilled labor, the number and typology of postgraduates.
- *Cultural risk*
  Deep cultural differences between the outsourcer and the delocalization

country are transformed directly into costs related to language difference, social system, openness to innovation and workers' flexibility.

ELECTRONICS OUTSOURCING

Profit margins in the electronics sector have grown in relation to the use of innovative technologies and, more generally, according to the intellectual property content embedded in the products. The sector was initially characterized by property production processes and technological patents; most of the Intellectual Property (IP) rights were financed, generated and held by OEMs. Later, new players entered the supply chain, and carried out activities that were previously managed by OEMs. Beginning in the 1980s, the industrial sector has gone through a progressive change in the production supply chain, characterized by a growing trend towards de-verticalization and the use of outsourcing.

Alongside the automotive sector, information technology is a sector where this change was particularly clear from the beginning and where the steps to define the current business model are easy to recognize. With respect to this issue, it is interesting to focus on the main strategic decisions of IBM during the years of its success with personal computers as wide diffusion products. The evolution of its strategy can be observed as a guideline for other businesses involved in the manufacturing of products associated with electronics outsourcing. In particular, in the early 1980s, IBM had to face the risk resulting from the entry of new manufacturers into the market. With the aim of competing by reducing time-to-market, IBM designed a new business model for the manufacturing of its own products. Instead of designing all parts of their personal computers themselves, IBM started using components whose intellectual property was held by other companies, relying on outsourcing for microprocessors (Intel) and operating system (Microsoft), as well as for many other subcomponents.[3] Within a short time, this strategy allowed IBM to create a *de facto* standard for personal computers, whose construction was based on a wide range of electronic products purchased externally.

In recent world economic history, few strategic decisions like the one made by IBM opening up to external outsourcing have had such profound consequences: entrusting third parties with the job of supplying some base elements led to the migration of the intellectual property from their own system to third parties' components, such as the microprocessor and the operating system, thereby making such intellectual property available to anyone.

The birth of 'IBM-compatible' personal computers raised the level of competition, with a resulting reduction of costs. A new path to personal information technology and, more generally, to the diffusion of IT and digital communications was open, without which market globalization would have been extremely difficult. Descendants of the IBM PC compatibles make up the majority of computers on the market, although interoperability with the bus structure of the original PC architecture may be limited.

The diffusion of personal computers as products with an extensive intellectual property content belonging to companies different from the manufacturer was a significant change, not only in information technology, but for the entire electronics industry. Indeed choosing an open standard was the consequence of the use of 'not proprietary' hardware and software. The open standard architecture meant the growth of many new firms specialized in high-tech components for personal information technology, such as microprocessors, mass storage devices and peripherals. The electronics industry was deeply changed, allowing better performance with respect to the old vertically integrated model. Other product typologies within the electronics sector (digital cameras, mobile phones, peripherals) followed a similar standardization path, supported by focusing on core business by many OEMs.

Since the 1990s, the outsourcing process within the life cycle of electronic products has become very common in the OEM business model. OEMs have modified their organizational and production structure from a vertically integrated organization able to handle the whole product life cycle directly, to a horizontal configuration. Currently the outsourcing of electronic technologies (design, engineering, manufacturing of components, semi-finished products and electronic systems) is more and more often considered a strategic business solution that can improve competitive positioning, enabling the company management to be kept lean and more dynamic.

In particular, the outsourcing of electronic technologies, both in activities with a high content of intelligence, such as design and engineering, and in processes for the construction of components and electronic systems, is present in several sectors such as high-tech electronics, chemical, pharmaceutical, automotive industries. Along with a horizontal cooperation between companies belonging to the same production sector (sometimes even between direct competitors), a vertical collaboration is tied in within the supply chain, between suppliers and clients.

Initially, outsourcing involved the mere acquisition of standard components, not ownership (Figure 3.3). OEMs could benefit from a reduction of costs in terms of investments in specific manufacturing plants. Later, the same acquisition activity, at least for the simplest and cheapest components, was progressively delegated to EMSs, while the procurement activities related to strategic and valuable components were kept internal.

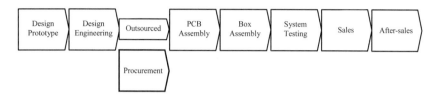

Figure 3.3   The 1980s: acquisition of standard components

During the period of rapid growth of the electronics industry in the 1990s the outsourcing practice was adopted extensively in manufacturing activities in order to cope with the extreme rapidity and variability of the demand. The nature of the agreement between OEMs and their subcontractors was that of pure transformation (contract manufacturing) and the economic value of transactions was related mainly to the labor costs and depreciation of plant, on which a certain profit margin was allowed.

Later, OEMs extended their agreements in order to purchase not only labor and the use of the plants, but also a considerable part of the electronic components from subcontractors. These were no longer supplied to be processed later, but their purchase was left to the supplier. Thus, outsourcing was extended also to procurement and to PCB assembly stages (Figure 3.4).

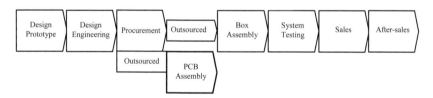

Figure 3.4   The 1990s: contract manufacturing

The growth of production volumes of external suppliers showed they were more efficient than OEMs, due to their increasing specialization and ability to more rapidly amortize the costs of their plants, allocating them over larger production volumes and more clients. Looking for improved efficiency and cost reduction, OEMs increased the outsourced parts, which were acquired already assembled, integrated and tested. Growth in the level of outsourcing led to the transformation of subcontracting relationships into further extended relations of electronics manufacturing services (EMSs) (Figure 3.5).

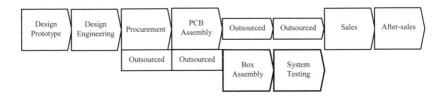

Figure 3.5   End of the 1990s: outsourcing of services (EMS)

The further extension to after-sales services was the natural result of the concentration of OEMs on activities considered to be strategic: R&D, marketing and sales (Figure 3.6).

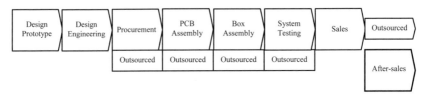

Figure 3.6   Early 2000s: further extension of services

In some industrial fields, particularly those with very high production volumes typical of consumer products such as ICT and mobile phones, the evolution that followed gave rise to a rapid growth of ODM firms (Figure 3.7), with a business model in which the products' intellectual property was taken away from OEMs, with an increased entrepreneurial risk and increased profits.

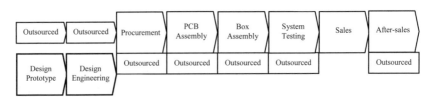

Figure 3.7   The 2000s: original design manufacturers (ODM)

The birth of ODM firms provides evidence of how OEMs, which initially governed the whole electronic product supply chain, have increasingly changed to outsourcing not only in manufacturing activities, but also in higher added-value services. Over the last twenty years, OEMs have changed from a vertically integrated model to a horizontally disaggregated structure; a growing number of processes have been outsourced to specialized suppliers who have shown their ability to carry out the same activities in a more efficient and qualified manner and at a lower cost.

As far as outsourcing companies are concerned, an increase in industry dimension was encouraged by the further extension to elements of the supply chain and the adoption of progressively more complex models in terms of intellectual property (from contract manufacturing to ODM). Nevertheless, at the same time the indirect cost structure has become less flexible compared to the previous situation. Indeed, in this new context, EMSs/ODMs have to bear the charges coming from the fixed costs associated with tangible and intangible investments, the management of human resources and the growth of the working capital. Therefore, the evolution in electronics outsourcing requires new metrics and new indicators to monitor the success of the underlying strategy. Traditional measures, based on cost reduction, on quality level and, more generally, on efficiency, are no longer adequate; they need to be integrated with new ones, among them organizational agility and flexibility, the readiness to handle the changes and the rapidity of the market dynamics.

Today's economic organization requires that all of the actors in the supply chain individually optimize their cost structure and be ready to adapt to the fast-changing demand. A shared metric is needed in order to reach excellent management of the entire value chain and it should include, in addition to the traditional indicators, other values that must be carefully monitored, such as:

- Time-to-market
- DFM performance (design for manufacturability)
- Quality performance (design for quality)
- Stock levels of the firms involved in the chain

OPERATING AREAS

The market where ODMs and EMSs operate includes several industrial sectors:

- computers
- consumer devices (mobile phones, LCD television sets, videogame consoles, MP3 players, cameras, etc.)
- servers and storage
- networking (wireless access points, switches, routers, etc.)

- telecommunications (infrastructure for mobile phones, optical fibers, Bluetooth devices, etc.)
- peripherals (monitors, printers, etc.)
- others sectors (automotive, medical and industrial electronics)

Table 3.5 shows that the sector where electronics outsourcing is used most is that of computers, with a share of about one third of the total (due to the high concentration of ODM activity in this segment), followed by consumer devices at 27 per cent. The medical, automotive and industrial sectors only reach 11 per cent of the total market, but show the highest estimated growth rates and are almost exclusively controlled by EMS firms.

Table 3.5   EMS and ODM operating areas

	Impact on EMS/ODM sales (%)
Computer	34
Consumer devices	27
Servers and storage	8
Networking	8
Telecommunications	6
Peripherals	6
Others (automotive, medical, etc.)	11

Source: IDC (2008).

AUTOMOTIVE ELECTRONICS OUTSOURCING

Currently the trend of electronics outsourcing is geographically global and pervasive across sectors to the same extent that the electronics technology is pervasive in current goods and services.

It may be particularly important to examine the automotive sector because it has historically been the catalyst for the use of outsourcing, especially for the machining of mechanical parts, and today it still has an important role among users of outsourcing.

The recent growth of electronic technologies in the automobile sector has had a remarkable affect on the electronic technological content of cars. They are supplied through outsourcing, mainly concerning control and safety devices as well as, more recently, entertainment and comfort features.

- Powertrain and transmission (powertrain controls, infinitely variable transmission (IVT), electromagnetic valve rain (EVT), ignition sensing)
- Chassis control (control-by-wire, brake-by-wire, adaptive cruise control (ACC), electronic stability program (ESP), collision avoidance)
- Safety (lane departure warning, tire pressure monitoring, blindspot detection, night vision, vision enhancement, driver conditioning and monitoring, safety event recorder)
- Entertainment and comfort (driver assistance, keyless entry, voice recognition, passenger position sensing, GPS car navigation, DVD readers)

The value of the electronic parts used in the automotive industry worldwide has grown from 50 billion dollars in 1994 to over 300 billion dollars predicted for 2010. The market value of electronic chips manufactured for this sector has been estimated to reach 25 billion dollars in 2009. The share of outsourced electronics, which is already high, is growing.

Figure 3.8 shows that the relationship between the value of purchases in electronics outsourcing (EMS, ODM), with respect to total purchases of automobile makers, has grown from 10 per cent in 2004 to 13 per cent in 2009. The same figure shows how the importance of the automotive sector is growing for EMSs/ODMs.

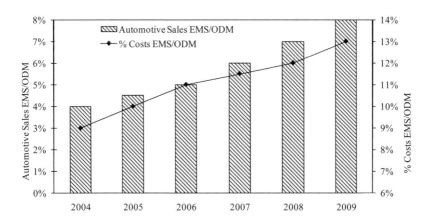

Source: Technology Forecasters.

Figure 3.8   EMS/ODM and the automotive industry

Considering that in the early 1990s electronics was approximately 10 per cent of the total cost of a car, while today it is estimated to be as much as 23 per cent and is expected to grow, there is still margin for a further growth of electronics outsourcing.[4]

Yet, the cost is not the only decisive factor for the selection of suppliers. To begin with, quality and reliability are very important; the performance of electronic devices in the automotive sector must comply with tremendous reliability requisites depending on dynamic vehicle conditions and environmental conditions.

The know-how expected for consumers' electronic applications is different from that expected in the industrial context. For this reason, the outsourcing of electronic technologies in the automotive sector is handled exclusively by a few large manufacturers. The consumer market has a higher level of tolerance as far as product defects are concerned because the consequences of a failure are substantially different. While in some consumer or industrial products a defect index of a few parts per thousand can be accepted, the zero defect concept is the standard in the automotive sector, especially where safety is concerned.

The basic EMS/ODM supplier selection factors in the automotive industry are the following:

- Quality and reliability
- Cost
- Technological level
- Compliance to the standards
- Production rate
- Flexibility
- Control of the supply-chain
- Information technology
- Culture

We should also consider factors related to the high cost investments on the design and the production of very complex components characterized by a high obsolescence rate. The outsourcing operators' interest in the automotive sector is growing at the same time, allowing the creation of new long-term collaboration agreements and partnerships with large manufacturers that allow the sharing of risk.

GLOBAL ELECTRONICS MANUFACTURING

Economic globalization has fostered the growth of the world economy in many manufacturing sectors, despite a remarkable differentiation in the growth rates of some geographic areas. Asia has benefited from the globalization of markets with an increase in gross domestic product (GDP) two to three times higher than in Western economies and in the USA in particular.

Despite some problems of measurement, an increase in gross domestic product of a country is generally taken as an increase in the standard of living of its inhabitants. A comparison between the GDP increases in India and China shows annual growth rates of 8–10 per cent, while the same factor is around 3–4 per cent in the USA (Figure 3.9). In 2007, the world's GDP was as high as 4.9 per cent.

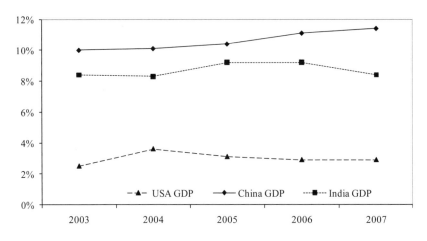

Source: International Monetary Fund.

Figure 3.9   GDP growth in China, India and the USA

As far as the whole of the electronics outsourcing activities is concerned, the revenues of Asian EMS and ODM businesses are estimated to be increasing. The most involved sectors are those of information and communication technology and consumer electronic devices. The growth of electronics outsourcing in Asia can be credited to the continuous search for optimization of the cost structure by OEMs, therefore encouraging outsourcing to low-cost labor areas, mainly China and India. Other areas, such as Thailand and Vietnam, are significantly emerging, at the expense of China.

The expansion of EMSs in Asia is mainly due to low labor costs, but also to the presence of an increasing number of component suppliers and of companies dedicated to the manufacturing of semi-finished products following the delocalization of their clients.

OEMs continue to leverage the cost structure of EMS players and outsource their manufacturing to low-cost centers in Asia. In key Asian markets, OEMs have persuaded EMS players to establish their local operations so they can capitalize on the domestic demand well.
Source: Mayank Jain, In-Stat (2007).

Due to the growing production rate of these countries, a sizeable segment of European and American factories dedicated to electronics manufacturing has become obsolete, resulting in their closure and/or heavy conversion of production processes.

The EMS expansion in Asia also shows some difficulties. Besides the unsurprising problems related to linguistic and cultural differences, EMSs have to bear high costs for the training of the workers and for global logistics. Furthermore, the risks related to the intellectual property rights of technologies and products being delocalized are real. The protection given by the patenting process is not always satisfactory to prevent a commodity product from being copied, technological products from being reverse engineered[5] and luxury products from being counterfeited. It should also be taken into account that the transfer of almost all of the productive capacity into a single country can be hazardous due to geopolitical turmoil.

The existing problems can be summarized as follows:

- Lack of infrastructure
- Lack of skilled labor
- Problems associated with productivity and quality
- Efficiency of the logistics organization
- Protection of intellectual property rights
- Cultural differences
- Language difficulties
- Communication difficulties due to different time zones
- Geopolitical risks

In the past, these issues have discouraged smaller firms from delocalizing; they have also considered that the saving derived from a lower labor cost is less meaningful if the production volumes are low, while, on the other hand, the transportation and operation costs generated by remote delocalization are much higher.

Despite this, a large number of EMSs have moved their production divisions to Asia, convinced mainly by their bigger customers who, in turn, have found it convenient to move to regions with a lower labor cost. The desire not to lose their important clients, to keep their market share and to have a new end market and a better competitive position led even small companies to invest in production units in China and India.

CHINA

The importance of China as a low-cost production country has grown exponentially and has involved several sectors, among them electronics. OEMs, in their permanent search for efficiency, have invested in China, especially since 2001 when China entered the World Trade Organization. Table 3.6 lists the main Chinese OEMs by their 2006 revenues and shows a remarkable growth rate of 20 per cent on average.

Table 3.6   Main Chinese OEMs

	Sales ($M)	Sales growth (%)
Lenovo	13 250	23
Huawei	6 150	33
TCL	5 970	17
Haiter	5 400	8
ZTE	2 190	21
Hisense	2 826	16
Gree	2 688	23
Midea	2 230	18
Changhong	2 004	12
Skyworth	1 910	30

Source: iSuppli.

In the supply chain logistics, investments made in Asia by OEMs are followed by those of electronics outsourcing companies, both EMSs and ODMs, that have outlined their own strategies to delocalize and have a new approach to their clients' new production plants. The EMSs growing interest towards China not only represents an answer to the solutions adopted by OEMs, but more broadly is an opportunity for strategic diversification. The possibility to seize higher margins, sharing the advantages with their customers, implies an improvement in their own competitive position.

Evolution in the competitive context, however, makes it necessary for China's EMSs/ODMs to grow, also because of the limited increase expected in the next years for these sectors in Western countries. China represents a competitive solution for the production of commodity electronic products, with high volumes and low mixing, such as in the case of mobile phone devices. Also, China is a large end market. The on-site management of the process is less difficult, the requested quality standards are less rigorous, and the problem of duties on imported goods is not present.

As far as the electronics industry is concerned, since the 1990s, China-based companies have run along the curve of experience in the production of semi-finished and end-products, shifting from the production of printed circuits to the assembly of medium-complex integrated subsystems and related services. The trend of increasing manufacturing skills towards more complex applications and systems is still in progress.

- 2000: Low-technology electronic boards and electronic consumer components, with a limited know-how requested by the producer (e.g. videogames consoles), are manufactured. Delocalizing in order to reach the lowest possible cost is the determinant of the investments made in China by larger EMSs.
- 2002: More attention is paid to the technological level involved in the production of electronic boards, although the driver is still the price. Some EMSs begin to invest in the Chinese market aimed at gaining a position in segments that are characterized by mass production.
- 2004: The production of systems with a high level of know-how grows. Many OEMs start to outsource the production of large volumes targeted to the Chinese domestic market; the level of services available in China increases by design and testing.
- Since 2006: China gains a position as a strategic area for highly complex and technological production lines. Also increasing is the number of EMSs based in China that produce middle volumes.

During 2000–2005 China substantially increased its production capacity in the electronics sector. In 2003, the Chinese government declared an increase in the turnover of the companies operating in electronics manufacturing 34 per cent higher than the previous year; in 2004 about 56 per cent of Asian electronic products were produced in this country; all of the biggest EMS companies globally invested in China.

The delocalization of the productive capacity of all goods that need to be manufactured in large volumes is probably meant to further growth, turning China into one of the most suitable areas to place plants and industrial assets. The Chinese government has also considerably encouraged investments in projects on semiconductors and in electronics manufacturing facilities. It is therefore strategic to develop and expand operational bases in the area. This is most crucial for businesses that are also investing into the ODM's typical activities within the design and engineering process. To stay competitive, EMSs need to be able to perfectly integrate Chinese plants, characterized by low labor wages, with other added-value activities in order to implement global sales and distribution strategies at competitive prices.

China is an important strategic outsourcing option for firms within the electronics industry; despite the growing competition level coming from other low labor cost areas, it maintains its own attractiveness not only in terms of costs, but increasingly as a final market.

INDIA

China is not the only country available for EMSs and the electronics market in general. The low cost of labor and of land, together with the fast growth of domestic consumption, are leading business organizations to evaluate the opportunities of investing in India as well.

As far as the IT sector is concerned, which is strictly associated with EMSs, Taiwanese manufacturers of electronic equipment are showing a growing interest in moving their production to the Indian market. Indeed, Taiwanese companies are aiming to strategically reduce their dependence on China's plants; in fact, they had invested approximately 200 billion dollars in China up to 2005. More than 70 per cent of the Chinese industries involved in electronics outsourcing services are dependent on investments by Taiwanese companies.

> We closely monitor the breathtaking technological developments taking place on the subcontinent and we are interested in forging closer ties with India, which is not only the world's most promising market but also an attractive potential manufacturing site for Taiwanese products.
> *Source*: Wu Tao-yuan, Taiwan Semiconductor Industry Association (2007).

In the past, cultural differences had limited the interest in delocalizing to India. Yet recent changes in the macro-economic scenario have led many Taiwanese companies to increase their investments in the sub-continent. In February 2005, for example, Foxconn announced an investment of 110 million dollars for a settlement in Chennai, the fourth biggest Indian city, where the Indian factories of world-leading companies in IT and electronics are located. Even the Taiwan Institute for Industrial Information established an R&D branch facility in the same city.

Among the factors behind India's growth we can identify:

- Increase in consumers' trust, due to the increase in individual spending allowance
- Availability of financial instruments to obtain credit
- Increase in local production
- Great expansion of local distribution networks

The growth of the Indian economy, with a great increase in the demand for electronic goods, is an opportunity for EMSs and ODMs to enter a market with a very high expansion potential. The following growth in the demand for electronic components in both the business and consumer segments, aside from import-related constraints, is an incentive for the construction of production units in India also directed to the domestic market. It has been estimated that the average annual income of a family which approaches the electronic consumer market is about 4500 dollars; in 2006 about 18 million Indian families reached or topped this threshold level, that means about 100 million people. This quota is going to double in the next five years.

The strategic decision to delocalize to India is influenced by the opportunity of entering into a market that, when compared to the industry life cycle model, features the typical characteristics of the growth phase. The growth in the demand for electronic products has therefore not only sparked the attention of global OEMs, but also that of the main EMSs, primarily in telecommunications and consumer electronics industries, followed by computing and industrial areas.

India is one of the fastest growing markets with sizeable growth potential. Mobile phone production revenue is expected to reach $13.6 billion by 2011 from $4.9 billion in 2006, a CAGR of 26.6 percent. Many major OEMs have already seen the great opportunity and have a business development plan there, e.g. LG, Ericsson, Motorola, Nokia, Samsung and Siemens, etc. About 59 per cent of the telecom equipment requirement of about $5 billion in India is still imported. It's vital to have electronics manufacturing capacities to support OEMs to develop hardware manufacturing in India.
Source: Carsten Barth, Elcoteq (2008).

There are several reasons that lead electronics outsourcing companies to invest in the Indian market.

- Access to local market
- Low labor cost
- Diversification with respect to China

- Spread software-related competence
- Pervasive technical competence
- Knowledge of the English language

Regarding production, low labor cost is one of the main determinants for investment in India, especially compared to the Chinese market, where the salaries are growing and where there is still a problem of lack of technically skilled workers.

Referring more specifically to EMSs/ODMs, besides the labor cost issue, investments in India are interesting for the technological competence, especially in information technology, traditionally supported by government policy. The Indian IT sector, located around the district of Bangalore, has shown a growing trend and has attracted foreign companies: more than one third of the US multinationals' software has been developed in India. Also, the policy on protection of patents and intellectual property is encouraging new investments because the level of protection has reached Western standards.

The strategy implemented by EMSs to enter the Indian market seldom implies the creation of startup companies, but rather involves purchasing local Indian companies operating in the same field or production factories that were previously owned by an OEM. An example is given by the four local businesses purchased in 2005 by Flextronics with the aim of manufacturing electronic components for mobile phones, or by the acquisition of the production plants of Philips India by Jabil Circuit in the consumer electronics arena.

Yet, there are still some difficulties related to the lack of infrastructure, which is inadequate to support rapid growth, and to management of the supply-chain because of the lack of world-class component suppliers. The situation requires EMSs and ODMs to import components and to bear customs duties and charges.

SOUTH-EAST ASIA

Although China is the global center of electronics manufacturing, beyond Taiwan and India, countries such as Singapore, Thailand and Vietnam play an important role. There are different factors that may support growth in these areas, among them:

- Diversification of the risk taken by OEMs, compared to China alone
- Availability of a work force with a good level of education
- Global production capacity and production mix

- Government incentives
- Infrastructure and public and private research centers

Some ODMs decided early on to relocate plants that were based in China because of the increase in the Chinese labor costs and because of a change in the incentive policy on investments, with respect to what had been promised by regional and central Chinese authorities in the decade of 1995–2005.

EAST EUROPE

Besides the emerging countries in South-East Asia, Eastern European countries have also acquired a competitive position in the electronics global market.

Belarus, Bulgaria, the Czech Republic, Croatia, Estonia, Latvia, Lithuania, Malta, Poland, Romania, Russia, Slovakia, Slovenia, Turkey and Hungary have been involved recently in important investments in every kind of high-tech industry.

> The electronics manufacturing services market in Eastern Europe will grow from about $9 billion in 2006 to nearly $24 billion in 2013. This is not a surprise. Eastern Europe has a culture and infrastructure conducive to volume manufacturing and EMS companies have been established there for many years.
> *Source*: 'Electronics manufacturing grows in Eastern Europe', James Carbone, *Purchasing* (2007).

The reasons for this remarkable growth in Eastern European countries are essentially found in the excellent level of education offered and through production costs that are lower than in Western countries.

NOTES

1. An agreement was signed at Chrysler in October 2007 with the union representatives of the United Auto Workers on the stability of wage levels in exchange for a reduced use of outsourcing. Similarly, in the same period, an agreement at General Motors ratified the taking back of two company divisions which had previously been outsourced.
2. After a 15-year negotiation, the agreement for the access of China into the WTO was signed on September 17, 2001. China committed to ensuring the international operators easier access to the domestic market, and abolition of local protectionism, preferential relationships between the authorities and local firms, and the arbitrary norms imposed by local officers.

3. On August 12, 1981, IBM announced the commercial availability of its first personal computer, with two key components that were acquired from the market: the 4.77 MHz Intel 8088 microprocessor and the Microsoft MS-DOS 1.0 operating system. IBM's strategic decision has since influenced the personal computer domain and has generated the neologism 'Wintelism', referring to the widespread diffusion of the binomial Windows and Intel in the area of personal computers.

4. In 2006, some important partnership agreements were signed between big automotive industries and electronics outsourcing companies (General Motors and Lite-on Technology); the same year some agreements with car component suppliers (Anthai and Foxconn, Quanta and TomTom) also came into force.

5. The term 'reverse engineering' refers to the detailed analysis process of the structure of a device, usually an electronic component or a software package, with the purpose of manufacturing a new device or program which is functionally equivalent to the original. In the case of electronic devices, the activity starts with breaking them down into their component parts to study their design and interoperability. A software package, instead, is disassembled with the aim of studying its parts or removing its protection or anti-counterfeiting techniques. Reverse engineering activities are often illegal and are criminally sanctioned in many countries as a violation of intellectual property rights.

PART TWO

Global Electronics Supply Chain

4. Component Suppliers and Distributors

MANUFACTURERS OF ELECTRONIC COMPONENTS

Manufacturers of electronic components of both active semiconductor devices (e.g. microprocessors and memory units) and passive components (e.g. resistors and capacitors) are at the beginning of the electronics supply chain with the basic elements allowing the manufacturing of all electronic products. Due to the high technological content of semiconductor devices, their manufacturers show a strong bargaining power. The merging process has led to large global American, European, Japanese and South-Korean firms (Intel, ST Microelectronics, Toshiba, and Samsung). The small number of active component suppliers is the cause of a recurring criticality in the availability of electronic components, with periodic shortage problems and price increases typical of a speculative market.

ELECTRONIC SEMICONDUCTOR DEVICES

Semiconductor devices are the most used electronic components in electronic applications. They are used to generate, amplify and control signals and they include microprocessors, interface devices and signal amplifiers. The characteristics of these components are related to the use of semiconductor materials, principally those with an electric conductivity intermediate between metal conductors and insulating materials.

The reference semiconductor is silicon, particularly in polycrystalline form. Component suppliers use silicon in the form of a wafer, which is thin cross-sections (around 0.5 mm thick) of silicon cylinders, with a diameter between 24.5 and 500 mm. These wafers are the base on which integrated electronic circuits are produced.

The world market of silicon manufacturers is oligopolistic and controlled by only a few large suppliers (Table 4.1). Consistent with this type of market, silicon manufacturers have very high profit margins.

Table 4.1   Main manufacturers of silicon wafers

	Sales 2007 ($M)	Variation in sales y/y	Market share (%)	Headquarters	Stock market
Shin–Etsu Handotai	4 058	23.8	32.5	Japan	not listed
Sumco	2 708	24.7	21.7	Japan	Tokyo SE
MEMC	1 848	29.2	14.8	USA	NYSE
Wacker Siltronic	1 216	3.5	9.7	Germany	not listed
Sumco Techxiv	959	11.9	7.7	Japan	Tokyo SE
Total market	12 486	22.5			

Source: Gartner (2008).

The high level of concentration causes the rationing of polycrystalline silicon and a subsequent price strain. The situation is made worse due to an increase in demand by the remarkable growth of the renewable energy business through the photovoltaic technology (with an estimated annual increase of 40 per cent).

The oligopolistic form, combined with a constantly growing demand, generates an increase in the silicon manufacturers' profitability. For example, with MEMC and Sumco Techxiv, the EBIT margin is respectively 57 per cent and 20 per cent (2007). The annual world production of silicon is about one million tons and it is mainly used by aluminum, glass and ceramic industries, while the semiconductors and photovoltaic markets receive 42 thousand tons. Forecasts estimate that this value is growing, with the trend led mainly by Asian operators.

The whole production of semiconductor integrated circuits, which is highly diversified and in continuous development, is based on silicon wafers. Every electronic device is characterized by specific process technologies, integration levels, functional and design specifications. The main industrial processes used in the production of semiconductor devices are, historically, the bipolar and CMOS processes, with development starting in the 1970s: the former is applied to produce very fast devices, while the latter is utilized with low-power consumption devices. CMOS technology allows a very high integration of a number of transistors within single silicon chips, which makes it the dominant technology for personal computer and consumer applications. The classification of semiconductor devices requires a subdivision between discrete devices (diodes, transistors, and resistors) and integrated circuits (ICs), which are made of more transistors diffused on the same chip. The market of discrete products shows a lower growth rate because of a minor level of innovation and differentiation.

THE SEMICONDUCTOR MARKET

Growth in the semiconductor market is related to the continuous expansion of electronic applications over the last 40 years, consistent with the so-called 'Moore's Law' (Figure 2.2). The expression of an endless technological evolution, Moore's law has allowed an exponential growth in the performance of electronic devices and a similar decrease in costs. The single transistor incorporated in today's electronic devices costs as much as the printing of one single character on this page. As the size of transistors shrinks, their speed increases, so it is common to mention Moore's law to refer to the rapidly advance in computing performance per unit cost, because increase in transistor count is also a rough measure of computer processing performance. If a similar relationship to Moore's law were to be applied to another technology, for instance to air transportation, the improvement of the performance would make it possible to fly between Milan and New York in less than 1 second at the price of 1 cent, with an aircraft not bigger than a small car.

From an industrial production process standpoint, the level of miniaturization required by the market and the continuous search for production efficiency have driven research towards the reduction of the dimensions of semiconductor devices. There is a convergence of technologies towards the miniaturization, because it allows an increase in the intrinsic speed of the device and a reduction of the cost per unit.

It is estimated that a semiconductor manufacturer invests on average as high as 15 per cent of its revenues in R&D activities. The high investments have erected natural barriers, as well as strong selection for the entry of manufacturers in the market; and this has also caused the closing of the smaller manufacturers of integrated semiconductors to the bigger ones' advantage. Technological innovation is one of the most important competitive variables in this field. From the early 1990s, the growth rates of the expenses related to R&D have increased more rapidly than turnovers; they have increased at a CAGR of 12.7 per cent between 1990 and 2007, compared with a growth of the semiconductor market at a CAGR of 9.9 per cent. As a consequence of the trend towards production outsourcing, the fabless model has also become common. This model identifies the manufacturers of integrated circuits that control the design process and who holds the related know-how, but do not necessarily own the production plants. Fabless firms have developed a highly specialized business model that focuses its resources in the development of devices and microelectronic technology, and outsources the production process to other companies (silicon foundry), based mostly in Asia.

Table 4.2 shows the trend of R&D expenses of some of the most important electronic component suppliers. Consistent with the implemented business model, R&D investments made by silicon foundries are less significant than those made by the firms who design their own devices (integrated devices manufacturing (IDM) and fabless).

Table 4.2   Sales and R&D expenses of component suppliers

Company	Business model	Sales 2007 ($M)	Sales growth (%)	R&D expenses 2007 (%)	Headquarters
Intel	IDM	38 334	8.3	15.0	California (USA)
Samsung	IDM	19 951	15.3	21.4	South Korea
Texas Instruments	IDM	13 309	−3.0	16.2	Texas (USA)
Toshiba	IDM	11 850	12.2	17.0	Japan
STM	IDM	9 966	−6.8	18.1	Netherlands
TSMC	foundry	9 813	15.1	5.6	Taiwan
Renesas Technology	IDM	8 001	3.0	17.0	Japan
NXP	IDM	6 026	2.8	22.3	Netherlands
AMD	IDM	6 013	6.4	30.7	California (USA)
Infineon Technologies	IDM	5 772	−3.1	18.5	Germany
Qualcomm	fabless	5 619	17.9	21.6	California (USA)
NEC Electronics	IDM	5 593	7.2	18.6	Japan
Freescale	IDM	5 447	1.7	20.9	Texas (USA)
Broadcom	fabless	3 754	3.0	35.9	USA
UMC	foundry	3 247	n.a.	8.9	Taiwan
Marvell	fabless	2 895	29.4	34.2	Texas (USA)
SMIC	foundry	1 550	n.a.	6.3	China
Chartered	foundry	1 458	−9.0	11.0	Singapore

Source: IC Insight.

Integrating the effects of the cyclic trend of this sector, the world's semiconductors market has been constantly growing, with a CAGR of 15 per cent in the period 1982–2007.

Figure 4.1 shows the reduction experienced by the semiconductor market, as in the whole electronics supply chain, between 2000 and 2002, associated with the economic downturn. The following crisis that has hit the economy since 2008 has also caused a volume reduction due to the decrease in demand in the mobile phone and personal computer segments.

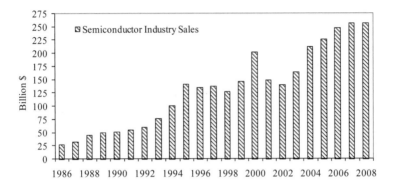

Source: Semiconductor Industry Association.

Figure 4.1   Sales in the semiconductor industry

As a consequence of the fast technological evolution, electronic components are subject to a high rate of obsolescence, which forces manufacturers to make continuous investments in new plants and to face the problem of their right dimension. As a consequence, during demand reduction periods the installed productive capacity is excessive, causing a fall in the price of semiconductors and in the manufacturers' profits.

The cyclic nature, which frequently alternates stages of growth and fall is typical of this sector, partly because of the variation in the final demand and partly because of an overestimate of the same with a subsequent excessive increase in the production capacity.

Economic shocks cause unpredictable changes in aggregate demand and short run aggregate supply which lie outside normal macroeconomic models. The 2001 recession was caused simultaneously by the demand side and the supply side; the 'dot-com bubble' burst and the 9-11 attack occurred at the same time as the supply excess, due to the existing high production capacity. The main differences with the 2008–2009 downturn can be found in the fact that now semiconductor manufacturers have limited the problems of overcapacity and have been able to stem excessive supply and reduce stock. Figure 4.2 shows the trend of the semiconductors industry over the last 60 years, highlighting many declining stages, eight of which have culminated in periods of sales decrease. The semiconductor industry has entered a new downturn phase concomitant with the 2008–2009 financial crisis.

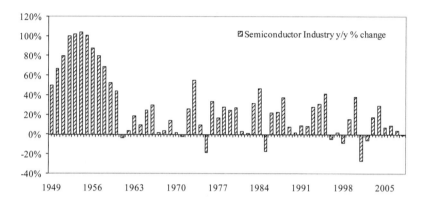

Source: Semiconductor Industry Association and Future Horizons.

Figure 4.2   Declining periods in the semiconductor industry

Figure 4.3 shows three different periods characterized by different average growth rates: the periods 1988–1995, 1995–2000 and 2000–2006. The figure shows the change of the number of semiconductors manufactured during the last three cycles of the semiconductors industry; it points out how the average annual growth dropped from a CAGR of 16 per cent during the development stage of the sector (1988–1995) to 5 per cent (2000–2006). The comparison with the growth of the world gross domestic product shows that the semiconductor sector is moving towards maturity. In fact the rate of growth of demand and/or supply of the semiconductor industry is similar to the growth of GDP.

The sales of semiconductors, in terms of volume, are about 500 billion units per year, and the market is starting to show the first signs of maturity in areas like the USA and Europe, with reduced growth rates compared to those of other areas, like Asia, as shown in Figure 4.4. An increase in Asia's turnover is estimated (50 per cent), while the revenues coming from Europe and Japan have shown a reduced variability over the last ten years, with a market share of 18 per cent and 16 per cent, respectively.

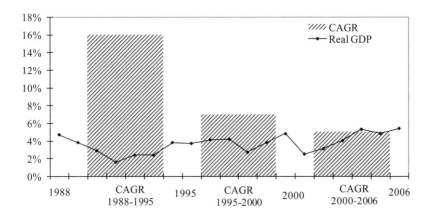

Source: World Semiconductor Trade Statistics, International Monetary Fund.

Figure 4.3   Change in the number of semiconductor devices produced

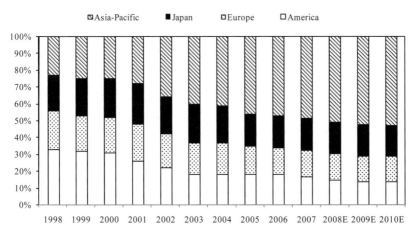

Source: Semiconductor Industry Association.

Figure 4.4   Semiconductor sales by geographical area

Table 4.3 lists the main component suppliers, characterized by a sales level above five billion dollars.

Table 4.3   Main electronic component suppliers

Company	Sales 2007 ($M)	Sales growth (%)	Employees	Headquarters	Stock market
Intel	38 334	8.3	94 000	California (USA)	NASDAQ
Samsung	19 951	15.3	84 721	South Korea	Seoul SE
Texas Instruments	13 309	−3.0	30 175	Texas (USA)	NYSE
Toshiba	11 850	12.2	190 706	Japan	NYSE
STM	9 966	−6.8	52 180	Netherlands	Milano
TSCM	9 813	15.1	2 749	Taiwan	NYSE
Hynix	9 614	22.2	15 200	South Korea	Seoul SE
Sony	8 040	13.1	n.a.	Japan	NYSE
Renesas Technology	8 001	3.0	25 000	Japan	not listed
NXP	6 038	2.8	30 000	Netherlands	not listed
AMD	6 013	6.4	16 420	California (USA)	NYSE
Infineon Technologies	5 774	−3.1	43 079	Germany	Frankfurt SE
Qualcomm	5 619	17.9	12 000	California (USA)	NASDAQ
NEC Electronics	5 593	7.2	23 982	Japan	Tokyo SE
Freescale Semiconductor	5 447	1.7	n.a.	Texas (USA)	not listed

Source: iSuppli, Gartner, Thomson One Banker.

The list also includes firms that operate at multiple levels of the electronics supply chain, such as Samsung, Sony and Toshiba, controlling the chain both upstream as component suppliers and downstream as OEMs, then interfacing with end-users.[1]

The leader is Intel, having a 2007 turnover of almost 38 billion dollars, an 8 per cent increase relative to 2006, largely thanks to microprocessors. A major part of the sector's growth in the years 2006–2007 can be attributed to the diffusion of memory units (Hynix).

Even in the supply chain area of electronics manufacturing, a clear segmentation is revealed, as the market players are focused on different business segments. The profits of the players are different and it is hard to identify a common trend in the sector. For example, Intel, which operates in the CPU segment for personal computers in an almost monopolistic way, shows a margin level always higher than that of ST Microelectronics, whose products, although highly technological, are positioned in a segment which is more easily contended by other manufacturers (automotive applications, mobile phones, memory units, etc.) (Table 4.4).

Table 4.4   EBIT margin of Intel and ST Microelectronics

EBIT (%)	1998	1999	2000	2001	2002	2003	2004	2005	2006	2007
STM	13.7	14.9	24.2	6.8	10.1	4.6	8.2	3.3	8.2	−4.2
Intel	34.9	38.3	45.0	8.4	16.0	24.9	30.6	32.5	20.0	24.0

Source: Thomson One Banker.

Aimed at the continuous reduction in semiconductor size to improve functional integration and speed, the manufacturing process affects the costs sustained by the sector for the production of semiconductor devices. The miniaturization of devices has become a market priority because it provides several advantages, such as the improvement of production output with the following reduction of costs and power consumption, and the opportunity to integrate a higher number of transistors, thus improving processing power. The design of new technologies, though, is very complex: the costs to start up a silicon foundry dedicated to the diffusion of semiconductors are estimated to have gone from 200 million dollars in 1993 to 2.5 billion dollars in 2003.

The commitment to changing and creating new products and processes gave rise to an average investment in R&D of 10–15 per cent of the turnover, as well as the costs for upgrade of production plants as high as 25–30 per cent per year. The high investments required for the construction of a new semiconductor factory on the one hand have marked the end of the typical small manufacturer of integrated semiconductors, encouraging the concentration of this sector, and on the other hand have helped the birth of the fabless model, in which the device manufacturer carries out its own initial research and design while the actual production is carried out through outsourcing, usually to low-labor-cost countries.

Innovation is still the dominant competitive factor in the sector of electronic components. The technologies available on the market evolve at a considerable speed and, in order to reach a leadership position, it is necessary to keep developing new solutions. New innovations must reach the market quickly, allowing for exploitation of the economies of scale necessary to amortize the huge investments before the technology becomes obsolete, causing a subsequent erosion of the margins.

SEMICONDUCTOR EQUIPMENT SUPPLIER

The industry of component suppliers is tightly connected to that of semiconductor equipment suppliers; they are the suppliers of the equipment dedicated to the production of electronic components. Due to the tight client–supplier link, the trend of this market is affected by the trend that characterizes the component suppliers.

In 2006, the worldwide sales of equipment for the production of chips reached 45 billion dollars, with a growth of 24 per cent relative to 2005. Table 4.5 summarizes the main manufacturers of plants for silicon production in order of 2007 revenues.

Table 4.5   Main manufacturers of plants for semiconductor production

	Sales 2007 ($M)	Sales growth (%)	EBIT (%) 2007	Headquarters	Stock market
Applied Materials	9 735	6.2	25.8	USA	NASDAQ
Tokyo Electron	9 103	26.2	18.7	Japan	Tokyo SE
ASML	5 255	15.4	23.7	USA	NASDAQ
Dainippon Screen Manufacturing	2 811	10.2	3.5	Japan	Tokyo SE
KLA-Tencor	2 522	−7.7	22.6	USA	NASDAQ
Lam Research	2 475	−3.6	23.8	USA	NASDAQ
Advantest	1 836	−7.8	12.9	Japan	Tokyo SE
Novellus	1 570	−5.3	20.5	USA	NASDAQ

Source: Thomson One Banker (2008).

COMPONENT SUPPLIER: INTEL

Intel Corporation is the leader company in the sector of electronic component manufacturers, with a turnover of more than 38 billion dollars and more than 94 000 employees (2007).

Founded in 1968 by Robert Noyce and Gordon Moore, the author of the so-called 'Moore's Law', the company originally produced semiconductor memory components. The turning point occurred in 1971 with the first microprocessor (Intel 4004), which led to the progressive shifting of the company's core business towards the new application area of digital processing units.

The technical development and improvement in performance continued over the years; in 1975 the Intel 8080 processor was integrated in one of the first personal computers, the Altair 8800, and its next version 8088 was used in IBM PCs (1981).

In 1986, Intel went public on NASDAQ and since the 1990s the 'Intel Inside' logo has been visible on personal computers worldwide; Intel became the first component supplier known on a global level. The large size reached by the company over the years has made it possible to exploit economies of scale and knowledge and to make sizable investments in research and innovation.

INTEL AND ITS SECTOR

Figure 4.5 shows the revenues achieved by Intel from 1998 to 2007, characterized by an average compound annual growth of 4.3 per cent. This growth trend stopped twice, corresponding to the years 2001 and 2006.

Source: Company reports.

Figure 4.5   Sales of Intel

In 2001, the decrease was caused by the aforementioned economic downturn that has characterized the entire market of electronics. In 2006, however, the negative situation was due to intense competition and to the weakening of the IT sector, causing a price decrease. The company, however, was able to deal with the situation by carrying out a cost reduction plan and introducing new products, bringing the 2007 sales back in line with the trend of the sector.

The negative performance that characterized the years 2001 and 2006 is also reflected in terms of profitability (Figure 4.6). The data show that there were larger decreases in profit than in revenue (–85 per cent in 2001 and –43 per cent in 2006).

Furthermore, as highlighted by the historical series related to the 1998–2007 period, there has been a reduction in the value of the net operating profitability that has decreased, although not with a constant trend, from 35 per cent in 1998 to 24 per cent in 2007.

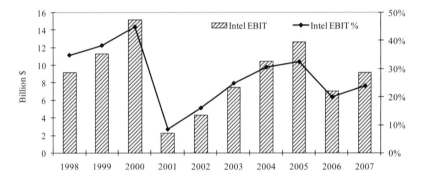

Source: Company reports.

Figure 4.6   EBIT and EBIT margin of Intel

The progressive profit loss can be linked to a structural trend, consistent with the sector life cycle of semiconductor devices, which is characterized by an increase in the costs for development and innovation of products, as they are subject to ever-increasing miniaturization and complexity. The above considerations are supported by the chart in Figure 4.7 (total assets turnover vs. EBIT margin).

The most complex situation was associated with the economic downturn that hit the sector in the years 2001–2002, with a decrease of EBIT margins and efficiency. Production over-capacity, generated by excessive investments and over-estimation of the sector's growth, seriously affected the production system and the whole EMSs' value chain. However, examining the data for the whole period, even excluding this two-year period, does not reveal any detectable trend that is constant over time.

Intel's revenues arise from different main business segments, namely digital enterprise, mobility and flash memory.

- *Digital Enterprise*
  The segment includes microprocessors, microcontrollers, chipsets and motherboards, workstations and network infrastructures. The products are directed to the computer market, as well as the automotive, industrial, consumer electronics and telecommunications industries.
- *Mobility*
  The segment includes microprocessors and chipsets created for integration into products in the ultra-mobile market, characterized by energy efficiency and wireless connections, like notebook computers.
- *Flash Memory*
  The segment involves the production of flash memory components, used in cameras, audio-digital readers, mobile phones, PC boards and USB flash drives.

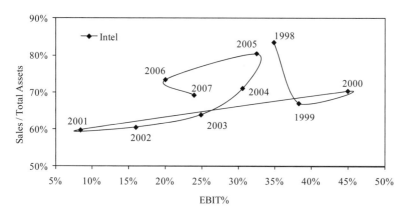

Source: Company reports and Datastream.

Figure 4.7   Total assets turnover vs. EBIT margin of Intel

Table 4.6 shows the evolution of the turnover generated by each of Intel's business segments in the five-year period 2003–2007. Although the digital enterprise share has always been the main turnover source (over 76 per cent in 2003 and 53 per cent in 2007), the mobility segment is growing (CAGR higher than 30 per cent), compared to the digital enterprise's negative figure (−3 per cent).

The flash memory segment has also been marked by a remarkable growth trend (CAGR of 18 per cent in 2003–2007), although this group represents only a fraction of Intel's total revenue.

Moreover, in 2008, the flash memory segment was assigned to Numonyx, a joint venture between Intel and STMicroelectronics. Intel had previously entered into two other joint ventures with Micron Technology.

The creation of new independent companies to whom the production of flash memories are delegated is a strategic choice made by the main firms operating in this sector, operating in alliance to achieve better economies of scale in both production and technology investments.

Table 4.6   Sales of Intel by business segment

	2003 ($M)	2004 ($M)	2005 ($M)	2006 ($M)	2007 ($M)	CAGR 2003–2007
Digital Enterprise	23 059	24 778	25 137	19 814	20 317	−3.1
Mobility	5 086	6 981	11 131	12 384	14 567	30.1
Flash Memory	1 608	2 285	2 278	2 952	3 183	18.6
Other	388	165	280	232	267	−8.9
Total	30 141	34 209	38 826	35 382	38 334	6.2

Source: Company reports.

Table 4.7 lists Intel's main competitors, grouped by product category, in particular microprocessors, chipsets, memory units and connectivity products.

Table 4.7   Main competitors of Intel

	Main competitors
Microprocessors	AMD, VIA, IBM, Sun Microsystems, Freescale
Chipset	AMD, NVIDIA, Silicon Integrated Systems (SIS), VIA
Flash memories	Hynix, Samsung, SanDisk, Spansion, STM, Toshiba
Connectivity product	Atheros Communications, Qualcomm

Source: Company reports.

The semiconductor sector shows strong competition, based on performance, availability, quality, price and brand identity parameters. Moreover, the sector is highly concentrated and affected by rapid technological progress and the introduction of new products with an increasingly shorter life cycle, less than one year in some cases.

Intel's main competitor is AMD, and although much smaller than Intel (6 billion dollars vs. Intel's 38 billion), it is nonetheless the second biggest manufacturer of microprocessors in the world after Intel. AMD is listed as a competitor in both the microprocessor and chipset sectors. Intel and AMD also compete as the sole microprocessor manufacturers for Wintel personal computers (with a microprocessor derived from the 8088 and Microsoft's operating system).

Intel has a dimensional superiority that allows making bigger investments in R&D activities, in the setting up of the production process and in the necessary tests for the manufacturing of the products.

The firm has a competitive advantage generated by the direct ownership of the facilities where assembly and testing operations are carried out, and is therefore able to have direct control over processes and related efficiency and quality levels.

INTELLECTUAL PROPERTY

R&D activities are a basic element for consolidating and increasing Intel's market share. Such activities range from the design and development of new products to the optimization of production technologies in terms of performance, quality and efficiency. Figure 4.8 highlights that the R&D expenses have increased both in terms of absolute value and as a percentage of the annual sales.

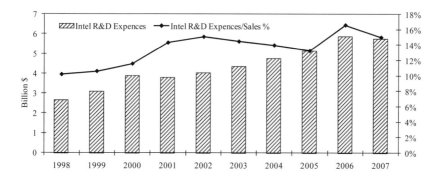

Source: Company reports.

Figure 4.8   R&D expenses of Intel

Intel's dimensions enable the company to make large investments, larger than those made by most of its competitors. Although AMD has assigned a better fraction of its revenue to research activities (more than 30 per cent of the 2007 turnover, while Intel's R&D range has been between 10 and 16 per cent), the absolute value of AMD's investments have never exceeded two billion dollars, compared to Intel's six billion.

The capital invested in research stayed high during the 2001–2002 downturn, highlighting the importance of innovation for Intel. The research is based on an international organization, with more than 7 000 researchers all over the world, in a network that includes universities, scientific research centers, governmental organizations and joint ventures with other companies in the same sector.

A TECHNOLOGICAL BRAND

Intel has always communicated the value of its products through intense marketing activity targeted to the end-user. The company has indeed held the communication of its own brand to be very important, signing agreements with OEMs and ODMs to give evidence to the 'Intel Inside' logo. Together with its lead position within the sector, over the years Intel has thus been able to associate its products with an image of quality, in turn gaining customer loyalty.

Many co-branding campaigns based on the logo 'Intel Inside' created a market advantage for both the company and for ODMs and OEMs using the logo. That strategic choice has allowed Intel to differentiate from its main competitors, especially AMD, also generating switching costs to the customers.

DISTRIBUTION CHANNELS

Along with the electronics manufacturing supply chain, the distribution channels of electronic components allow an aggregation of the demand coming from the different players (OEMs, EMS and ODMs) redirecting towards the manufacturing firms. The main task of the component distributor is maintaining a many-to-many connection.

Some OEMs buy the most expensive electronic components directly from the manufacturers, while relying on distribution channels for the best part of the low-cost components. They buy from the distributors also in case of unexpected demand from the market.

The electronics distribution network plays an extremely important role in the supply chain of electronic products in maintaining the connections between the medium-volume market, the smaller component manufacturers and EMSs/ODMs.

Concerning electronics manufacturing, the interest is mainly focused on electronic devices, such as semiconductors and passive devices. In this area, the sector has been the target of a merging process that has led to the creation of a few world-class groups that are active in the sale of electronic components. These are mostly companies that operate in similar ways, with good profitability and organizations focused on efficiency, giving special attention to the critical variable of goods and inventory management. The most important global distributors have established tight relationships with the largest EMSs and ODMs, working closely with the clients and suppliers of logistic services.

A strategic choice for electronic component distributors was the decision to rely on information technologies to manage not only the daily logistics, but also the setting up of more advanced demand forecasting procedures in the short–medium period. In fact, to meet the rapid changes in demand, EMSs and ODMs have implemented stock optimization procedures (material requirement planning) and supply contracts towards the distributors to reduce the inventory.

An accurate stock management is a crucial element for the supply chain. Through an electronic infrastructure able to keep a direct link between customers and suppliers, electronics distribution generates benefits despite the minor margins allowed with electronics components.

Even the electronics distribution sector was affected by the world recession of 2000–2002; nevertheless, since 2002 the sector seems to be growing again (Figure 4.9), similar to the two other reference sectors, EMS and ODM. Economic effects have been less evident in the sector of the value chain representing distribution because it is not tied to a few important customers or suppliers, as is normally the case with EMSs and ODMs, which can be heavily affected by the default of even a single customer in terms of revenue and economic results.

During 2007 the growth in the electronics distribution sector was as high as 8.4 per cent with a turnover of about 63 billion dollars, while the average growth between 2002 and 2007 was about 9 per cent.

Table 4.8 shows the composition of the distribution sector listed by world market shares; of note is the concentration of the two US companies Avnet and Arrow Electronics.

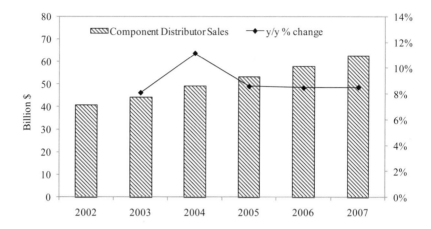

Source: Datamonitor.

Figure 4.9   *Growth of the electronics distribution channel*

Table 4.8   *Main electronic component distributors*

	Sales 2007 ($M)	Market share 2007 (%)
Arrow Electronics	15 985	25.5
Avnet	15 681	25.1
WPG Holding	4 670	7.5
Future Electronics	4 416	7.1
Bell Microproducts	4 050	6.5
Other	17 798	28.3
Total	62 600	100.0

Source: Datamonitor.

The dominating positions allow Arrow Electronics and Avnet to establish long lasting and profitable relationships with the main semiconductor manufacturers worldwide. However, the situation does not encourage competition since the entry of new players is made practically impossible and it is extremely difficult for smaller distributors to grow. In the period

2002–2006 the growth of the ten most important independent distributors in the American market has been almost nonexistent.

As far as sector profits are concerned, Figure 4.10 shows the trend of sales and profits cumulated by the largest three distributors of components (Arrow Electronics, Avnet and WPG). A growing trend in sales in electronics distribution is clear, with maximum values recorded in the year 2000, followed by a drop during the downturn of 2000–2002; the revenues returned to 2000 values only five years later.

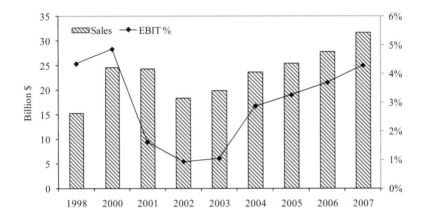

Source: Company reports.

Figure 4.10   Sales and EBIT margins of the three main electronics distributors

The increase in sales volumes of the main distributors has been supported by a strong exogenous element, through a specific policy of mergers and acquisitions by the leading companies; the targets were distributors of micro-electronics and high-tech components in geographical areas where the leading distributors were not yet present. For example, in the case of Arrow Electronics, the first acquisitions date back to the late 1960s, followed by more than 40 significant acquisitions. According to a strategy that favors the speed of growth, the acquisition activity allows direct access to the clients' portfolios and to maintain those relationships, instead of opening new green-field locations.

The concentration process has not yet reached its conclusion. The relationship between large distributors and clients is more than the simple distribution of components and includes important services such as stock management, often outsourced by the client, which makes it impossible or very costly to change the supplier to a smaller distributor. Furthermore, the bargaining power of the large distributors is so strong that they can put pressure on the costs and delivery terms of the semiconductor manufacturers. Small-size distributors, instead, are not able to bias the industrial policy and planning of electronic manufacturers, and are therefore in a less competitive position making them takeover targets.

About 50 per cent of the revenues of the distribution are from North America, 31 per cent from Europe and the residual 19 per cent from Asia (Table 4.9).

Table 4.9   Electronics distribution by geographical area

	America	Europe	Asia	Total
% Arrow sales	50.4	32.1	17.5	100
% Avnet sales	50.7	30.7	18.6	100
% Total sector	50.3	31.0	18.7	100

Source: Datamonitor (2006).

The lower than expected figure attributed to Asia is not surprising given that not all of the sales of electronic components occur within the distribution channel. In particular, in the case of very large clients, the manufacturers often sign a contract directly with ODMs and EMS, with a disintermediation of the distributors. The majority of these sales takes place in Asia; even in other areas a part of the component sales is brought directly to the large OEM clients without the use of distribution channels.

COMPONENT DISTRIBUTOR: AVNET

Avnet is one of the most important world distributors operating within the electronics supply chain, with revenues exceeding 15 billion US dollars in 2007 and about 13 000 employees. As a consequence of its position in the sector, it is a link between different players, mainly between component suppliers and EMSs, ODMs and OEMs.

Founded in 1921 by Charles Avnet, during the last century the company has to face macro-economical and historical events, such as the 1929 financial crisis and WWII, that have obliged it to reconsider, from time to time, its own business and strategy. In 1959, Avnet was listed at the NYSE and in the following years it started a process of exogenous growth through acquisitions of companies such as Hamilton Electro (1960), Fairmount Motor Products (1963), Carol Wire & Cable and Time Electronic Sales (1968). In 1973, Avnet became the official distributor of Intel, thus accessing the activities related to the world of computers.

In 1990 Avnet completed a centralization and automation plan and set the stage for a spate of acquisitions that would redefine the global technology distribution industry. Avnet's sales and market shares have constantly grown over time thanks to strategic partnerships (for example IBM, entered in 2000) and acquisitions policy.

AVNET AND ITS SECTOR

Figure 4.11 shows the trend in Avnet's revenues in the decade 1998–2007 during which there was growth slightly greater than the distribution sector. Like the rest of the electronics industry, Avnet was affected by the 2002 downturn when sales dropped by more than 30 per cent with respect to the previous year, yet the growth process did not stop, and during the decade Avnet nearly tripled its revenues.

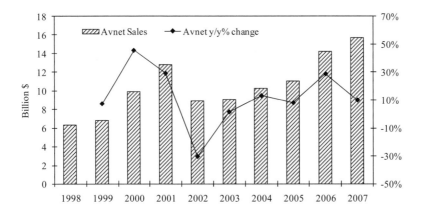

Source: Company reports.

Figure 4.11   Sales of Avnet

Figure 4.12 compares Avnet's revenues with those of the semiconductors market from 1973 to 2007: there is a strong correlation between the two series. The negative percent values are caused by macro-economic shocks such as the oil crisis, the Gulf war and the Internet bubble. It is also

particularly interesting to note that Avnet's trend is similar, even though
delayed, to the trend of the semiconductors market.

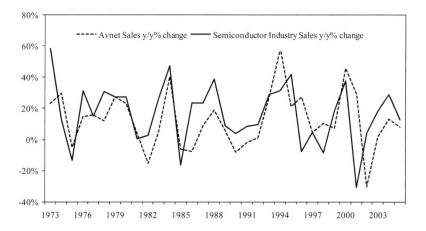

Source: Company reports, Semiconductor Industry Association, World Trade Statistics.

Figure 4.12   Change in sales of Avnet and the semiconductor industry

Regarding profitability (Figure 4.13), a reduction is clear in the pre-crisis
period culminating in an almost zero profit in 2002, later followed by a new
growth.

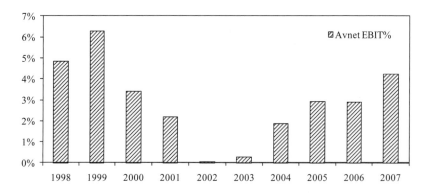

Source: Company reports, Datastream and Fortune 500.

Figure 4.13   EBIT margin of Avnet

THE AVNET–ARROW DUOPOLY

As described above, the sector of electronic distribution is highly concentrated, since the first four businesses, in terms of turnover, cover more than 65 per cent of the market. Arrow and Avnet hold a share higher than 50 per cent. The sector, even if it includes several competitors, has a *de facto* duopolistic market configuration, where the two largest companies face off and compete for the leading position.

Arrow and Avnet's prevalence has grown with time, as shown in Table 4.10. The market share held by Arrow and Avnet highlights a growth trend to the disadvantage of smaller businesses. The two companies are similar in terms of their dimensions, since they both pursue an exogenous growth strategy aimed at the acquisition of smaller competitors.

Table 4.10   Market shares of Avnet and Arrow

Year	Arrow (%)	Avnet (%)	Others (%)	Arrow and Avnet (%)
2000	23.5	16.6	59.9	40.1
2001	22.1	27.9	50.0	50.0
2002	17.6	21.3	61.1	39.0
2003	19.1	20.0	60.9	39.1
2004	21.1	20.4	58.5	41.5
2005	20.5	20.2	59.3	40.7
2006	23.5	24.7	51.8	48.2
2007	25.5	25.1	49.4	50.6

Source: Datastream and Datamonitor.

There are similar traits also from an organizational viewpoint. In fact, Arrow and Avnet are both divided into two divisions: Electronic Marketing and Technology Solutions for Avnet and Electronic Components and Enterprise Computing Solutions for Arrow. As far as the geographical reference areas are concerned, there is a substantial overlap (Table 4.11).

Both companies operate mainly in America and in the EMEA area and, to a lesser degree, in the Asian market. The situation can be traced back to the presence of large OEMs, EMSs and ODMs in Asia that interface directly with the component supplier market without the need for the distributors' intermediation. Recently both Avnet and Arrow have been trying to consolidate their role in this area too, paying special attention to newly industrialized countries, such as China and India, involved in the more recent acquisitions.

Table 4.11   Sales by geographical area of Avnet and Arrow

Market	Avnet	Arrow
America	50	54
EMEA	31	31
Asia-Pacific	19	15

Source: Company reports (2007).

Figure 4.14 compares Avnet and Arrow in terms of total assets turnover (Sales/Total Assets) vs. EBIT margin, showing a convergence trend.

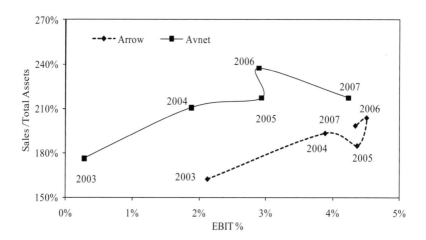

Source: Datastream.

Figure 4.14   Total assets turnover vs. EBIT margin of Avnet and Arrow

Arrow was able to capture a higher margin with respect to its main competitor, with an EBIT margin not far from 4 per cent since 2004, while Avnet reached this value only during the year 2007. Nonetheless, Avnet has been more efficient because, with the same sales figures, it engaged fewer assets.

GROWTH BY ACQUISITIONS

The growth strategy pursued by Avnet focuses on the exogenous path and M&A operations; this choice ensures the entry into new markets, on both a geographical and product type level. Moreover, through the acquisition of smaller competitors the level of competition is reduced.

Table 4.12   Main acquisitions of Avnet

Year	Acquired company	Headquarters	Transaction value ($M)
2000	Cosco Electronics	Hong Kong	30
2000	Marshall Industries	USA	647
2000	SEI Macro Group	UK	61
2000	Savoir Technology Group	USA	140
2001	VEBA Electronics Group	EMEA	740
2005	Memec Group Holdings	USA	663

Source: Company reports and Datamonitor.

Among the strategically important transactions is the acquisition of the Savoir Technology Group, one of the main distributors of IBM products. A different strategic goal was the one pursued by M&A transactions in 2000–2001, which enabled the company to develop the Asian market to take advantage of the significant growth in that area. After these operations, the revenues generated in the Asian area have doubled between 2000 and 2003. Furthermore, the acquisition of Memec Group Holdings allowed the company to control the Japanese market.

EFFICIENCY IN LOGISTICS

Infrastructure management is an element that deserves great attention, both in the case of Avnet and for all large component suppliers, because it requires the implementation of an efficient global logistics network, with warehouses placed in strategic positions that take into account proximity to clients and suppliers as well as transportation services. Avnet has its own warehouses, or logistic centers, based in the US, in the EMEA area and in Asia. Avnet uses centralized warehouses, with subsequent higher transportation costs, but at the same time they can ensure a better overall efficiency level.

Since 1987, this infrastructure management policy has given rise to large logistics centers, with more rapid order management; structures of this size have a higher level of automation and are located in strategic areas. To guarantee higher standards of service all over the world, Avnet has entered partnership agreements with fast delivery agencies.

Table 4.13 shows two indexes associated with the logistics efficiency: namely the inventory turnover (average days to sell the inventory) and the resulting inventory turnover ratio (number of times, on average, the inventory is sold during the period). There is a decreasing trend in inventory turnover days, due to improvement with time and a more correct forecasting of the demand and market cycles. Also the inventory turnover ratio shows an increase in efficiency, from 5.5 in 2000 to more than 8 in 2007.

Table 4.13   *Inventory turnover indexes of Avnet*

	2000	2001	2002	2003	2004	2005	2006	2007
Inventory turnover (days)	66.8	63.4	79.1	58.6	50.9	49.5	42.0	45.1
Inventory turnover ratio	5.5	5.8	4.6	6.2	7.2	7.4	8.7	8.1

Source: Company reports (2007).

Information systems play a fundamental role in logistics management because they enable transmission and sharing of information with clients and suppliers for the supply chain coordination.

Recently the role of logistics in the electronics industry has evolved from the conventional execution of the orders to the integrated management of the supply chain and of the client's pipeline. Accordingly, Avnet has implemented a logistics system which overturns the traditional ordering cycle. In the usual supply relationship it is the client who, based on his inventory and expected demand, sets the quantity and the schedule of his orders; with the new implementation, the supplier is fully responsible for these activities and autonomously manages the whole process of the client's warehouse provisioning.

The client, therefore, shares and defines his sales forecast with the distributor, and entrusts the inventory management. In this way, Avnet resizes the threat of non-intermediation, or rather, of a direct relationship between its clients, EMSs, ODMs and OEMs, and its suppliers, the component manufacturers.

NOTE

1. For companies operating at more than one level of the electronics supply chain, such as Samsung, Sony and Toshiba, the turnovers refer to their specific semiconductors divisions.

5.　Electronics Manufacturing Services

ELECTRONICS MANUFACTURING AND OUTSOURCING

During the early diffusion of electronic technologies, most of the supply chain activity, from design to after-sales support, was carried out almost entirely within companies, with no activity being outsourced. The business model was highly integrated vertically and the internal organization was in charge of the planning, construction and testing of the final product, managing both returns and maintenance servicing.

The feasibility and the actual development of every electronic product were dependent on the ability of each firm to preserve a satisfactory profit and to sell a product volume adequate to generate enough revenue to bear the R&D costs.

The increasing trend to outsourcing has changed the structure of the electronic supply chain significantly. The market segments occupied by the firms involved in outsourcing are becoming increasingly important, from R&D to product engineering, from the manufacturing of semi-finished products to the supply of end-products, from technical support to the management of after-sales services (Figure 5.1).

Prototype Design	Engineering Design	Procurement	PCB Assembly	System Assembly	Final Testing	Sales	After-sales Service
R&D and design activities of new products	Engineering of efficient products and productive processes	Sources for the supply of electronic components	Assembly of electronic boards (printed circuit boards)	Assembly of entire systems	Automatic functional and quality test	Market sales by OEMs	After-sales and repairing service

Figure 5.1　Electronics industry supply chain

The businesses known as electronics manufacturing services (EMSs) provide outsourcing services in the design, product engineering, production and after-sales segments. EMSs do not normally operate directly with their own brand name, but through their OEM clients, who assign them the control of one or more steps of the supply chain.

PROTOTYPE DESIGN

EMSs offer their technical support for the design and the development of electronic systems and products, based on technical and functional specifications as well as on target costing. EMSs' added-value services include co-design activities in partnership with the client's R&D department:

- Development of electronic know-how and transfer to the client of the intellectual property
- Studies on new products and innovative solutions
- Preliminary cost analysis by means of target costing techniques

In most cases the non-specialization of EMSs in a specific field and the pervasive nature of the electronic applications in different industrial areas allow them to apply the specific skills acquired in different sectors to added-value design activities. Thus, for instance, the very high reliability level expected by their customers in the aerospace field has a positive influence in production processes, bringing benefits to customers in the industrial sectors as well. Similarly, the solution given by an EMS for the problems associated with electromagnetic compatibility, typical of electronic power solutions, can also be useful in the electro-medical area. In other words, cross-fertilization among different sectors can enrich single industrial fields without impoverishing others.

ENGINEERING DESIGN

Often, OEMs entrust the process of electronic design and the construction of a prototype to their own R&D department, and then assign the task of transforming the prototype into a product to external firms; they have the responsibility to tune the product design details for mass production.

This implies the use of competences related to modern engineering methods, namely DFM[1] (design for manufacturability), DFT[2] (design for testability) and DFQ[3] (design for quality). Very often, re-engineering activity on existing products is carried out through the change of parts to improve quality and manufacturability, or by changing electronic components with newer or less expensive ones. The re-engineering of the projects is most often left to the EMSs, due to the cross-industry competence that they have acquired.

PROCUREMENT

In the cost classification of electronic equipments, the biggest fraction of the overall cost is usually generated by a limited group of electronic components. The knowledge of the global markets sourcing and the ability to purchase large quantities become crucial elements within the bargaining process. Often, the competences on the procurement activity are more developed by EMSs/ODMs than by the single OEM, because of the additive function related to a large client portfolio.

PCB AND SYSTEM ASSEMBLY

The evolution in electronics technology, in terms of functional complexity, size reduction and improved performance of the components, implies a growing complexity also from the manufacturer's viewpoint. For this reason, the assembly of electronic boards was historically the first outsourced activity as contract manufacturing.

FINAL TESTING

Unlike the first and simplest contract outsourcing activities, which only involved assembly labor, now the agreements with EMSs also assign the responsibility for full working tests through testing procedures checking the construction process (automatic optical inspection and X-ray tests during the welding process), the proper functioning (e.g. parametric tests and active stress tests), as well as environmental tests (e.g. temperature and humidity changes to detect any problems related to early defects in the components).

AFTER-SALES SERVICE

EMSs are sometimes required to take care of the after-sales support in terms of service or repairs of faulty or not perfectly functioning products. This task, if properly handled, guarantees the gathering of information that allows the investigation of specific aspects for continuous improvement of the product.

FACTS AND FIGURES

EMS firms establish business-to-business (B2B) relations with other industrial firms leaving them the relationship with the end-user. EMS companies function as strategic partners to original equipment manufacturers (OEMs) by providing them with a full range of services from contract design and manufacturing to post-manufacturing services. By using the services of EMS providers, OEMs can concentrate on their core competences such as research and development, brand building and marketing.

For instance, the microprocessor electronic system of a security system can be manufactured by an EMS firm for the company that installs security integrated systems. Or, the electronics in a vending system can be supplied by an EMS to the company actually working in this sector, who then incorporates its own systems as an added-value element to ensure the functioning, reliability and higher performance. Furthermore, an EMS can take on the construction of the electronic systems of modern elevators that, besides being versatile and reliable, respond to the increasingly strict safety norms. Within the wider electronics outsourcing industry, the economic values of the EMS segment (sales volumes, revenues, margins, investments, etc.) have largely changed over time, consistent with the outsourcing evolution.

REVENUES AND PROFITS

It has been estimated that during the 1990s the EMS sector achieved an annual aggregate turnover of approximately 10 billion dollars. Despite a reduction in the sector's sales associated with the world downturn of 2000–2002, the EMS sector has grown up to 180 billion dollars in the last decade before the 2008 credit crunch (Figure 5.2).

The end of growth is related to the world's economic recession. However, the 2000–2002 problematic situation involved the whole electronic equipment supply chain and was caused by many endogenous as well as exogenous factors related to the reference market. An increase in internal competition arose with the parallel development of the ODM model, which was just starting to consolidate and was detrimental to the margins of EMS firms. From a macro-economic standpoint the bursting of the Internet bubble, followed by the consequences of the September 11, 2001 tragedy, affected the economic growth. Leaving out the conjuncture, the strong growth in the EMS sector is not surprising since it has been supported by the great diffusion of electronic products over recent decades.

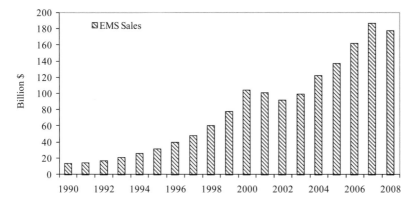

Source: iSuppli, Technology Forecasters.

Figure 5.2   Sales of EMSs

The development of the EMS sector was also positively affected by the contribution of the world's largest EMS, Foxconn, a Taiwan-based business whose turnover was less than 200 million dollars in 1994 and, with a 1994–2007 CAGR as high as 54 per cent, reached 52 billion dollars in revenue in 2007. Figure 5.3 shows the effect of Foxconn on the EMS global revenue trend; it is evident that the growth of this sector is directly linked to that of the leader company as the 2001–2007 CAGR of the EMS sector was as high as 10.7 per cent, while the growth was equal to 5.6 per cent after deducting the contribution of Foxconn. Over the same time period the US GDP had an average growth of 2.6 per cent and the world GDP grew by about 4 per cent. From these figures we can deduct that the position of the EMS sector along the life cycle is near that of the most important mature industrial sectors (automotive, personal computing, large-scale retail trade, etc.).

The analysis of several indicators highlights how electronics outsourcing, three decades since its birth, has concluded the typical fast development stage of the startup period of new activities and has entered a stage of more stable moderate growth. However, firms like Foxconn have shown that new growth is possible even in mature contexts. New entrepreneurial ventures, different business models, development strategies consistent with opportunities coming from technological innovations, and new consumers' trends can lead, if not the entire industry, at least single entrepreneurial companies to a renewal phase.

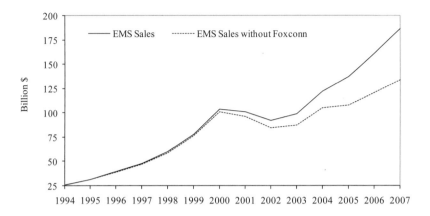

Source: Orbis, iSuppli, Technology Forecasters.

Figure 5.3   Sales of EMSs without Foxconn

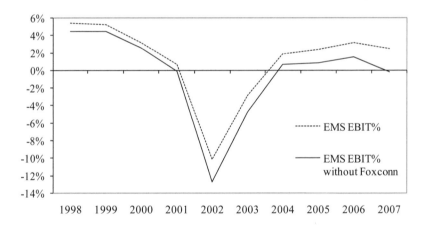

Source: Orbis and Lexis Nexis.

Figure 5.4   Cumulated EBIT margin of Top Class EMSs

The trend of economic profits cumulated by the nine largest EMS firms (Top Class EMS) highlights a positive outcome after the 2000–2002 downturn and shows the following recovery (Figure 5.4). Profitability and sales have also been positively affected by the incidence of Foxconn.

EMS providers are assuming an increasingly important role and making a significant impact on manufacturing concerns worldwide. The action areas for EMS businesses are continuously evolving across many industries:

- Industrial automation
- Industrial computers
- Automotive
- Home and building automation
- Traffic control
- Consumer devices
- Railways and transportation
- Machinery and tools
- Personal and industrial computers
- Aerospace systems
- Security and alarm systems
- Medical and life-support systems
- Electronic instruments
- Professional appliances
- Utilities and power
- Telecommunications
- Vending machines

The pervasiveness of electronic applications explains the fast growth that occurred in the electronics outsourcing sector in the 1990s as well as the development and diffusion of products related not only to the manufacturing and electronics industries, but also to services, telecommunications and IT.

Table 5.1 highlights the contribution given to the EMS sector by the information technology industry (personal computers, peripherals, etc.) and by consumer devices (digital cameras, MP3 players, GPS portable navigators etc.). The level of outsourcing in the cost structure is related to the specific sector, as highlighted in the right column of the abovementioned table, showing the share of the costs associated with EMS services compared to the total costs of the sector.

Concerning localization, there is a visible trend towards a change in the end markets and an increase of revenue coming from Asian businesses. In early 2000, US EMSs achieved a turnover of almost half of the total revenues, then decreased to 30 per cent (Figure 5.5). However, the simultaneous growth of the sector has allowed US businesses to preserve a positive trend, with an average annual growth of 4.4 per cent from 2002 through 2008 (Table 5.2). In Europe the world-based share has remained stable, growing in absolute value.

Table 5.1   Sales of EMSs by business segment

	EMSs' sales ($M)	EMSs' costs on sector total costs (%)
Information technology	49 819	20.7
Consumer devices	13 634	6.9
Industrial applications	10 580	5.6
Wireless communications	27 138	22.3
Cable communications	24 847	39.5
Automotive	2 737	4.7

Source: iSuppli (2006).

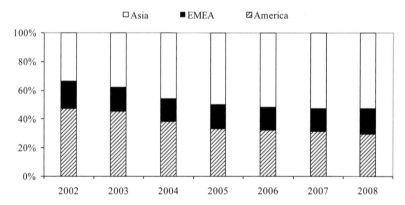

Source: iSuppli and Technology Forecasters.

Figure 5.5   EMS market shares by geographical area

The development of the sector is due largely to Asian EMSs, who experienced a CAGR of 21.8 per cent from 2002 to 2008. The main reason was the growing openness to international trade and to the development of emerging economies, especially those of China and India. Other factors, such as the availability of low-cost labor and the specific capability in electronic manufacturing, have helped Asian-based EMSs to achieve a share of up to 50 per cent of the electronics outsourcing market.

Table 5.2   Sales of EMSs by geographical area

Sales ($M)	2002	2003	2004	2005	2006	2007	2008	CAGR (%)
America	43 200	44 600	46 500	45 200	49 600	54 700	55 900	4.4
EMEA	17 500	16 800	19 600	23 300	24 800	28 200	34 700	12.1
Asia	31 300	37 600	56 300	68 600	80 700	93 600	102 200	21.8
Total	92 000	99 000	122 400	137 100	155 100	176 500	192 800	13.1

Source: iSuppli and Technology Forecasters.

DIMENSIONAL CLUSTERING

The growth of electronics outsourcing is promoted by the pervasiveness of electronic technologies in many industrial as well as consumer products. The trend of many manufacturers to assign a growing number of activities to EMSs has increased dramatically. Manufacturing contracts have become more and more specific and include electronic engineering services, manufacturing activities, integration into more complex sub-systems and after-sales services.

Due to the heterogeneity of their target sectors, the focus of EMSs on the production of specific goods with similar features is strategic. Actually, because of the variety of products requested with respect to performance, planning, volume and delivery times, EMSs have differentiated and specialized over the years, focusing on the demand suited to their structural and dimensional characteristics. A dimensional clustering is based on the sector concentration and the turnover of the single EMSs.

Table 5.3   Dimensional clustering of EMSs

	Sales ($M)	Main characteristics
Top Class EMSs	> 1000	Mass market productions, intellectual property
Global Class EMSs	10–1000	Intermediate volumes, intellectual property, flexibility
Local Class EMSs	< 10	Limited volumes, contract manufacturing, flexibility

Table 5.3 shows three dimensional industry segments (Top, Global and Local Class), each of them showing its own characteristics in terms of production rate, management flexibility, contribution of intellectual property.

TOP CLASS EMSs

Top Class EMSs include firms with revenues exceeding 1 billion US dollars. According to 2007 data, the largest segment includes the EMS firms listed in Table 2.4, which all together represent about 70 per cent of the world's EMS turnover. The clients of Top Class EMSs are among the world's largest companies involved in information technology, mobile communications, consumer devices and automotive. They all operate in mass markets and in sectors with extremely high production volumes.

Top Class EMSs have also grown as a consequence of the M&A process and have subsequently attained strategic positions in domains that are characterized by economies of scale and product standardization. Their fast growth has been favored by the incorporation of factories and plants previously owned by OEM clients. Among the last decade's many growth-by-acquisition operations, in 1998 Jabil Circuit, an EMS multinational, acquired the US and Italian Hewlett-Packard factories dedicated to the assembly of electronic boards for laser printers, obtaining a three-year contract for the supply of these products. In 2000, the European Commission authorized the operation through which Celestica, an EMS Canadian firm, acquired IBM's activities in Italy dedicated to the production of printed circuits, to the assembly and testing of servers and IBM's activities in Rochester, USA, dedicated to the assembly of electronic boards and to the related test services.

GLOBAL CLASS EMS

There are a large number of EMS firms that are of relevant size though they generate revenues less than a billion dollars a year. They have implemented a different growth strategy from that of the Top Class EMSs. They have a turnover exceeding 10 million dollars and are dedicated to the production of complex electronic boards and systems, at medium and medium–high volumes, for the industrial sector and the medical, building automation, railway, safety and vending industries. Both from demand side, in terms of potential customers, and supply side, in terms of capability to propose products and services, the differences between Top Class and Global Class EMSs are significant.

The main firms within the Global Class segment are listed in Table 5.4.

Table 5.4   Main Global Class EMSs

	Sales 2007 ($M)	EBIT margin (%)	Employees	Headquarters	Stock market
Kinpo Electronics	841	4.7	8 298	Taiwan	Taiwan SE
Nam Tai	781	5.5	n.a.	Hong Kong	Hong Kong SE
CTS	686	5.2	4 746	USA	NYSE
Jurong	661	5.4	n.a.	Singapore	Singapore SE
Alco	655	4.9	9 600	Hong Kong	Hong Kong SE
Beyonics	604	3.4	n.a.	Singapore	Singapore SE
Multi-Fineline	508	0.3	16 021	USA	NASDAQ
Sypris Solution	436	−0.1	n.a.	USA	NASDAQ
Wong's Intl.	432	3.0	6 700	Hong Kong	Hong Kong SE
Neways Electronics	412	7.5	776	Netherlands	Euronext
RadiSys	397	2.3	24 300	USA	NASDAQ
Info-Tek	355	0.9	n.a.	Taiwan	Taiwan SE
Ngai Lik	325	−6.7	n.a.	Hong Kong	Hong Kong SE
SMTC	256	2.7	2 238	USA	NASDAQ
LaBarge	235	10.8	1 500	USA	Nyse AMEX
Raven	218	17.9	1 260	USA	NASDAQ
Keytronic	202	3.4	1 200	USA	NASDAQ
Sparton	200	−3.2	900	USA	NASDAQ
DDI	181	1.5	n.a.	USA	NASDAQ
Sigmaton	166	3.1	1 300	USA	NASDAQ
Simclar	136	4.1	2 470	USA	NASDAQ
Noretech	118	3.0	n.a.	USA	NASDAQ

Source: Datastream.

Although smaller than Top Class EMSs, Global Class EMSs have a global dimension both in terms of offerings (procurement and manufacturing in

different geographical areas) and demand (international clients). They have
chosen a strategic position that focuses on service and added value over large
volumes, and acquire factory facilities often delocalized in low-labor-cost
countries in order to maintain an extremely high competitiveness.

Unlike Top Class EMSs that have based their growth on exogenous
processes through mergers and acquisitions, Global Class EMSs have
preferred organic expansion strategies. The growth comparison of the two
segments (Figure 5.6) clearly shows that they have applied different
expansion strategies.

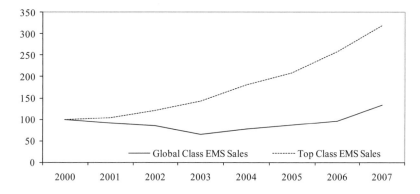

Source: iSuppli, Technology Forecasters.

Figure 5.6   Growth of Top Class and Global Class EMSs (2000=100)

Global Class EMSs have played a very important role in the diffusion of
electronic technologies in non-mass markets. For example, the supply of
electronic components for electro-medical and life support equipment does
not require a high production capacity, such as in the case of mobile phones,
but rather a superior level of quality and engineering. A similar remark could
be made with reference to the sectors that deal with traffic control, railway
transportation, tool machinery and aero-space systems.

The trend in manufacturing partnership has been growing steadily as
OEMs strive to reduce time-to-market, time-to-volume, flexibility and
quality in the advanced technology evolution services and strategic business
solutions to maintain their competitive advantages.

Global Class EMSs have established their relationships and processes
focusing on flexibility, a crucial feature when production lines need to be
equipped for low volumes and frequent product changes. Historically, the
flexibility has allowed higher margins than Top Class EMSs, though a

convergence trend between the two sub-segments is clearly evident (Figure 5.7).

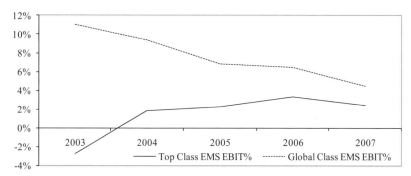

Source: iSuppli, Technology Forecasters.

Figure 5.7   EBIT margin of Top and Global Class EMSs

LOCAL CLASS EMSs

Local Class EMSs have a turnover below 10 million US dollars and they operate in small and local domains, which are in geographical areas not far from their facilities. Their client portfolios are usually restricted, and often include a single firm, normally located nearby, with whom they have a reduced bargaining power.

Often, Local Class EMSs' activity is similar to that of contract manufacturing, typical of small enterprises that process raw materials (electronic components), subcontracted by OEMs. Occasionally, they are paid for labor costs and the depreciation of production plants. Normally, they give no added value in terms of product intellectual property. Only in some cases, characterized by high specialization and small production volumes, do small enterprises acquire all the traits of an EMS and also offer added-value services. Despite the large number of small and micro enterprises, their influence on EMS sector total revenue is negligible.

TOP CLASS SEGMENT: FOXCONN

Hon Hai Precision Industry, known by the commercial brand Foxconn, is the leader in the electronics manufacturing services sector in terms of turnover and growth rate. In 1974, Terry Guo, chairman of the company, founded the

Hon Hai Plastics Corporation in Taiwan in order to start the production of plastic components for televisions. In 1981, Foxconn also started manufacturing connectors for the computer industry; this decision turned out to be successful as it generated a turnover increase in a rapidly expanding sector, allowing the company to establish business relationships with the most important computer manufacturers worldwide.

In the early 1990s, the Taiwan company consolidated its position by investing in production plants in China, thereby taking advantage of low labor costs. It also founded research centers in Japan and in the USA and approached the financial markets going public on the Taiwan Stock Exchange. In the same period, Foxconn started to manufacture components for personal computers and soon became the world leader in this sector, thanks to low production costs and satisfactory quality standards. At the end of the 1990s, the company invested in new production facilities in the UK, Ireland, the USA and the Czech Republic.

While maintaining its leadership in the personal computers sector, in 2001 Foxconn diversified its portfolio by also starting to manufacture components for the mobile phone sector; the strategic approach of that period was focused on computers, communication and consumer electronics. In 2003, Foxconn started a process of external growth through some acquisitions that ensured the company its leadership position in terms of turnover in the EMS sector. In February 2005, the Taiwanese company acquired Antec Electronic Systems, one of the main manufacturers of car electronic components, which allowed it access to the automotive industry. In 2006, with the acquisition of Premier Image Technology, a leader company in the sector of digital cameras, Foxconn further extended its areas of action.

Between 1998 and 2000, Foxconn was the sixth company in the EMS sales ranking. In 2004 the company had already become a market leader, widening the gap with its competitors year after year. In 2005, it was in 371st position in the Fortune 500 world classification and in 14th position in the electronics industry. In 2007, it had already reached the 154th position worldwide and the 9th in its sector. Again, according to Info Tech 100, the company is in 3rd position for its 2004–2005 turnover growth (corresponding to 63 per cent), immediately following High Tech Computer (HTC) and Google.

Foxconn is focused on motherboards for personal computers, PC elements, notebooks, LCD monitors, MP3s, videogame consoles and cellular phones for the major international OEMs, such as Apple, Ford, Intel, Nokia and Sony. In little more than twenty years Foxconn has become an EMS world leader, with a turnover exceeding 52 billion dollars and 550 000 employees.

FOXCONN AND ITS COMPETITIVE SCENARIO

Figure 5.8 shows Foxconn's sales trend from 1998 to 2007: in ten years the company has grown from an annual turnover slightly above 1 billion US dollars to more than 52 billion. The annual growth is always above 28 per cent; Foxconn's average CAGR, calculated from 1998 to 2007, reached as high as 51 per cent, an important figure taking into account that the whole EMS sector has grown, over the same years, by 13 per cent. Foxconn, therefore, stands out as a real outlier in the competition scenario of electronics outsourcing, able not only to redefine the sector limits but also to condition its evolution.

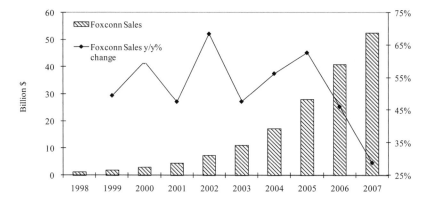

Source: Orbis.

Figure 5.8   Sales of Foxconn

Table 5.5 shows the list of the main EMS firms in order of their 2007 turnover: Foxconn's revenues were 70 per cent more than Flextronics', the second EMS provider, and five times that of Jabil's and Sanmina–Sci's revenues, which were in third and fourth position, respectively. The dominance of Foxconn in this sector is evident also in the analysis of the 30 per cent growth in its 2007 turnover. Only Flextronics had an apparently higher growth, due to its 2006 merger with Solectron. In terms of market form, a transformation towards a duopoly with a competitive fringe seems to be taking shape. In fact, in 2007, the top businesses of the sector owned more than 70 per cent of the market – Foxconn held 28.1 per cent while Flextronics, by the time it merged with Solectron, held a 15.7 per cent share; the two figures correspond to 43.8 per cent of the whole market.

Table 5.5   Main competitors of Foxconn

	Sales 2007 ($M)	Sales growth (%)	CAGR (%) 1998–2007	EBIT (%) 2007	Average EBIT (%) 1998/2007
Foxconn	52 495	29.6	52.3	6.3	6.8
Flextronics	29 336	51.7	36.7	0.6	0.4
Jabil Circuit	12 291	19.7	28.6	1.5	3.0
Sanmina–SCI	10 384	−5.2	34.5	−9.2	n.a.
Celestica	8 684	1.5	11.9	0.9	−1.2
Elcoteq	5 911	4.6	32.7	−2.6	0.6
Benchmark	2 916	0.3	21.0	3.6	3.7
Venture Manufacturing	2 690	32.1	22.2	8.0	7.8
USI	2 008	23.0	n.a.	3.8	n.a.

Source: Orbis.

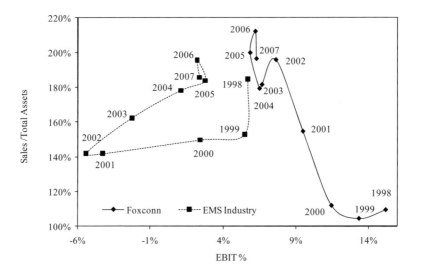

Source: Orbis.

Figure 5.9   Total assets turnover vs. EBIT margin of Foxconn

Foxconn has significantly higher economic results compared to other competitors, who in some cases even show negative performances. It is clear, therefore, that the company's impressive dimensional growth has not been carried out as a result of the loss of its margins, but on the contrary, operational efficiency is crucial for Foxconn's paradigm.

Both Foxconn and the whole EMS sector diminished their margins in the 2000–2002 period (Figure 5.9); however, while for Foxconn this reduction was minimal, the EMS market experienced a negative EBIT margin. Improvement in terms of asset utilization is remarkable, highlighting an extraordinary increase in the efficiency of the whole sector also in relation to the highly competitive pressure that, despite improvements in the processes, has generated a reduction in the margins.

FOXCONN: EMS OR ODM?

At the beginning of the new century, the ODM segment acquired part of the revenues that were formerly intended for the EMS segment. For this reason several Top Class EMS, among them Foxconn, have completed some acquisitions with the aim of maintaining a strong competitive position in the mass-market business areas specific to the ODM segment. It is therefore difficult to clearly distinguish between EMSs and ODMs, since a convergence of the two sectors is currently taking place. Considering the large dimension of Foxconn, the classification as an EMS or an ODM is the origin of major changes in growth figures and in subsequent considerations about strategy.

Table 5.6   *Economic data of the EMS and ODM industries (Foxconn as ODM)*

	EMS 2006 (%)	ODM 2006 %
Sales growth	7.7	23.1
Net profit/sales	1.5	3.3
Return on assets	2.6	4.1
Return on invested capital	4.4	6.2
Inventory turnover	8.5	12.8

Source: Technology Forecasters.

Should Foxconn be considered as an ODM, Table 5.6 shows that 2006 would have been characterized by an even better performance of the ODM segment relative to the EMS. In particular, the average turnover growth in 2006, compared to the previous year, is limited to 7.7 per cent for the EMS sector, while it is more than 23 per cent for the ODM sector. The profitability of the ODM sector is more than double that of the EMSs, and every index listed in the table shows that the ODM sector is more attractive than the EMS one, so much so as to persuade EMS companies to adopt the typical ODM strategies and business models.

Had the above data been processed including Foxconn in the EMS category, variations would be substantial, as we can easily infer from Table 5.7 that shows the results of a double simulation; in the first one Foxconn is considered as an ODM, in the second, an EMS. If Foxconn is considered an EMS the results of the two segments appear to be more balanced.

Table 5.7   *Comparison between the EMS and ODM industries (Foxconn as ODM or EMS)*

	Foxconn as ODM (2006)	Foxconn as EMS (2006)
ODM sector		
Growth in revenues	23.1	21.7
Net profit/revenues	3.3	2.4
EMS sector		
Growth in revenues	7.7	12.2
Net profit/revenues	1.5	2.7

Source: Technology Forecasters.

The remarkable importance of the Taiwanese company in the EMS sector is not surprising, considering the data shown in Figure 5.3, which compares the growth of the EMS sector sales with and without Foxconn. Starting in the year 2000, the results of the whole EMS sector strongly depend on those of the market leader.

Foxconn's strategy, due to its particular business model and to a less clear distinction between the Top Class EMS and the ODM sectors, can be referred to by the wording 'Joint Design Manufacturing', an emerging model where the OEM client and the electronics outsourcing firm cooperate with their distinct competences on the project of a product.

STRESS ON SERVICE AND ACQUISITIONS

A distinctive element of Foxconn's strategy is customer service, achieved also through an acquisition policy focused on the clients they want to serve.

In 2003, Foxconn acquired Eimo, a Finnish firm closely linked to Nokia. In doing so, it not only ensured access to the market of mobile phones, but also increased the level of service to one of its most important clients. A similar statement can be applied to the acquisition of Motorola Mexican Mobile and to subsequent agreements with Motorola.

In 2004, with the acquisition of Ambit Microsystems (routers, modems, network components), Foxconn aimed to reinforce its relationship with Cisco, thanks to the vertical integration in that sector.

In 2005, the Taiwanese company purchased Chi Mei Communications Systems, a manufacturer of mobile phone equipment linked to Motorola. In this way, Foxconn enhanced its competitiveness with respect to the other Motorola suppliers, ensuring not only production activity, but also the added value of design. Another meaningful operation, with a value exceeding a billion dollars, was the acquisition of Premier Image Technology, the largest Taiwanese business in the production of digital cameras. Through this acquisition, Foxconn, in addition to entering a new market, set out to satisfy Olympus's and Sony's requests.

Also, the 2007 acquisition of G-Tech offered Foxconn an opportunity to expand; the acquired business, based in Taiwan, operates in the LCD screen field and had planned its own presence in the growing market of touch screens.

All this activity clearly shows that Foxconn wanted to seize new opportunities in order to expand its business. After confirming its position in the computer and consumer device sectors, it is now trying to emerge in the domains of communication devices and digital cameras, two business areas that are still growing.

CHINA: THE FIRST-MOVER ADVANTAGE

Low labor costs led many companies to start production units in China, Malaysia, Philippines and Korea. Indeed, 75 per cent of the 2007 production of Taiwanese ODMs was done in China.

Among electronics outsourcing businesses, from both the ODM and the EMS sectors, Foxconn was one of the first companies to set up production facilities in China, gaining a large competitive advantage thanks to the low cost of labor. The company started its first plant in 1993, and later built five industrial parks with a shared purchasing base. Foxconn has therefore been able to compete more effectively than its competitors. In 2004, 75 per cent of its production was done in China, while Flextronics and Solectron manufactured only 40 per cent and 27 per cent, respectively, of their products in China. Foxconn also benefits from delocalization in terms of domestic sales, as 20 per cent of the 2007 production was directed to China, one of the world's fastest growing countries.

At the beginning of 2007, Foxconn owned 23 production plants: one in Taiwan, representing its headquarters, and the others in China, the Czech Republic, Hungary, Mexico, Brazil, India and Vietnam. The locations outside of China respond primarily to the logic of service needs in terms of global logistics, because they serve plants that have already been set up by the clients in those same countries.

VERTICALIZATION STRATEGY

In order to pursue a growth strategy, Foxconn seems to grasp any opportunity offered by the market to enter into new business areas even through acquisitions. The latest acquisitions were consistent with this plan, where the final purpose is to become a fully integrated EMS firm.

Foxconn's vertical business model is very attractive to its clients since it allows them to have a single supplier for the entire production, whose fast reaction is guaranteed over the control of all the technologies and the production processes involved. The goal is to offer a wide range of customer services and assistance in order to avoid the problems associated with the coordination of outsourcing suppliers, such as unclear responsibilities, delays and misunderstandings.

What distinguishes Foxconn, therefore, is its high level of verticalization: the company's aim is to carry out end-to-end operations, from design to production and after-sales service and repairs.

THE ENTREPRENEURIAL DIMENSION

The growth and success of Foxconn is also due to the entrepreneurial talent of its founder and Chairman, Terry Guo. Over the years, his ideas, charisma and ambitions have been crucial to the success of the company. At the age of

24, Guo founded a small company with ten employees and started to manufacture plastic parts for TV sets. But his ability to predict market evolution soon persuaded him to invest in the new personal computers industry. From the very beginning, one of Foxconn's characteristics was the obsession with costs, which led Guo to become one of the first Taiwanese businessmen to delocalize his production plants to China with the aim of benefiting from the low labor costs.

One of the particular entrepreneurial characteristics of the Foxconn phenomenon is represented by the relationship between ownership and control, in other words by the overlapping of the two functions in the figure of Terry Guo. In most of the Top Class EMS competitors, the company often has a spread ownership, and therefore the running of the activities is left to the managers, who do not always have shares or stock options.

SUSTAINABLE GROWTH

The crucial issue about Foxconn's strategy, which includes 'first mover' traits, is to maintain a sustainable long-term advantage within a growing market, cost leadership, relationships with big clients and technological competence. It is useful to evaluate the scenario of extended competition, according to Porter (1980).

- *Direct competitors*
  The competitors' strength is certainly not to be ignored, especially after the Flextronics–Solectron merger. In the EMS sector, OEMs can always replace their suppliers. However, Foxconn's growth is superior to the growth of the electronics outsourcing industry, thus highlighting that the company's market share is still growing, thanks to cost and competence levels. The set of competences described seem to be at the base of the increase in the competitive advantage with respect to direct competitors.
- *Clients' bargaining power*
  The clients' contractual power is quite high and will remain as such, at least as long as OEM clients hold the competency involved in the production process entrusted to EMSs. Also, the limited number of clients grants each of them a strong negotiating power with Foxconn that would have to give up a significant part of its revenues should it lose one client.
- *Suppliers' bargaining power*
  Foxconn benefits from the sales of components and modules as well as from the large volumes of EMS products that allows it to have a strong bargaining power with the suppliers. In the electronics outsourcing

industry usually the component suppliers hold a valuable position with respect to their customers; however, in the specific case of Foxconn, their position is different due to the company's production volumes, which can significantly affect the revenues of the component suppliers.

- *New entrants*
  There seem to exist high barriers preventing entry into the business of Top Class EMSs; it is a mass-market, low profit, capital-intensive sector which therefore requires highly efficient production processes. Due to its relationships with its suppliers, Foxconn holds a competitive advantage in terms of cost, also thanks to its significant experience curve, economies of scale and access to distribution. It is unlikely that the Top Class EMS segment can attract businessmen and investors, because of the large investments it requires and its limited profitability, not to mention the very high concentration already in place.

- *Threat of substitute products*
  A product made by an EMS can be replaced as a consequence of technological evolutions and of the migration of intellectual properties from the system to the component, making the product itself useless or obsolete. Foxconn, however, owns the competences to anticipate evolutions concerning its customers by means of new solutions that make the products cheaper and more effective.

Porter's analysis does not fully account for such a complex phenomenon, which is unique also in its growth trend. There are legitimate worries concerning the impact of another possible SARS epidemic in China, reduced growth in the world's economy due to the 2008–2009 recession, and about Foxconn's ability to act as a global EMS in terms of distribution. Another problem for Foxconn could be related to the founder's succession. The company has grown mainly due to the entrepreneurial view of its founder, who has run it with his personal vision and style; the change to a managerial organization might prove to be critical for the business.

One of the main criticalities of Foxconn lies in its ability to face the fast growth of the business and the increase in competences and human resources that such growth requires. An increase in staff productivity would not be enough to maintain the growth rate, but, on the contrary, it would be necessary to find new human resources, with training and integration problems related to the various ethnic groups, languages and settings of the company's different production sites. Moreover, recently the high growth rate has been difficult in terms of employee organization and education.

Furthermore, the issue of selecting clients has led to a somewhat risky concentration and to a dependence of the markets on the same clients. Therefore, there are many points in support of the sustainability of the long-term competitive advantage, but there are also as many reasons to doubt that Foxconn will be able to maintain such high development rates for a long period of time, apart from the macro-economic factors that could present difficulties in sustaining that growth.

GLOBAL CLASS SEGMENT: EUTRON

Eutron[4] is a European company operating in electronics outsourcing and, in particular, in the Global Class EMS segment, that is, in the intermediate dimensional class between Top Class EMSs (turnover one billion US dollars and more) and Local Class EMSs (turnover less than ten million US dollars). The company has chosen a strategic position that focuses on service and added value over large volumes, acquiring factory facilities in China in order to maintain an extremely high competitiveness.

It was founded in 1987 by a team of researchers[5] as an entrepreneurial venture in the field of advanced digital microelectronics applications (photonics, wireless digital transfer, and digital encryption). The company has since grown over the years through different evolutionary stages until reaching the position it holds in the domain of medium-sized firms within the electronics manufacturing services industry, with a special talent for the supply of added value services.

Eutron manufactures professional electronic equipment dedicated to special applications, mainly industrial ones; products are the result of specific designs and made for the single client's exclusive use. The company cooperates, from preliminary steps, in both the production of devices previously designed and industrialized by the OEM client and the supply of special products designed to meet specific functionalities.

For many sectors, such as tools and industrial machinery, vending systems, automation and domotics, Eutron manufactures 'embedded electronics'; microelectronic technologies are used to produce the electronic devices incorporated inside machines, processes, and in any other contexts.

TOWARDS THE EMS MODEL

Eutron's growth in its 20 years of business is consistent with the theories that attribute the renewal mechanisms to entrepreneurial factors which aim at overcoming the typical business maturity which every company predictably experiences. The strategic changes in the business models that the company has implemented over the years has allowed virtually non-stop growth (Figure 5.10).

Four different growth phases can be identified:

- Focus on R&D
- Product and process engineering
- Manufacturing
- Extension of services towards the EMS model

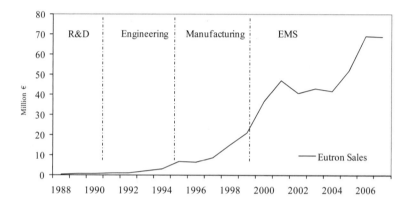

Source: Company reports.

Figure 5.10   Stages towards the EMS model of Eutron

- *1988–1992: Emphasis on R&D*
  In the years immediately following the foundation of Eutron, consistent with the fact that the founders were coming from research centers, the company offered electronic research and design services at an advanced level in both the industrial and the telecommunication sectors, supporting the transfer process of new electronic technologies and design techniques. In that period, the company had a dozen of employees, mainly electronic researchers and engineers; they achieved a turnover of one million euros. The added value, almost entirely intangible, was generated by technological design and consultancy activities. The manufacturing supply was limited to few prototypes of the electronic boards designed.
- *1993–1997: Product and process engineering*
  Along with R&D services, the company carried out a first transformation towards the EMS model, combining research with engineering competences. Customers would no longer be supplied only with the project for electronic devices or systems, but the company also

committed to develop the whole engineering know-how for the next industrial mass-market production. Product and process engineering, testing and pre-production activities were then associated with production activities, allowing the client mass production. Through this extension of client services, sales increased to ten million euros with approximately 50 employees.

- *1998–2002: Industrial manufacturing*
  In the late 1990s, through the acquisition of a manufacturing company and electronic production plants to support the expected growth, Eutron pursued a downstream integration to engage another segment of the value chain. The strategic goal was to reinforce and consolidate the growth path, gaining the profits associated not only with design activities, because they are interesting but occasional and not repetitive, but also the profits coming from production activities which, although lower in percentage terms, are more continuous and repetitive. Thanks to the availability to supply production services, Eutron became one of the few electronics outsourcing firms able to provide a range of services from research to design, product engineering, process engineering and production. The company's full responsibility up to the production phase allowed a further increase in revenues that exceeded 40 million euros with 200 employees.

- *2003–2007: Extension of services towards the EMS model*
  A new extension within the value chain through the widening of the services supplied has characterized the most recent period. The achievement of the electronics manufacturing services model was carried out downstream by means of fast prototyping project integrated services, automatic testing systems and, above all, after-sales services. The evolution allowed the customers to gain access to the latest equipment, process knowledge and manufacturing know-how without having to make substantial investments. The competitive advantage over the competitors has allowed the company to acquire large customers and further growth, in terms of volumes, of up to about 70 million euros. The increase in production, and at the same time the maintenance of a price competition level, was achieved through the localization of other production units in China, besides the existing ones in Europe. Based on the volume of its revenues, the internationalization of its offerings and the typology of its clients, Eutron can be listed within the segment of Global Class EMSs.

The growth of the company's turnover (Figure 5.11) is consistent with that of the EMS segment; a constant growth is shown over the two decades, with the exclusion of the downturn period from 2000 to 2002.

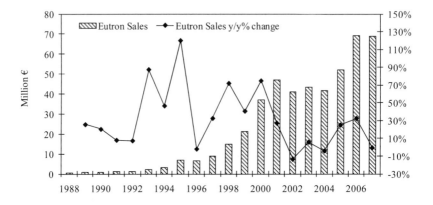

Source: Company reports.

Figure 5.11   Sales of Eutron

Although the EMS sector trend mainly characterizes the Top Class firms (eighty per cent of the total turnover), the industry effect also involves smaller firms that share several exogenous factors with them.

- Consistent with the trend expressed by 'Moore's Law', the evolution of microelectronic technologies in the years 1988–2008 has made a number of applications technically and economically possible, thanks to the reduction in the size and cost of electronic devices. The application range of electronics outsourcing services has expanded accordingly.
- The opening of new markets and the globalization of production factors have allowed access to countries with lower labor costs and to new markets for Western companies. Therefore, the demand for electronic applications has significantly increased in both mass-market products (Top Class EMSs/ODMs) and in specific and industrial applications (Global Class EMSs).
- Despite the downturn periods, the world economy is growing again. The electronics outsourcing sector also has positive growth forecasts through all its dimensional clusters.

Table 5.8 compares Eutron's annual growth rate with that of the reference sector and, for the sake of mere comparison, with the world's economy growth. It reveals that, with the exclusion of the most recent period, 2003–2007, the growth of the company has been significantly higher than that of the whole sector.

Table 5.8   *Growth rates of Eutron*

	Eutron sales CAGR (%)	EMS industry sales CAGR (%)	World GPD CAGR (%)
1988–1992	15.2	11.2	2.2
1993–1997	43.1	23.7	3.7
1998–2002	28.4	11.3	3.6
2003–2007	12.3	15.5	5.0
1988–2007	29.8	16.3	3.5

Source: Company reports, Amadeus, Technology Forecasters and International Monetary Fund.

It should be noted that the CAGR evaluation techniques do not consider the intermediate trend; nevertheless it is interesting to observe that in its twenty-year history Eutron has grown with an average rate of almost 30 per cent, that is, almost double with respect to the EMS sector, and about nine times the growth of the world's economy. A more meaningful comparison can be found in Figure 5.12, which compares the growth trends of the company and of the sector, both normalized with a base of 100 in 1998.

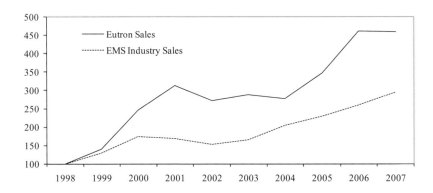

Source: Company reports, Orbis.

Figure 5.12   *Growth of Eutron and EMS industry (1998=100)*

Relating to economic margins, the profitability decrease trend in the EMS sector is shared by all segments, regardless of the dimensional characteristics. The EMS industry is close to maturity and its margins can grow only moderately because of both the effect of efficiency parameters and the market concentration. Furthermore, where Global Class EMSs are concerned, the net operational profit on the turnover (EBIT margin) has progressively decreased while it has remained higher than that of the EMS industry. These remarks are also valid for Eutron, which in 2000–2007 achieved an average economic result of 4 per cent; the margins have been higher than in the reference sector (Figure 5.13). The growing trend of the economic result confirms the validity of the strategic, organizational and dimensional difference of the company from that of Top Class EMSs.

It is interesting to note Eutron's relatively high profitability with respect to the sector, especially in the years 2000–2002, when the sector showed losses of around 10 per cent. This is partly due to the develop of intellectual property and supply design activities in alliance with the clients with the aim of finalizing shared projects with a common knowledge foundation.

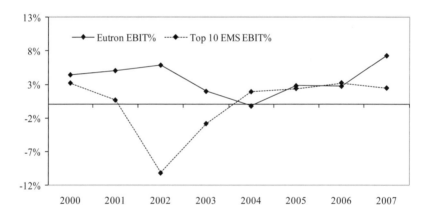

Source: Company reports, Orbis.

Figure 5.13   EBIT margin of Eutron and EMS industry

Figure 5.14 highlights the significant improvement of the data on the use of assets, as shown by the asset turnover trend. With growth in the asset turnover ratio from 105 per cent to 140 per cent, Eutron has shown a considerable increase in efficiency.

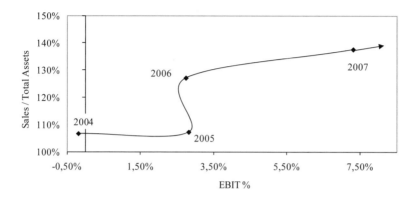

Source: Company reports and Orbis.

Figure 5.14   Total assets turnover vs. EBIT margin of Eutron

CROSS-FERTILIZATION EFFECTS

The electronics outsourcing allows growth and continuous improvement in the industrial field thanks to the cross-fertilization inherent in this activity. Having the opportunity to operate in different market segments (industrial, telecommunications, personal computers, automotive, etc.), the companies involved in electronics outsourcing can extend the competences acquired in a specific field to other domains. The presence in many areas is therefore a constant characteristic of electronics outsourcing and also its strength: the clients benefit from the specific know-how their suppliers have acquired in other sectors, and the suppliers decrease the risk arising from the volatility of few customer orders or of a single sector.

Eutron has a presence in many different areas (industrial, telecommunications, vending, tool machinery, etc.), so it is able to extend the competences gained in a specific field to other sectors. For example, the requirements of robustness to environmental conditions and vibrations accrued through electronics in the textile machinery sector create skills that can then be used in other situations. Similarly, the safety competences developed in the electro-medical context becomes part of the company's know-how and can be easily transferred to other applications.

Table 5.9 shows Eutron's action areas. It is clear how the company is consistent with the positioning of Global Class EMSs, or rather, with those customers characterized by medium intensity productions and far from the typical mass-market of consumer products. The industrial automation sector is one where the company has mainly directed its activity. An important segment in which the company displays world leadership is the control technology for the textile machinery. Other action areas of Eutron are electronic controls of elevators and lifting systems, electronic thermal control devices, home and building automation, food or beverages vending machines.

Table 5.9   Operating areas of Eutron

	Share on sales 2007 (%)
Industrial automation	56
Vending	11
Home and building automation	18
Professional applications	2
Telecom	2
Automotive	1
Computers and peripherals	1
Other sectors	9

Source: Company reports.

The percentage of sales relating to the top ten customers is around 90 per cent. This high concentration is associated with the willingness to establish a steady partnership with clients, an activity that requires a significant time investment to achieve a full operational affinity. Sometimes, the approach to the customers takes place during R&D activities, when Eutron designs the electronic devices dedicated to a specific application; later, through product and project engineering activities, pre-production is arranged as a necessary step before contracting the final production. Long-term partnerships, which extend from planning to after-sales, gain the clients' loyalty through the sharing of goals, operational methods and results in terms of excellence; this also makes subsequent switching costs expensive for both parties.

Revenue expansion can be implemented through the diversification of sectors characterized by specialization and intermediate volumes, and through an increase in the intellectual property of the products for which are anticipated noteworthy investments.

JOINT DESIGN MANUFACTURING: BEYOND THE EMS MODEL

Eutron acts as a Global Class EMS and operates in highly specialized sectors with an important level of intellectual property and with intermediate production volumes. In this context, the expansion of customer services extends along the entire value chain, as typically happens with electronics manufacturing services. Yet, while the majority of EMSs started by offering low-added-value services (typically, contract manufacturing) and only later changed to offer more valuable activities (such as product engineering), Eutron stands out for its genesis in research and development and, as a consequence, it naturally adds intellectual properties to its offer.

- Control over microelectronic know-how
- Cross-fertilization among different sectors
- Co-design and knowledge transfer
- Target costing methodologies
- Vertically integrated production model

The company is organized with teams dedicated to electronic design and it handles several types of contracts, from the common design contract paid by the client, to participating projects in which the intellectual property is shared and generation of knowledge is co-financed and shared with the customer.

In the latter case, the outsourcing model is named joint design manufacturing (JDM): the design services are expanded in order to develop systems and components in cooperation with the client. Implementing the JDM model, OEM clients bring their market knowledge and product specifications, while the outsourcing firm is in charge of the complete design and of the services to launch the new product. The intellectual property is shared and the production activity and after-sales service are given to the EMS (Figure 5.15).

Eutron is involved from the initial stage, when the specifications are defined, providing its own knowledge on electronic technology and ensuring for the client the benefit of technological cross-fertilization. The development of new products is carried out together with the OEM client. The companies define the terms of the intellectual property, sharing both the risk and the revenue that could occur from the project implementation. In this sense, the JDM extended business model ensures higher margins to the supplier and a significant differentiation from the competitors, together with an increased sharing of the market risk, whose complete evaluation can be carried out by the OEM customer only.

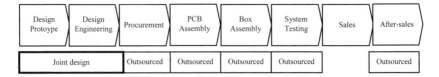

Figure 5.15   From EMS to joint design manufacturing

It should be noted that the increased competitiveness that comes from cost reduction due to low labor costs in Asian countries will reach its end in the medium term. To re-align a new global competitive mode it will be necessary to invest in intellectual property as Eutron is doing.

CHINA: SUPPLY-SIDE AND DEMAND-SIDE

Being closer to the industrial sectors, Global Class EMSs organize their structure in order to favor a highly complex and customized production. Consistent with this, their production plants are based in Western countries for those activities which imply a high level of automation, while the plants based in low-cost-labor countries are required for part of the products or processes in order to maintain their competitiveness.

Eutron has also defined a growth strategy to match the globalization trend both on the demand side, to satisfy the requests coming from the clients, and on the supply side, to satisfy the demand through plants based in new target markets characterized, at the same time, by low labor costs, like China.

Besides the mass-market products, that for some time have been of interest to the emerging Asian regions, several industrial production activities, as well, have also moved to Asia. One example is textile manufacturing firms that need machinery (looms, spinning machines and so on) that is more and more frequently built on site. Similarly, due to the real estate boom that has characterized China for many years now, new factories for the production of elevators and lifting systems were built, and they need a lot of electronic technology.

For this reason, Eutron has acquired a production plant in China through a second acquisition, having acquired its first plant in Europe in 2000. The availability of two production plants specializing in different volumes and product types not only widens the group of potential clients, but offers a greater level of security on supplies. Due to the customs duties and the high costs of importing electronic boards to China, the on-site plants serving the OEM China-based clients give a competitive advantage over their European competitors, turning the problem of customs duties into a market opportunity.

NOTES

1. 'design for manufacturability (DFM) is the engineering art of designing products in such a way that they are easy to manufacture. The basic idea exists in almost all engineering disciplines, but of course the details differ widely depending on the manufacturing technology' (Bralla, 1998).
2. 'design for testability (DFT) is a name for design techniques that add certain testability features to a microelectronic hardware product design. The premise of the added features is that they make it easier to develop and apply manufacturing tests for the designed hardware. The purpose of manufacturing tests is to validate that the product hardware contains no defects that could, otherwise, adversely affect the product's correct functioning' (Lavagno et al., 2006).
3. 'design for quality' (DFQ) (Huang, 2001).
4. The name Eutron (in Greek ευτρον) comes from the conjunction of the prefix ευ (good, well done) with the final part of the word ελεκτρον ('elektron' or 'amber', the root from which the terms 'electricity' and 'electronics' have originated).
5. The author of this book was one of the founders, president and CEO of the company and member of the Board of Directors for many years.

6. Original Design Manufacturers

ODM VS. EMS STRATEGIC MODEL

The heterogeneity of the outsourcing phenomena highlights a specific configuration made of a set of sectorial segments: each segment competes within the market in different ways and with different competitive advantages. This is the case for the segmentation between EMS and ODM firms.

Although the name ODM became common only in the 1990s, the EMSs' capability to handle their own products under private labels emerged at least one decade earlier. The phenomenon was caused mainly by explosive growth of the so-called IBM-compatible PCs, based on the Wintel platform.

The ODM outsourcing model is very developed in the mass-market sectors, because it allows a time reduction in the design phase and in the market introduction process, large economies of scale, access to distribution channels and a wide range of services including after-service. The ODMs' added value is related not only to the result of the reduction of costs tied with economies of scale, but also to the offering of specific technological competence and supporting infrastructure.

ODMs not only take care of the fabrication of the products they offer, but also take care of the planning and design definition. They are the owners of the intellectual property, providing both the direct sale and, more commonly, the sale to OEMs that represent the distribution segment.

Unlike EMSs, ODM firms are generally specialized in a limited range of products, and they are mostly focused on R&D and design activities. Sometimes, they are also the pioneers and the engines for the growth of specific segments, as in the case of notebook computers. Table 6.1 shows a comparison between the two electronics outsourcing models, EMSs and ODMs.

The comparison of the two models highlights the similarities and differences of the main traits in their relationship with the market.

Table 6.1   EMS and ODM models

EMS (electronics manufacturing services)	ODM (original design manufacturer)
Firms based in the USA and Taiwan.	Firms based mainly in Taiwan.
Services (design, manufacturing, etc.)	Products
'End-to-end' services, including design, manufacturing, assembly, direct order fulfillment, after-sales.	End products, ownership of intellectual property.
Global presence and services offered in proximity of the largest end-market areas.	Taiwan-based companies with large plants in China.
ICT, multimedia, defense, aero-space, medical, automotive and industry.	ICT, notebook and mobile phones.
The offer of production flexibility to OEMs, increasing their volumes without expanding the in-house capability.	The offer of new products with reduction in the investments and cost sharing to OEMs.
Bargaining power with component suppliers and ability of ensuring the supply of key components.	Decrease in product development cycle.

- Both models operate in an economic environment with a major concentration of big companies (sales more than one billion US dollars). However among the EMSs there are many small and medium-sized enterprises, so that there is a large turnover range.
- EMSs are diffused all over the world, mainly in Asia and in the USA. Europe has a high number of medium-size EMSs. Instead, ODMs are concentrated in a very limited geographical area for both their design activities (Taiwan, Hong Kong) and manufacturing operations (China).
- Both models allow access to production capabilities based on flexibility parameters. Yet, the use of owned technologies previously developed for other domains, enables ODMs to reduce the time needed for the development and introduction of their products in the markets. They can also use the same product base, adjusted to different clients in order to obtain the breakeven quantity and the advantages given by economies of scale.
- The cost structure is carefully monitored for both EMSs and ODMs; the latter often have access to a capital market that is more flexible and less regulated thanks to substantial governmental incentives.

- The use of cost-plus pricing techniques and the integration of quantity discount mechanisms are widespread. ODMs, however, play on intellectual property to differentiate themselves and pursue their breakeven levels to acquire market shares. They generally bring into their relationships a higher value with respect to EMSs and succeed at achieving higher profits.
- Sometimes ODM firms act in direct competition with OEMs, especially in the telecommunication and computer industries; EMSs have mere productive functions, always far from the end-user and therefore always subjected to OEMs.

The decision of the OEM customer as to whether or not to establish a relationship with an EMS or an ODM firm depends on many factors, among them strategic issues that are quite important. Table 6.2 summarizes the advantages and disadvantages for the OEM customer in a relationship with an ODM firm. Beyond the largely operational aspects, the strategic issues must also be taken into account.

Table 6.2   OEM–ODM relationship

Advantages for OEMs	Disadvantages for OEMs
Faster, lower costs, and easier access to OEMs' non-core areas	Loss of experience and know-how in the design
Rapid growth and expansion of OEMs' brand in new areas	Dilution of the brand and differentiation
Use of engineering experience in the development of complementary products	Loss of intellectual property and consequently of market opportunities
Better financial structure, reduction of both working capital and investments	Geographical risk and global management of the supply chain risk
Higher flexibility and shorter development time of new products	Maintenance cost for the quality control system

Table 6.3 shows the share values of ODM revenues. The most important sector is IT (computers and peripherals). Diversification has taken place in the adjacent sectors, i.e. telecommunications and consumer devices.

Industry data highlight the division in the two main areas of electronics outsourcing: while ODMs are in search of applications for mass products consistent with their mission and organization (IT, phones, consumer devices), EMSs, especially the smaller ones, are committed to industrial applications with smaller production volumes and often higher mission-critical functions (transportation, life-support systems, process automation).

However, there is a sort of convergence between Top Class ODMs and EMSs, since the two models share the organization and the production dimension. They compete in increasingly overlapping markets and the OEMs that are aimed to outsource design and production increasingly often need to choose between the two models. EMSs are attracted to the ODM's higher-added-value activities, so they increase their investments in R&D to achieve a greater amount of intellectual property.

The difference between the two is becoming increasingly blurred; a situation that is clearly revealed by their similar dimensional data and by their increasingly approaching margins. The convergence of the business models is typical of mass-market sectors, where the pursuit of economies of scale and the appropriation of the intellectual property are two important competitive advantages. This is a possibility that questions the EMS–OEM partnerships based on cost competition and time-to-market.

Table 6.3   Sales of ODMs by industry

	ODMs' sales (\$M)	ODMs' sales (%)
Computers	33 880	44
Computer peripherals	19 250	25
Consumer devices	10 010	13
Wireless telecommunications	9 240	12
Cabled telecommunications	3 850	5
Automotive	770	1

Source: Technology Forecasters (2005).

FACTS AND FIGURES

Figure 6.1 highlights the size and the growth of the ODM sector in the years 2002–2008. It is clear how the ODM model has experienced remarkable growth, higher than the growth of the majority of industrial sectors during the same period. Referring to the year 2008, the ODM market has had revenues of 120 billion US dollars and a share of 40 per cent of the total value of electronics outsourcing (i.e. of the EMS and ODM markets altogether).

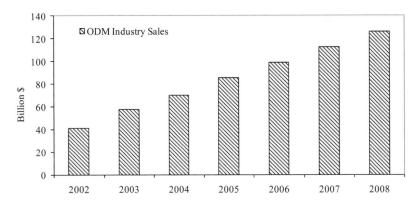

Source: iSuppli.

Figure 6.1   Sales of the ODM industry

The 2008–2009 financial crunch has reduced the forecasts on expected growth. The estimate shows a moderate recovery in the sales of the electronics outsourcing sector for both EMSs and ODMs. A slowdown in the growth process in latest years and in the near future is shown in Figure 6.2, which reveals a consolidation towards the maturity of this sector.

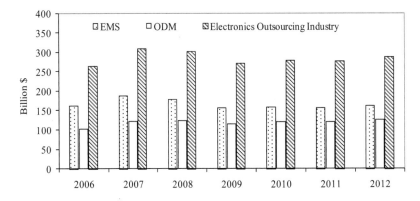

Source: IDC.

Figure 6.2   Sales of the EMS/ODM industries

Table 6.4 shows the average revenue growth in the years 2002–2007, specifically for the main ODM firms. Comparison of the growth with the sector average, which is about 24 per cent, is consistent with the trend towards concentration in the ODM sector. Through these figures, the market globalization and the spread of electronics outsourcing show the mutual support represented by the almost complete allocation of the production of electronic products in the Asian regions.

The ODM business model for IT products started in Taiwan, and today mainly serves the production segment of personal computers. Leading notebook manufacturers have relied on the cheap assembly costs and highly skilled electronics design engineers and wafer fabs to deliver cost competitive products. Local manufacturers have invested in research and development during the design and engineering phase, in order to develop competences in miniaturization, power saving and enhancement of technological standards. Following investments, 83 per cent of the notebook computers sold worldwide in 2007 were built in Taiwan, and one third of those were manufactured by a single ODM company, Quanta Computer.

Table 6.4   Average sales growth of the main ODMs

	CAGR 2002–2007 (%)
Quanta Computer	42.3
Asustek Computer	47.8
Compal Electronics	35.4
Wistron	30.7
TPV Technology	41.2
Inventec	28.0
Lite-on Technology	21.9
Tatung	10.2
Innolux Display	n.a.
High Tech Computer	43.8
Top 10 Total	32.4
ODM industry	24.3

Source: Company reports.

Table 6.5 lists the ten largest notebook manufacturers and the associated market shares. The names of the ODM companies, despite their size, are hardly known to end users. The reason is that the products manufactured by ODMs are distributed under the better known OEM branding. This is inherent to the strategic business model implemented by these ODMs, focused on product development, leaving all the costs related to sales and marketing to OEMs.

Table 6.5   Main ODM manufacturers of notebook PCs

	Market share (%)	Country
Quanta Computer	28.7	Taiwan
Compal Electronics	18.2	Taiwan
Wistron Corporation	9.2	Taiwan
Asustek Computer	6.9	Taiwan
Inventec	4.9	Taiwan
Elitegroup Computer	3.1	Taiwan
Mitac International	2.0	Taiwan
Foxconn	1.5	Taiwan
Samsung	1.5	South Korea
Arima	1.5	Taiwan

Source: iSuppli (2006).

Extending the analysis beyond the notebook segment, the ODMs' geographical localization elements remain unchanged. Indeed Table 6.6 shows that the Taiwanese firms are the world leaders, followed by Chinese, Japanese and European firms, while American ODMs play a marginal role. In particular, the absolute prevalence of Asian firms (95 per cent) identifies that continent as the world's factory of mass-market electronic devices.

Table 6.7 highlights the product diversification of the most important ODMs, that are used to operate with clients from different industries (computer, communications, digital commodity, television, automotive, entertainment, etc.), albeit to differing extents. Compal, for example, also due to the fall of the IT market, has diversified with respect to its original sector of computers and monitors, and has moved in the direction of the mobile phone industry.

Table 6.6   *Geographical location of ODMs*

	Share of ODM segment (%)	Value ($M)
Taiwan	77.4	76 433
China	12.1	11 949
Japan	6.1	6 024
Europe	3.5	3 456
USA	0.9	889

Source: iSuppli (2006).

Table 6.7   *Main ODM products*

	Notebook PC	LCD displays	Printers	PDA	Mobile phones	Cameras	Servers, routers	LCD/LED TV	MP3 players	DVD players	Communications
Asustek	X	X	X	X	X	X					
Quanta Computer	X				X		X	X			
Compal Electronics	X	X		X	X						
Inventec	X				X		X				
TPV Technology		X						X			
Lite-on Technology		X	X			X				X	X
Wistron Corp.	X				X	X		X			
Tatung	X	X			X	X	X		X		
Inventec Appl.				X	X			X		X		X

Source: Company reports.

Sales growth has a positive effect on the profits generated in this sector, even though the increase in the profits has been lower than the increase in sales (Table 6.8), demonstrating a clear reduction in the marginality due to an increase in competition within the sector. This also includes competition in search of better profitability by big EMSs, implementing an ODM model.

Table 6.8   EBIT margin of the main ODMs

	EBIT 2004 (%)	EBIT 2005 (%)	EBIT 2006 (%)	EBIT 2007 (%)	CAGR (%) 2004–2007
Asustek	6.3	6.1	4.3	5.2	−6.2
Quanta Computer	4.2	2.1	2.8	3.4	−6.8
Compal Electronics	4.9	4.7	4.5	4.1	−5.8
Inventec	2.0	1.5	2.4	2.6	9.1
TPV Technology	3.2	3.2	3.1	3.0	−2.1
Lite-on Technology	4.9	5.2	5.0	5.3	2.7
Wistron Corporation	0.8	2.5	3.4	3.1	57.1
Tatung	3.5	−3.1	−5.3	7.5	28.9
Inventec Appliance	3.6	3.6	3.0	4.1	4.4

Source: Company reports.

Additionally, the dimensional increase of the businesses and of the production quantities is usually associated with a decrease in marginality, due to customers' stronger bargaining power. Many ODMs have invested in production plants for personal computers and mobile phones, that is, in the domain of standard technologies and commodity products, where competition is more intense.

The main difference between the two electronics outsourcing segments, EMS and ODM, lies in the different intellectual property rights of their respective productions. For this reason, R&D activities are typical of the ODMs, so that they are remunerated by the market with higher margins than those of EMSs.

ODM VS. OEM DIRECT COMPETITION

To compensate progressive reduction in margins, the largest ODMs have increasingly extended their activity beyond the traditional products such as personal computers and mobile phones. Many ODMs were the first to develop and introduce smart phones; they decided to create their own brands in order to get directly to the end user, thus becoming a direct competitor of the OEMs. This is an extension of the business model defined as OBM (original brand model). OBMs compete directly with OEMs, especially for the products linked to mobile phones and notebooks. To follow this strategy, ODMs must invest in marketing to support their own brand; they compete with companies already well known to consumers by lower price. It is important to mention the case of BenQ, which changed from being a mere ODM supplier of Motorola to becoming one of its direct competitors.

The possibility of a conflict between client and supplier depends on their relationship and on the intellectual property quota incorporated in the product being negotiated. The two types of contracts that are normally applied and that reflect the OEMs' strategies are: the 'go shopping' and the 'design it' agreements.

In a 'go shopping' agreement, OEMs buy the end product (designed and manufactured) changing only some minor characteristics, sometimes only the label, but they bear the marketing and sales costs. In this case the ODM owns a stronger negotiation power and has the right to sell same products under its own brand, since it is the owner of the product's intellectual property.

If the relationship with the client is of the 'design it' type, OEMs give the task of designing some of the product parts but keep part of the intellectual property. In this case, it is unlikely that the ODM can act as a potential competitor of its own client, because the latter defines more binding legal terms within the contract.

It is clear that the relationship established by the OEM has to be consistent with its long-term strategies. The parties have to define all the contract terms in detail, evaluating the importance of the outsourced products to avoid their supplier from becoming a competitor. They also have to continuously re-evaluate the strategies within the relationship, taking into account the EMSs–ODMs' growth, trying to achieve a better overall view, and the highest level of control over the entire supply chain.

ORIGINAL DESIGN MANUFACTURER: QUANTA COMPUTER

The ODM strategic model is well represented by Quanta Computer, one of the largest firms worldwide in electronic industrial manufacturing. It was founded in Taiwan in 1988 by Barry Lam, offering contract manufacturing services in the information technology sector. Quanta progressively moved towards the ODM business model, acting mainly in the notebook sector. Consistent with an ODM strategic positioning within the electronic supply chain, the company operates in design and production in the areas of IT, mobile communications, and digital consumers on behalf of OEM clients that introduce their products into the market with their own branding and sales networks. Quanta's products include desktop and notebook computers, smartphones, and other electronic devices in the consumer area, with a turnover of around 25 billion US dollars and more than 60 000 employees (2008).

Quanta's strategic evolution can be related to Mintzberg's approach. That is a different strategy could result from the one initially and deliberately planned. During the course of action, the entrepreneurs learn and develop their knowledge, constantly adjusting their vision and actions, and seize the opportunities arising as described by Kirzner's theories on alertness.

It should also be remembered that at the end of the 1980s, the Taiwanese electronic industry was composed of companies operating as contract manufacturers, which were in fact offering low added-value labor with a consequent low marginality. Yet the rapidity of learning and the simultaneous evolution of the sector allowed the most dynamic firms to gain wider segments characterized by more intense engineering activities, such as product design and industrialization, within the supply chain. The turning point occurred in the 1990s, when Quanta and other manufacturers started to operate more and more as designers. The transformation process was supported by the policy of the Taiwanese government through fiscal incentives and investments.

A significant contribution to Quanta's growth was made possible by some US clients who started to ask not only for construction, but also for design and, more generally, the complete management of their notebook business, which also implied specialized know-how. The progressive increase in sales allowed the company to tackle world markets with a global strategy and new facilities in two crucial markets, North American and European.

One of the first world-class clients was Apple Computer, with whom, in 1995, Quanta shared the responsibility of the joint design of the Epic Powerbook series. Apple's goal was to reduce costs and time-to-market, two important factors in a field where the first signs of transformation from a consumer's viewpoint, appeared. The benefits derived from the operation persuaded the companies to renew the initial agreement granting Quanta most of the responsibility, including the design of the new generations of notebooks. In 1996, Quanta's first contract with Dell was signed, and the company soon became one of the most important clients in terms of volumes and turnover, for which some dedicated production plants were built.

Quanta underlined its vocation to grow in a technology-based mass-market, unfolding competences needed not only in the manufacturing process but also in design activity; its readiness to make significant investments in plants and infrastructure made possible the signature of agreements with the largest computer manufacturers of the time. At the end of the 1990s, Quanta's activity, like that of other 'ghost-manufacturers', started to play an increasingly important role in the growth of the world market of information and communication technology and, in particular, of portable PCs. The growth of the company, that in 1999 had a turnover of about 3 billion US dollars, was backed thanks to new financial resources coming from the IPO process.

Quanta succeeded in reinforcing its presence among the world's ODMs by outdoing the leader of the time, Toshiba, in terms of number of computers sold, achieving one seventh of the world's production. It is impressive that Quanta was able to obtain these results in a period of demand reduction in the electronics industry worldwide (2000–2002). The large production volumes typical of mass markets allowed Quanta to maintain production plants in its original locations in Taiwan, thanks to the high automation in the production process and to the subsequent low impact of labor costs. Yet, further volume growth and the search for a competitive advantage were pursued also by means of new investments in China-based plants. In 2004, the production of notebooks exceeded the threshold of ten million units, while annual revenue exceeded ten billion US dollars. The following years were characterized by a constant increase in sales, although the transformation process of the sector towards the mass-market typology caused a progressive reduction of the margins.

Within the convergence process between the Top Class EMS and ODM segments, the competitive scenario of Quanta Computer embraces both these electronics outsourcing segments ('simultaneously co-existing with ODM and EMS'). As a matter of fact, the company has also included typical EMS activities.

It should not be surprising that Table 6.9, which lists OEM clients of Quanta and its competitors, highlights an overlap of the client's portfolio with ODMs as well as Top Class EMSs. We can notice that the main world brands of the IT domain implement a business diversification in their provisioning activities to the point of involving more suppliers. The policy is aimed at keeping the competition level high in order to encourage price reductions and pressure towards the improvement of the products; secondly, diversification allows a reduction of industrial risks related to manufacturing problems.

Quanta's competition, in the case of ODMs as well as Top Class EMSs, is focused on mass markets, that is, notebooks, cellular phones, digital TVs and digital consumer goods. The production synergies that can be applied in the manufacturing process appear clear especially as far as digital technology is concerned.

Table 6.9   *Customers of the main EMSs and ODMs*

Company	2007 ($M)	Head-quarters	EMS/ODM	Products	Main customers
Quanta Computer	23 969	Taiwan	ODM	Notebook PCs, servers, mobile phones, digital TVs	Acer, Apple, Dell, Fujitsu-Siemens, Gateway, HP, IBM, NEC, Panasonic, Philips, Sony
Asustek	23 289	Taiwan	ODM	Notebook PCs, monitors, printers, PDAs, mobile phones, digital cameras	Acer, Canon, Dell, Fujitsu-Siemens, HP, NEC, Toshiba
Compal Electronics	15 362	Taiwan	ODM	Notebook PCs, LCDs, PDAs, mobile phones	HP, Dell, Toshiba, Fujitsu-Siemens, Acer, Apple, NEC, Hitachi, Motorola
Wistron Corporation	8 841	Taiwan	ODM	Notebook PCs, mobile phones, digital TVs	Dell, HP, IBM, Fujitsu-Siemens, Canon
Inventec	8 087	Taiwan	ODM	Notebook PCs, servers, mobile phones	HP, Toshiba, Apple, T-Mobile
Foxconn	52 495	Taiwan	EMS	Connectors, cables, desktop PCs, mobile phones, networking, game machines	Intel, Dell, Apple, IBM, HP, Cisco, Nokia, Motorola, Sony, Gateway, Acer
Flextronics	29 336	Singa-pore	EMS	Computers, IT infrastructures, consumer handheld devices, communications infrastructures, networking, automotive	HP, Sony-Ericsson, Alcatel, Casio, Dell, Ericsson Telecom AB, Microsoft, Motorola, Nortel, Cisco, IBM, Cisco, Sun Microsystems
Jabil	12 291	USA	EMS	Automotive, computing & storage, consumer mobility, displays, medical instrumentation, networking, telecommunication	Cisco, HP, Company, IBM, Motorola, Network Appliance, NEC, Nokia, Siemens, Philips Electronics

Source: Kishimoto (2005), Thomson Financial (2008).

COMPETITIVE SCENARIO

In the decade encompassing 1999–2007, Quanta sustained its growth path. Figure 6.3 shows the development of the company's sales starting from 1999, the IPO year, up until 2007, a period when the value grew from around 2.4 billion to almost 24 billion US dollars. The size of Quanta's business increased by almost one third of its value each year, a major result if we consider the period 2000–2002 and the well-known collapse that involved the whole electronics industry worldwide.

The comparison with the sector average figure in the same years (a little higher than 25 per cent) and with that of the main ODMs (about 36 per cent) confirms the high concentration of the market.

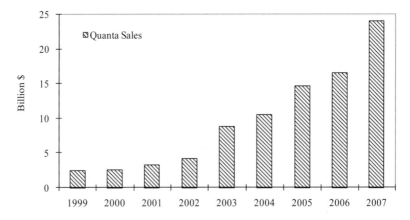

Source: Thomson Financial.

Figure 6.3   Sales of Quanta Computer

Table 6.10 shows some data about Quanta's main ODM competitors. Between 2006 and 2007, the annual growth of the total sample in terms of turnover was as high as 27 per cent, while in the period 2004–2007 the same parameter showed a CAGR of 30 per cent. In both periods, Quanta achieved a higher than average performance, registering a 45 per cent increase with respect to 2006 and a 2004–2007 CAGR equal to 32 per cent.

Figure 6.4 reflects the relationship of profitability, in terms of EBIT margin, with the efficiency indicator in the use of assets, calculated as a ratio between annual sales and assets value. Considering the period of 1999–2007, there is a major reduction in the profits, which went from 12.6 per cent in 1999 to 3.4 per cent in 2007. Meanwhile, the ability of Quanta to increase revenue through a reduced use of assets is manifested and highlights how the company, like other ODMs, implements the efficient use of available assets to compete.

Table 6.10   Main competitors of Quanta Computer

	Sales 2007 ($M)	Sales growth (%)	CAGR (%) 2004–2007	EBIT (%) 2007	Employees 2007
Quanta Computer	23 969	45.3	32.0	3.4	67 291
Asustek Computer	23 289	35.5	43.4	5.2	8 885
Compal Electronics	15 362	30.9	28.4	4.1	38 656
Wistron	8 841	30.3	33.9	3.1	31 682
TPV Technology	8 459	18.0	31.2	3.0	27 320
Inventec	8 087	2.5	23.1	2.6	26 447
Lite-on Technology	8 074	18.4	6.0	5.3	68 127
Tatung	7 060	21.0	26.5	7.6	39 140
Innolux Display	4 846	49.4	230.1	11.6	29 300
High Tech Computer	3 645	12.7	47.0	27.3	7 179
Elitegroup Computer	2 912	30.6	32.4	1.1	15 493
Inventec Appliances	2 857	−11.5	4.6	4.1	18 566
Cal Comp Electronics	2 785	29.6	24.2	3.7	12 677
Mitac International	2 782	−1.2	14.0	8.0	12 878

Source: Company report.

The increase in margins being less than the increase in revenues characterizes a trend in line with the entire ODM sector, confirming the profit reduction; this is shared with the largest ODMs and is a consequence of increased competition. Furthermore, notebooks, mobile phones, and digital consumer devices are the product categories through which the company has most of its revenue; these are standard technologies applied to commodity products where the competition is strong.

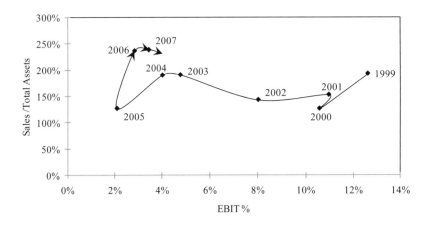

Source: Company reports, Thomson Financial.

Figure 6.4   Total assets turnover vs. EBIT margin of Quanta Computer

Figure 6.5 compares the reduction of Quanta's EBIT margin, which progressively declined from 12.6 per cent in 1999 to 3.4 per cent in 2007.

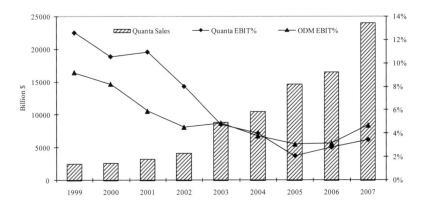

Source: Datastream.

Figure 6.5   Sales and EBIT margin of Quanta Computer

This is a structural trend, aligned with the trend of the ODM sector life cycle, which seems to have concluded its rapid growth expansion beginning the transition towards a maturity period, or a lower growth rate of margins. This observable fact has involved the majority of the largest ODMs and for many of them could represent a sign of future achievements of their efficient dimension.

The company has identified all aspects related to costs, quality and flexibility as indispensable elements of its policy. The assignment of commercial distribution to the OEM customer is reflected in the cost structure that is almost totally associated with production processes, while the costs for the marketing and sales activities are negligible. A specific company function has the responsibility of the efficiency of production processes and product engineering, with planning of constant reductions of the total costs according to target-costing methods.

Quanta's production organization follows the principle of 'worldwide profile with deep roots in Taiwan'. Since 2002, while keeping its headquarters in Taiwan, the company delocalized part of its production to China with the aim of a significant reduction in unit costs. At the beginning of 2008, the construction of a new plant was started in Vietnam.

GROWTH STRATEGIES

As happens with many first-generation entrepreneurs, the founder's spirit is reflected into Quanta's strategies, whose growth expectations are based on the continuous innovation of process and technologies. The entrepreneurial approach, the ability to seize and exploit the opportunities and a dynamic learning organization have allowed a sequence of strategic events consistent with new competences matured over time in a constantly evolving economic and industrial context.

Quanta's initial growth has been led by the surrounding conditions, such as, for instance, its entry in the electronics market, its rapid growth at the beginning of the 1990s, as well as by its entrepreneurial ability to identify the specific characteristics of this sector just before its competitors. Timing is crucial to preserve a competitive advantage and in particular:

- time-to-technology: time needed to develop or acquire a new technology
- time-to-volume: time needed to achieve the optimal production volume
- time-to-market: time needed to introduce a product on the market
- time-to-end-user: time between the acquisition of a new technology and the delivery of the product to the client

Due to the ability to anticipate the mass market needs, Quanta has often been able to enjoy the typical first-mover advantages in the definition of both new technologies and products with a high intellectual property protection.

During the first years of activity, the strategy to focus around emerging technologies aimed at satisfying the growing demand for portable PCs was supported by the specific skills of the company's founder. Where the main competitors had diversified their offer, Quanta specialized in the large-scale design and production of notebooks, achieving excellence on one side and focus on the other, able to satisfy the requests of different customizing and product configuration specifications.

From an organizational standpoint, the company has followed a progressive verticalization path along the supply chain, especially through several acquisitions. The reasons for this extension along the supply chain are consistent with the strategic goal of gaining a better control of the costs and the time needed in the use of new technologies, for the introduction of the products on the market and for the achievement of optimal volume levels.

Since 2004, after a decrease of the growth rates in the notebook segment in a natural transition towards the maturity stage, Quanta's management decided to widen their product range. The company explored new business opportunities in the areas of LCD TV sets, smartphones, Internet and GPS technologies. Strategically the decision was made in a fit-to-the-environment context that could take advantage of a very good position on the experience curve where digital electronics are concerned. Quanta decided to increase the variety of the offer, supported by the competitive advantage resulting from a technological cross-fertilization.

The company's entry in the market of mobile phones and smartphones occurred exogenously, through the acquisition of the Chinese company Tech-Yeh in 2004. The sector of smartphones was at the starting stage of the life cycle and experienced a rapid growth with attractive profit expectations, so the decision of Quanta was followed by other direct competitors such as Compal and Foxconn.

The convergence process between IT and mobile phones, attributing many functions of the notebook to cellular phones, allowed Quanta to use its technological know-how to also grow rapidly in this new segment. The competences accumulated in the mobile phones domain eventually pushed Quanta towards further widening its business and to act as an EMS for the world manufacturers of mobile phones (Motorola, Nokia and Sony Ericsson, and later Apple).

An agreement signed with Toshiba, in 2006, for the production of LCD TV screens, started the diversification within the LCD sector, in its growth phase and having the traits of a mass market. In the same year, Quanta Storage, controlled by the Quanta group and the second largest manufacturer of optical storage products, partnered with the technological R&D group of the Sony–NEC joint venture to access the emergent Blue Ray technology, giving the production capability needed to satisfy the demand of a fast growing market to the joint venture.

The availability of more technologies and the skills to integrate them have persuaded Quanta's management to delineate a new strategic approach, called Design Manufacturing System Solution and Move, to supply customized solutions that require the integration of different technologies. This is an extension of the ODM model from the products to the systems, that is a move towards solutions that are based on more than one product, connected to or integrated with one another, with specific software applications. For example, due to the increase in the use of electronic devices in the automotive sector, solutions to infotainment by integrating GPS, DVD and mobile phone technologies are offered.

GROWTH AND M&A ACTIVITIES

As with the majority of its competitors in the ODM segment, Quanta Computer's growth has benefited from acquisitions, participations and strategic alliances aimed at widening its product range. ODMs require specific knowledge in product design and manufacturing that is not easily accessible or replicable. Through the acquisition of companies, Quanta has pursued its objective of sustaining its growth and the penetration of markets beyond notebooks, obtaining the advantages of the cross-fertilization process.

A growth strategy based on M&A activities is also associated with quickly reaching a size that favors economies of scale. In the ODM segment the dimensional factor plays an important role in the cost reduction process, both in terms of the distribution of investments over large production quantities and in terms of an increase in bargaining power with the suppliers. The acquisitions of subjects that are part of the supply chain are an important element of an ODM's growth strategy, because they are carried out with the aim of controlling cost and time variables.

Table 6.11 lists some of the acquisitions carried out by Quanta in the years 2004–2006, oriented towards the notebook, mobile phone and LCD segments.

In 2004, a minority share in Alpha Networks was acquired: a company operating in networks and telecommunications. In the same year, the acquisition of the Chinese company Tech-Yeh was completed, and this allowed Quanta to consolidate its presence in the notebook sector and to approach the mobile phone sector. In 2006, two operations were completed at the same time – the merger with AU Optronics and the Joint Venture with Sanyo Electric – with the aim of reaching a leadership position in the manufacturing of LCD flat TV screens. The merger between AU Optronics, the first Taiwanese manufacturer of LCD-TFT panels, and Quanta Display enabled the Quanta group to become the world's first manufacturer of both large-screen LCD's and LCD monitors for PCs. The alliance with RoyalTek, signed in 2006, had the goal of keeping a high level of know-how related to the most recent GPS technologies. The applications of these technologies can also generate key opportunities in the automotive, computer and communication sectors. At the beginning of 2008, Quanta acquired a minority share of Kontron Asia, the Asian branch of the German company specialized in the production of industrial computers, with applications also in the communications, automation, transportation and aviation sectors.

Table 6.11   M&A activity of Quanta Computer

Target	Country	Products	Deal	Closing
Alpha Networks	Taiwan	Networking equipment	Acquisition	2004
Tech-Yeh	China	Notebook, mobile phone and peripherals	Acquisition	2004
Sanyo Electric	Japan	Flat screen televisions	Joint Venture	2006
AU Optronics	Taiwan	LCD panel	Merger	2006
RoyalTek	Taiwan	GPS	Acquisition	2006
Kontron Asia	Taiwan	Industrial computer	Acquisition	2008

Source: Zephir.

R&D ACTIVITIES

The need to implement the strategic plan to support such long-term growth has required an intense R&D program in the electronics and high-tech sectors. In particular, the aim to widen the product mix and to expand the business limits in the mobile phone, LCD TVs, and network and communication sectors has made the company's experience and technological know-how crucial.

In 2003, Quanta Research & Development Complex (QRDC) was founded. QRDC is one of the largest research and technological innovations centers in Taiwan where all the technological resources and knowledge coming from Quanta's different action areas have been integrated. The center carries out research activities aimed at several time horizons and cooperates with many universities, MIT among them.

As already mentioned in the previous chapters, the difference in competition between the two electronics outsourcing segments, EMSs and

ODMs lies in the different level of intellectual property rights of their respective productions; this is achieved also through deeper R&D activity performed by ODMs. Figure 6.6 highlights the trend of Quanta Computer's R&D expenses.

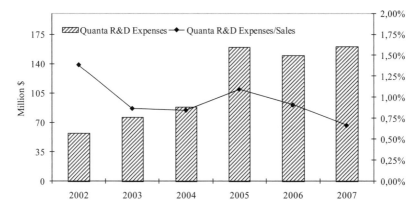

Source: Company reports.

Figure 6.6   R&D expenses of Quanta Computer

Although marginal, the investments aimed at improving the products and processes are higher than those expressed by the EMS sector, differentiating them from the ODM sector due to the absence of product design activities.

PART THREE

Growth Strategies in Outsourcing

7. Growth through Mergers and Acquisitions

The development of a company or an industry normally runs along a dual path of endogenous growth, such as through investment in infrastructure and labor, and exogenous growth through acquisitions or mergers with existing companies. Within electronics outsourcing business models, fast dimensional development and concentration processes have been significantly encouraged by the exogenous component in the development strategy of the EMS and ODM sectors through mergers and acquisitions (M&A). In acquisitions a company buys the majority share of another company or, if the latter has a spread ownership, a share to gain control of it. In mergers two or more companies are joined through an agreement, creating a new organization.

M&A processes have been very important for the growth of the electronics industry. An analysis of M&A operations in the EMS and ODM sectors in the 1997–2007 decade makes the strategic policy evident. The marked preference for exogenous growth, especially in the case of the main players, is related to its rapidity compared to endogenous solutions; in fact, infrastructures, human resources and technological skills do not need to be developed from scratch, but are already present in the company's targets.

M&A transactions from 1997 to 2007 are the main factor underlying the high concentration in the EMS and ODM sectors. From a strategic point of view, both acquisitions and mergers have a similar effect: they do not widen the overall dimension of the reference market but cause a concentration process that reduces the number of competitors.

The most important M&A operations have involved Top Class EMSs and ODMs; they are classified as such when they reach sales volume exceeding one billion US dollars. Table 7.1 summarizes the main M&A transactions carried out between 1997 and 2007 by Top Class EMSs firms, with the associated announcement dates and the economic values of the completed transactions.[1] The choices to pursue growth through acquisitions have followed different strategies. The sector leader Foxconn concluded a lower number of operations compared to its main competitor, Flextronics, which pursued intense M&A activity with a sequence of operations, the most important of which was the acquisition of Solectron.

Table 7.1   *Main EMSs' M&A operations 1997–2007*

Acquiring company	Acquired company	Head-quarters	Acquired share (%)	Announcement date	Transaction value ($M)
Foxconn	Ambit Microsystems	Taiwan	100	06/11/2003	1 112
	Premier Image Technology	Taiwan	100	20/06/2006	934
	Eimo	Finland	from 24.3 to 100	21/08/2003	85
	CMCS	China	56.48	12/05/2005	78
Flextronics	Solectron	USA	100	04/06/2007	3 600
	Nortel Network	various	Assets	30/06/2004	725
	JITHoldings	Singapore	100	10/08/2000	632
	Chatham Technologies	USA	100	31/07/2000	588
	NatSteel Broadway	Singapore	100	20/05/2002	369
	Orbiantgruppen	Sweden	91	29/10/2001	317
	International Display Works	USA	100	05/09/2006	243
	Hughes Software Systems	India	55	08/06/2004	227
	Xerox	various	Assets	02/10/2001	220
	Arima Computer	Taiwan	100	20/09/2007	203
	Microcell	Finland	100	14/08/2003	200
	Neutronics Electronic	Austria	100	03/11/1997	136
	Kyrel EMS	Finland	100	15/07/1999	100
	Wave Optics& Fiber Optics	USA	100	09/02/2001	100
Sanmina–SCI	SCI Systems	USA	Merger	16/07/2001	4 000
	Segerstromm & Svensson	Sweden	100	26/01/2001	512
	Altron	USA	100	07/09/1998	220
	Essex Holding	Sweden	100	01/06/2000	127
	E-M-Solutions	USA	100	24/09/2001	111
	Pentex-Schweizer	Singapore	100	28/06/2004	79

Solectron	C-Mac Industries	Canada	100	09/08/2001	2 700
	NatSteel Electronics	Singapore	100	31/10/2000	2 400
	Singapore Shinei Sangyo	Singapore	100	24/05/2001	260
	Centennial Technologies	USA	100	23/01/2001	108
Jabil Circuit	Taiwan Green Point	Taiwan	100	23/11/2006	871
	Marconi—Factories	United Kingdom	Assets	13/01/2001	369
	GET Manufacturing	Hong-Kong	100	11/08/1999	243
	Koninklijke Philips- Plants	Nether-lands	Assets	29/08/2002	231
	Varian Manufacturing	USA	100	07/02/2005	195
	Celetronix International	India	100	17/01/2006	185
	Hewlett-Packard — LaserJet asset	USA Italy	Assets	11/05/1998	76
Celestica	Lucent — Facilities	USA	Assets	24/07/2001	650
	IBM — Operations and asset	USA Italy	Assets	12/01/2000	500
	Omni Industries	Singapore	100	14/06/2001	494
	Manufacturers Services	USA	100	15/10/2003	279
	Primetech Electronics	Canada	100	01/06/2001	173
	Avaya	USA	Assets	20/02/2001	130
Elcoteq	Tellabs	Finland	Assets	15/11/2003	126
Benchmark	Pemstar	USA	100	17/10/2006	300
	Avex Electronics	USA	100	02/07/1999	289
Venture Manufacturing	GES International	Singapore	100	26/07/2006	962
Viasystems	Wirekraft Industries	USA	100	24/02/2000	210
	Marconi — Network business	China	Assets	25/01/2000	115
	Zincocelere	Italy	100	13/03/1998	100

Source: Zephir, Thomson Financial.

Unlike Top Class EMSs, Global Class EMSs have, at least in the past, pursued mainly endogenous dimensional growth strategies. Finally, as far as Local Class EMSs are concerned, they generally operate at a local level and their activities are similar to those of a contract manufacturer; their growth paths are seldom carried through M&A operations.

Table 7.2 lists the most important M&As that have characterized the ODM segment. The use of exogenous growth operations is less than that in the EMS segment, both quantitatively and in terms of the value of individual transactions.

Table 7.2   Main ODMs' M&A operations 2003–2007

Acquiring company	Acquired company	Head-quarter	Acquired share (%)	Announcement date	Transaction value ($M)
Asustek	Elite Group	Taiwan	Assets	28/03/2003	86
Compal Electronics	Trinity Communication	Taiwan	50	24/04/2000	42
	Toppoly Optoelectronics	Taiwan	n.a.	20/03/2005	41
	Arcadyan Technology	Taiwan	69	25/08/2006	30
TPV Technology	Koninklijke Philips	Nether-lands	Assets	16/12/2004	358
Lite-On Technology	Perlos	Finland	100	30/08/2007	377
	Li Shin International	Taiwan	from 20.83 to 100	11/01/2007	157
	BenQ — Optical storage operations	Taiwan	Assets	10/04/2006	129
	Leotek Electronics	Taiwan	72	03/09/2007	59
	Antek Semiconductor	Taiwan	100	01/06/2005	40
Mitac International	Tyan Computer	Taiwan	100	22/03/2007	57
Elite Group Computer	Uniwill Computer	Taiwan	100	10/07/2006	99

Source: Zephir, Thomson Financial.

It should be noted that the ODM segment has developed only recently; the dynamics and consolidation of M&As within the ODM segment will be part of its future development strategy. The convergence of Top Class EMSs' and ODMs' growth paths might also be favored by M&A operations that involve both subjects.

M&A IN THE EMS INDUSTRY

In the decade of 1997–2007, the EMS segment was characterized by intense operational activities aimed at exogenous growth. An M&A policy was adopted for the most part by Top Class EMSs. Figure 7.1 shows the trend of the number and the annual cumulated value of the 178 M&A operations completed by Top Class EMSs between 1997 and 2007, divided according to their closing dates.[2]

The important growth of the electronics industry that characterized the end of the 1990s generated the need for a very fast increase in electronics outsourcing production volumes. Growth through aggregation processes allowed EMS firms to increment their production capacity rapidly, thus answering the increased demand for electronic boards and systems from OEMs.

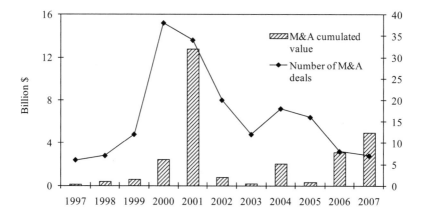

Source: Zephir, Thomson Financial.

Figure 7.1   M&A activities by Top Class EMSs

The M&A activity between the years 1997–2000 reflects the trend of the sector revenues. This positive period was followed by a declining phase during the years 2000–2002, characterized by a general slowdown in the economy. The electronics market experienced a demand fall, also due to the bursting of the dot-com bubble based on non-sustainable business models. It is not surprising that the entire EMS industry was affected. The main EMSs, in fact, suffered a strong reduction of profits. In 2002, the EBIT margin of the largest companies was negative, with percentage values around 10 per cent, with sharper peaks referred to some businesses. The exogenous growth strategy, adopted by Top Class EMSs in the historical context before the recession, had actually generated very high fixed costs as well as an excess in production capacity, with a subsequent negative effect on the firms' economic performance. The low saturation rate of the plants implied that EMSs, in their attempt to recover at least the fixed costs, accepted contracts with an unavoidable reduction in the final product price and, as a consequence, lower profit margins.

From a strategic standpoint, the intense M&A activity in 2001 was the natural continuation of the dimensional development started several years before. Several M&A transactions have therefore contributed to emphasizing the subsequent period of economic downturn. In 2001, the first stage of the exogenous growth had ended. One year later with respect to the overall revenue trend of the sector, M&A activity regarding the Top Class EMS group suffered a decisive reduction. In 2004 the EMS sector began to resume the growth process, which led to a total turnover estimated to be 180 billion US dollars during 2007. Furthermore, in the five-year period from 2002 to 2006, the market share held by the top ten companies grew from 63 per cent to 73 per cent.

After the period of sales decrease, many Top Class EMS companies again resorted to M&A as a tool in developing their production capacities to respond to the needs of a market in which demand was once again increasing and undergoing a renewal phase of acquisitions. The overall value of the related M&A activity grew from two billion US dollars in 2004 to more than five billion US dollars in 2007.[3] However, the number of transactions decreased progressively over the same four years, highlighting a trend to conclude only a few valuable operations while the impact of asset acquisition transactions was almost reset.

In the middle of 2006, Foxconn announced the acquisition of Premier Image Technology, with the proclaimed purpose of widening its range of products and services to its customers, reinforcing its structure and group competitiveness and reducing the relative production costs. Foxconn concluded the first acquisition carried out by a Top Class EMS firm over a Top Class ODM firm. Again, in 2006, Venture Manufacturing acquired GES International, an EMS firm focused on the planning and design of electronic systems and listed at the Singapore Stock Exchange. The acquisition was aimed at reinforcing competences in design R&D.

Among the most important M&A undertakings in 2007, Flextronics, the second largest EMS company, made a takeover bid to acquire Solectron, one of the three US companies competing for the world's third place position in the EMS industry. The transaction was positively closed after having been approved by the antitrust commissions in the USA and in the European Union. Flextronics aimed at changing the competitive scenario of the EMS sector, creating an organization able to generate about 30 billion US dollars in revenue as opposed to the leadership of Foxconn. The Flextronics–Solectron acquisition was the most important M&A operation ever to have occurred between two companies in the EMS industry.

Acquisition endeavors are often directed towards targets located in geographical areas with particular elements of interest. Many operations are carried out with firms based in countries with a low cost of labor, such as China and India, or by those aiming towards the acquisitions of technologically advanced companies based in Taiwan. Figure 7.2 shows the geographical distribution of companies that were acquired by M&A operations from 1999 to 2007.

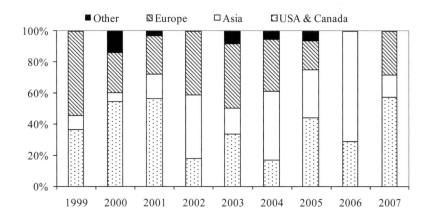

Source: Zephir, Thomson Financial.

Figure 7.2   M&A geographical distribution by Top Class EMSs

A univocal trend is not emerging; acquisitions were characterized by a high level of geographical variability from year to year. This variability may be due, at least in part, to the fact that EMSs provide support to their OEM clients following them in the localization process that they have chosen.

In the years 2000–2002, when most of the acquisition activities occurred, the number of closed operations on Asian targets was rather small, while later, the occurrence of M&A operations in Asia became more significant, underscoring how the Eastern market represents an unrivaled long-term opportunity, thanks to the growth potential of the local markets.

With reference to Foxconn, about 95 per cent of the acquisition investments were connected to transactions with Asian-based organizations, highlighting the Taiwanese company's focus in that area. Solectron shows a parallel situation; before its acquisition, the US firm concentrated mainly on domestic targets, almost neglecting Asia. Other Top Class EMSs have implemented a different strategy for their geographical localization, showing a more widespread distribution of acquisitions, in both numerical and geographical terms. Seventy per cent of the 48 operations involving Flextronics took place in Europe and North America, while only 23 per cent took place in Asia.

Figure 7.3 shows the total value of the M&A operations carried out by each Top Class EMS from 1997 to 2007, as well as the number of operations that occurred to obtain each value.

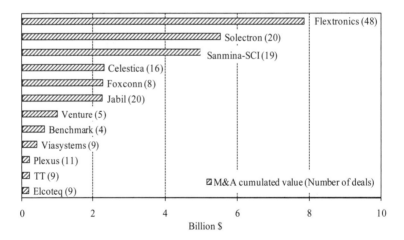

Source: Zephir, Thomson Financial.

Figure 7.3   M&A distribution of Top Class EMS

A high level of heterogeneity in the selected operations is clear, both for the number of such operations and for their value. Half the operations were completed by Flextronics, Solectron and Sanmina–SCI. The main company that promoted the aggregation processes that have characterized the EMS industry in that decade is Flextronics, which alone contributed more than 25 per cent of the M&A operations of the Top Class group. Also, Solectron and Sanmina–SCI have largely resorted to acquisitions to promote rapid dimensional growth; these are the same firms that were more heavily affected by the 2000–2002 recession.

The figures on the sector leader company, Foxconn, are surprising for the limited number of M&A operations, considering a 59 per cent CAGR calculated for the period from 1997 to 2006. Almost identical figures were allocated to the exogenous process of dimensional development by the American company Jabil Circuit and by the Canadian company Celestica. Each transaction carried out by Foxconn implied an average expense of 381 million US dollars,[4] higher than the average price paid by the two North American companies (Jabil, 207 million dollars and Celestica, 289 million dollars).

The trend to allocate significant financial resources to different growth strategies is clearly shown primarily by the comparison with Solectron and Sanmina–SCI, which invested an average of 790 and 638 million US dollars in the acquisition of each target. Flextronics' position appears to be more balanced, though the Singapore company based the process of dimensional development specifically on M&A operations; the average value of these operations was 357 million US dollars, in line with the data considered for Foxconn.

A preliminary analysis obtained by crossing revenue data (Table 7.3) showed an inverse relation between the profitability and intensity of M&A operations. This could be a sign of the difficulties involved in rapidly achieving pre-established synergies in business plans concerning acquisition operations.

The companies that resorted more to exogenous growth activities (Flextronics, Solectron, Sanmina–SCI) actually showed lower operational performances than other EMSs that concluded a limited number of operations (Foxconn) or operations of lower value (Jabil Circuit). This has no statistical value because of the limited number of observations, yet there are operational aspects, such as the costs associated with the restructuring need to implement synergies, as well as financial aspects, namely the payments of the debts derived from acquisition operations.

Figure 7.4 shows the most important EMSs based on the importance they placed on exogenous growth strategies and to the actual overall dimensional development they achieved. The two axes of the chart are defined respectively as the total value invested in M&A operations in the years 1997–2007 and as the annual growth rate calculated in the period 2001–2006,[5] while each circle area is proportional to the turnover achieved in 2006.

Table 7.3   EBIT margin of the Top Class EMSs

	EBIT (%) Foxconn	EBIT (%) Flextronics	EBIT (%) Jabil Circuit	EBIT (%) Solectron	EBIT (%) Sanmina–SCI
1998	15.2	3.8	5.8	6.0	5.6
1999	13.4	3.6	6.1	5.3	7.5
2000	11.5	−3.7	6.0	5.0	8.5
2001	9.5	−1.1	3.8	−0.7	1.5
2002	7.6	−0.4	1.5	−31.4	−31.6
2003	6.6	−1.6	0.6	−23.9	−0.8
2004	6.5	2.4	3.5	−0.5	0.7
2005	5.8	2.2	3.3	0.7	−4.2
2006	6.2	2.3	2.8	0.9	−0.3

Source: Orbis.

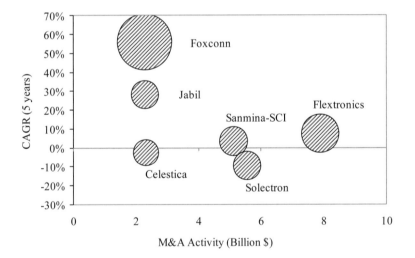

Source: Orbis, Zephir, Thomson Financial.

Figure 7.4   Growth vs. M&A activity of Top Class EMSs

Foxconn is the company that achieved the greatest growth, even though it invested only a little more than one fourth of the resources allocated by Flextronics in its own M&A activity. The very fast development of the Taiwanese company represents an anomaly within the EMS industry, whose net growth rate was reduced to 3.4 per cent without Foxconn.

Although its revenues were a little higher than 10 billion US dollars, Jabil too follows a development trend close to 30 percentage points; yet, against a total investment in M&A operations that recalls the growth strategy implemented by Foxconn, the American company has proved to be one of the most dynamic as far as M&A operations are concerned, having concluded 20 transactions over the last ten years.

Among the EMSs more active in M&A operations, Flextronics is the only company that was able to achieve an annual growth (CAGR 7.8 per cent) greater than that of the sector (not including Foxconn). Sanmina's sales, after having more than doubled between 2001 (4.1 billion US dollars) and 2002 (8.8 billion US dollars) following the merger with SCI, have remained almost unchanged during the last five years. Conversely, during the same five-year period, Solectron's revenues underwent a significant reduction (CAGR −9.5 per cent)

ACQUISITION TYPES

Different strategic policies can be identified in order to stimulate M&A activities. There are also many determinants that have encouraged Top Class EMSs to increase their size through successive aggregation processes. Factors that often contribute to the conclusion of one specific M&A operation are associated with the achievement of a better competitive position in the reference market. They can therefore be outlined by different objectives and acquisition typologies.

- EMS consolidation
- Vertical convergence
- OEM divestiture
- EMS divestiture

EMS CONSOLIDATION

The need to rapidly increase their production capacity pushed EMSs towards an acquisitive growth process, especially at the end of the 1990s when the demand for electronic products and services jumped. The acquisition of

existing production plants allowed the companies to reduce the necessary
time for a green-field development of the resources needed to satisfy the
OEMs' requests.

Table 7.4   EMS consolidation M&As

2007	Acquiring company	Acquired company
January	Benchmark	Pemstar
January	IPTE	Barco Manufacturing Service
February	Kimball ElectronicsGroup	Reptron Electronics
March	AWS Electronics	Cemgraft Electronic Manufacturing
April	Sierra Proto Express	PC Boards
April	Delta Group Electronics	Singletec
May	Incap	TVS Electronics
June	Adeptron Technologies	Pacific Circuit Assembly
June	Nu Visions Manufacturing	Veritek Manufacturing Services
June	Worldwide Manufacturing USA	Shanghai De Chuang Electric and Electronics Company
August	Creation Technologies	SMC
August	Creation Technologies	Taytronics
August	AWS ElectronicsGroup	Instem Technologies
October	Flextronics	Solectron
November	Note	Ionics EMS
December	Foxconn	Carston
December	Asteel	Flash Electronics
December	Beyonics Technology	Senai Seagate Industries
December	Hansa Electronics	Elektromekan I Årjäng

Source: Lincoln International (2008).

Where the two companies involved in the transaction are using the same
production technology, the increase in production volume generates a
reduction of the costs, thanks to the exploitation of economies of scale and to
the operational synergies. Meanwhile, the acquisition of a target enables the

acquiring company to widen its range of products, optimizing the original offer with the incorporation of complementary products or services, or acquiring skills in business areas previously not under its control, but characterized by a strong attractiveness in view of the company's future development.

The geographical position of the targets can be decisive in expanding the market served by the acquiring company and optimizing the production supply chain. Recently many EMSs have moved towards a geographical arrangement in order to keep the R&D and after-sales service divisions close to their main clients, and delocalizing the production capability to low-labor-cost countries. Acquisitions and mergers completed with the aim of achieving these results are classified as EMS consolidations; this category includes the two most important operations in the history of the sector, Sanmina–SCI and Flextronics–Solectron.

Table 7.4 shows the main EMS consolidation operations that occurred in the entire sector in 2007. It is interesting to highlight how M&A activities have also become somewhat important for Global Class EMSs. Of the nineteen transactions carried out in 2007 and listed in the table, 16 can be credited to Global Class EMSs, while three belong to Top Class EMSs (Benchmark, Flextronics and Foxconn).

VERTICAL CONVERGENCE

Over the last decade, EMSs have progressively evolved to add many added-value services to their original contract manufacturing activity. Several M&A operations were encouraged by the need to access the know-how to implement new services, such as the engineering of electronic systems or maintenance and after-sales service. Acquisitions of this kind can be identified as vertical convergence operations since they enable the acquiring companies to integrate vertically, upstream or downstream.

Among the most important operations was the takeover of International Display Works, a company specialized in the design and creation of LCD Displays, by Flextronics in 2006. As far as downstream integration is concerned, in 2001, Solectron closed the first acquisition carried out by an EMS towards a distributor of customer relationship management, the American firm Stream International. Four years later, Solectron likewise completed the acquisition of Service Source Europe, with the aim of widening its logistics and after-sales services.

This type of operation is similar to the exogenous growth strategy implemented by Foxconn; the Taiwanese firm concluded its two main operations with the aim of widening its end markets and integrating in the supply chain in areas qualified by higher margins. The two main M&A operations involving Foxconn, Ambit Microsystem (2004) and Premier Image Technology (2006), gave way to the control of the two ODMs.

Table 7.5   EMS vertical convergence M&As

2007	Acquiring company	Acquired company
January	Jabil Circuit	Taiwan Green Point
January	Jaltek Systems	Wavesight
February	Flextronics	Webraiser Technologies
March	Design Solutions	Paradigm Manufacturing Partners
April	Tellumant	Rhomco Electronic Assemblers
April	Partner Tech	Labyrint Development
April	Heatterm	Elektropoint
April	Jurong Technologies	Amould Plastic Industries
August	Jurong Technologies	SEB Corporation

Source: Lincoln International (2008).

OEM DIVESTITURE

The resorting to outsourcing of an ever increasing number of production activities and added-value services has transformed the OEM business model, allowing OEMs to reduce the number of plants and the associated quantity of physical assets. As a consequence, several EMSs have pursued a growth strategy that implied the acquisition of industrial plants, production units, and generic assets left by their clients.

These M&A operations, classified as OEM divestitures, are frequently associated with contracts that anticipate a long-term supply of the same electronic systems that used to be manufactured by the same OEMs, and of added-value services.

Falling into this category was the transaction in which Flextronics acquired Xerox Corporation's production activities located in Canada, Brazil, Mexico and Malaysia in 2001. Then Jabil Circuit concluded the acquisition of the French plant of Alcatel dedicated to the production of electronic components and systems for the telephone industry, obtaining a contract for the supply of the same products. Four years earlier, Jabil Circuit completed a similar operation by taking the Italian and US factories for the assembly of laser printer electronic boards from Hewlett-Packard; contemporary to the transfer of the assets, the two companies signed a three-year supply contract.

It should be noted that often these operations are carried out due to the OEM's bargaining pressure, with the EMSs' goal of obtaining supply contracts of 3–5 year periods, rather than for strategic-structural reasons. Frequently, when the contract expires, OEMs may entrust the electronics outsourcing services to other EMSs, ensuring lower costs.

From this point of view, we can understand the data about the number of asset acquisitions showed in Figure 7.5. It is not surprising that the highest number of M&A operations of this group happened within the 2000–2002 crisis of the sector. In order to get large-volume supply contracts to pay back their fixed costs, EMSs were ready to acquire their clients' production plants.

A trend seems to emerge, where this kind of operation is becoming less frequent, a sign of the stability reached by the OEM business model: from 2005 to 2007, only five asset acquisition operations were completed and the trend became marginal. The peak from 2000 to 2002 can also be interpreted as the period that forced the OEMs to rely more pervasively on the electronics outsourcing model.

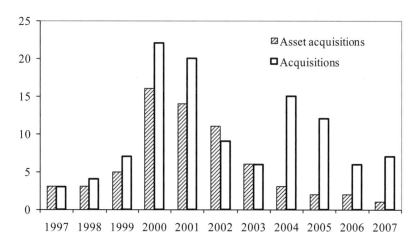

Source: Orbis, Zephir, Thomson Financial.

Figure 7.5   Asset acquisitions on M&A operations for Top Class EMS

Table 7.6 summarizes the main OEM divestiture operations completed during 2007. Even in this category, we find that the Top Class firms' contribution is limited.

Table 7.6   OEM divestiture M&As

2007	Acquiring company	Acquired company
February	TBP Electronics	Alcatel-Lucent
February	Jurong Technologies	Orcom International
July	Benchmark	Quantum Storage
September	Kitron ASA	UAB Kitron Elsis
September	Elecsys Corporation	Radix International
November	Jurong Technologies	i-Sirius
November	Jabil Circuit	Nokia Siemens Networks
December	Sanmina–SCI	Powerwave Technologies
December	Nam Tai Electronics	Jetup Electronic

Source: Lincoln International (2008).

EMS DIVESTITURE

Sometimes EMSs, like OEMs, with the aim of a major focus on their specific business segment, also choose divestiture operations, selling their production plants to other EMSs. The link between EMS suppliers and OEM clients is very important in this operations typology. A change in the localization strategy of OEM manufacturing plants often causes EMSs to close down factories located in areas that are no longer considered strategic.

Table 7.7   EMS divestiture M&As

2007	Acquiring company	Acquired company
February	Nortech Systems	Suntron
March	Prevas	Flextronics
July	Venture Corp	VS Electronics
July	Startronics Group	Sanmina–SCI
August	Red Rocket	Celetronix Power India

Source: Lincoln International (2008).

Table 7.7 lists the EMS divestiture operations for 2007. With respect to other M&A types, they are lower in number and were concluded by Global Class EMSs only.

DETERMINANTS OF MERGER AND ACQUISITION ACTIVITY

Consistent with the theories that assign a recurring trend (M&A Wave) to the merger and acquisition activity, two periods stand out for their intense aggregation activity, shown at the beginning of the year 2000 and in the years 2006 and 2007. The first period is associated with the growth of the sector (growth wave), while the second is more steady (maturity wave). A correlation between the intensity of M&A activity and the positioning with respect to the industry life cycle is evident; the two waves indicate different market dynamics and different strategic plans.

In the case of the 2000–2001 period, the strong increase in M&A activities was mostly motivated by an aim to rapidly increase production capability following demand growth. From another standpoint, the operations of this period could be evaluated as a sign of the strategic need to maintain or expand the company's presence in the rapidly expanding electronics outsourcing market. Another contribution to this first wave, especially as far as asset acquisitions are concerned, comes from the OEMs which, in a phase where their business model is changing and outsourcing is spreading, have sometimes forced EMS firms to purchase their plants to obtain supply contracts, which later negatively affected the profit performance. The end of the 2002 growth wave was related to the market drop.

The second wave (2006–2007) lies in a different strategic context because the sector seems to have been showing the first elements of maturity. To compete in a market that grows with the world economy, M&A operations facilitate economies of scale, aggregating knowledge and technology with the goal of achieving a stronger bargaining power. The main acquisition activities were no longer focused on an increase in production capacity but on the control of companies, usually medium enterprises, with a growth potentiality to offset the decreasing margins.

The Flextronics-Solectron case was different in that the aggregation process seemed to be motivated by an attempt to oppose Foxconn in dimensional terms.

The acquisition trend in the sector was also justified by the position of EMSs firms who were in an intermediate position along the supply chain, and have the component suppliers and distributors as suppliers, and OEMs as clients. Their main suppliers, be they manufacturers or distributors of electronic components, have remarkable dimensions that contribute, together with the high degree of concentration and the absence of substitute products, to enhance their bargaining power. Also due to the structure of the semiconductor market, cycles are often presented that affect both costs and supply chain timing.

The OEM clients' bargaining power is high, not only because of their large dimensions, but also for the EMSs' cost structure that make them accept orders even with very low margins to achieve an adequate plant saturation rate and pay back their fixed costs. M&A operations thus represent a reaction to the competitive pressure from both the suppliers and the clients. As far as EMS consolidation operations are concerned, they respond to a double function: on one side, they increase the company size and its market power with a consequent increase in the margins due to the EMSs' better position during the negotiation and to the larger economies of scale. On the other, the high degree of concentration reached by the EMS market represents a credible threat for the OEMs, because the aggregation processes have reduced the number of large-size EMS firms that were able to guarantee both the production capacity requested by the OEMs and the necessary level of know-how.

As far as vertical convergence operations are concerned, they represent an attempt to reduce the competitive pressure brought by the players close to the EMS industry, catching higher margins while at the same time ensuring access to new competence in order to reach a higher degree of diversification.

EXOGENOUS GROWTH FOR GLOBAL CLASS EMSs

The aggregation process among EMSs can be summarized in different stages, each of them showing specific traits. Recently M&A operations seem involve more significantly medium and small players, like the Global and Local Class EMSs.

- The 1980s and 1990s: The sector was highly fragmented and the first aggregation operations referred to consolidation procedures directed towards geographical, technological and service aspects. This stage was characterized by a high number of potential targets and limited competition among the bidders.
- Late 1990s: In this second stage, the exogenous growth strategy spread and the number of companies that chose this strategy was very high. The number of potential targets decreased, causing a higher level of competition among the bidders and an increase in the price of the companies to be acquired.

- 2000–2004: In the third stage, the EMS industry was more concentrated and the market leaders started to focus on the integration of the acquired companies, orienting towards their endogenous growth. The number of M&A operations decreased and the competition among the bidders increased, but the value of the target companies started to decrease.
- 2004–2008: The companies promoting acquisition processes displayed their strategies; they reached a critical mass, exploiting economies of scale and exerting a strong competitive pressure on the other companies. M&A activities were minimal for the larger companies and the value of the firms that had not aligned their business models to compete efficiently was decreasing. The consolidation processes within the EMS sector also started to involve smaller companies. In the year 2007, the majority of the operations, approximately 80 per cent of them, were carried out by Global Class EMS.

To take advantage of the consolidation processes and to avoid their criticalities, Global Class and Local Class EMS must carefully choose a strategy that enables them to react to and adjust to changes within the competitive scenario.

- *EMSs as acquiring companies*
  Although being the acquiring company is an attractive option for many EMS firms, it is not always a practicable one. To pursue an acquisition strategy, a company must have a competent and experienced management team. Exogenous growth requires a set of skills distinct from those needed for the company's operating management. Furthermore, the companies must have access to the capital needed to finance M&A operations. The capital comes from various sources, such as banks, investment funds, and private equities.
- *EMSs as companies being acquired*
  Many EMSs cannot consolidate through acquisitions. These companies can choose to be acquired by the sector leaders of the market. To maximize the value for the target company's shareholders, it is important that the transaction is planned while taking into account the latter's specific needs and objectives.
- *EMSs that reposition their business without M&A operations*
  This is a risky option because the market, after its consolidation process, will very likely experience major changes. The Top Class EMS segment will be large, well exploited and focused on eroding the smaller competitors' market shares. Many Local and Global Class firms might find it difficult to 'survive'. Those who succeed in implementing this

solution are the ones that address a more specialized market and that are able to differentiate themselves from their big competitors.

Medium sized EMSs belonging to a consolidated industry should develop and implement a strategy to fit to the environmental changes. Another stage of M&A operations is expected to take place mainly owing to Global and Local Class EMS. The companies that decide not to implement exogenous growth strategies should develop a sustainable business model that can compete in the post-consolidation market, such as through technological specialization in areas without major competitors.

M&A IN THE ODM INDUSTRY

The ODM business model was developed in the early 2000s, stimulated by the growing extend of the outsourcing of added-value products and services among OEMs. In the years 2002–2006, the sector had a significant dimensional development, together with an equally rapid concentration process that has allowed Top Class firms to represent a cumulated market share that exceeded 95 per cent of 2006 revenues. Unlike the EMS firms, ODMs have not carried out a high number of operations aimed at exogenous growth.

Figure 7.6 shows the M&A activity carried out by Top Class ODMs in the years between 1997 and 2007.[6] The overall volume of the transactions achieved an aggregated value a little higher than 1.6 billion US dollars; this is about 6 per cent of the total amount invested by Top Class EMSs in exogenous growth operations.

Due to its most recent development, the ODM sector did not have to react to the growth of the electronic market that occurred during the 1990s, nor to the following sales contraction period of 2000–2002. On the contrary the 2002 cumulated industry revenues exceeded the threshold of 50 billion US dollars. In particular, until the year 2005 the M&A activity attributed to Top Class firms was limited to one or two transactions per year, not a significant figure in terms of the related economic values. Later, the number of M&A operations progressively increased, totaling 12 transactions in 2007; their total value contributed a 60 per cent value to the total aggregated value invested by Top Class ODMs in exogenous growth operations.

It is surprising to note the extraordinary growth of the main firms in this sector that were able to increase their turnovers with a progression that can be compared to the trend covered by the EMS Foxconn. In particular, the first two ODMs, Asustek and Quanta Computer, achieved a turnover of approximately 47 billion US dollars in 2007, after a four-year growth with a CAGR of 43 and 32 percentage points, respectively.

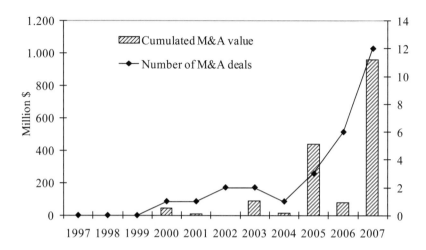

Source: Zephir, Thomson Financial.

Figure 7.6   M&A activities by Top Class ODMs

The availability of low-cost labor in their regions and the possibility of achieving higher margins by exploiting economies of scale have encouraged ODMs to expand their production activities through the establishment of several subsidiaries and the green-field creation of new industrial plants. They also applied a growth policy that promotes the creation of strategic alliances as well as signing joint ventures mainly with other companies within the same sector.

FLEXTRONICS–SOLECTRON MERGER

The operation of the purchase of Solectron by Flextronics was concluded in October 2007. This agreement will have an effect on mutual competitive relationships among the market players for years to come.

In the EMS competition scenario, Flextronics was in second position in 2006 in terms of sales revenue, with 19 billion US dollars and an average growth of approximately 8 percent per year for the previous five years. Meanwhile, Solectron was in fourth position, with a turnover of approximately 10 billion US dollars. Some of the main competitors were

Foxconn (sector leader with revenue exceeding 40 billion US dollars), Jabil Circuit and Sanmina–SCI.

Figure 7.7 contains data on the normalized turnovers and shows the high growth rate of Foxconn, followed by Jabil Circuit, while the other players show almost constant normalized turnovers from 2002 to 2007.

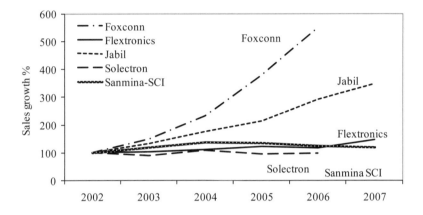

Source: Orbis (2007).

Figure 7.7   Top Class EMSs' compared sales growth

Figure 7.8 instead highlights the trend of operating profit vs. turnover. Foxconn stands out for its higher margin that remains around 6–7 per cent. In the years 2000–2002 the other EMSs, Solectron in particular, showed relevant losses.

FLEXTRONICS

Flextronics was founded in 1969 by Joe McKenzie with the entrepreneurial idea of offering an external service for the assembly of electronic boards to Silicon Valley companies that had a limited production capability. In 1970, the firm was bought by Bob Todd, Joe Sullivar and Jack Watts who set up extreme technological innovations, such as highly automated assembly plants, with the aim of reducing the impact of labor while increasing the quality of the manufactured boards. In the 1980s, Flextronics started to offer design services and, thanks also to the opening of new production plants in Asia, it increased its production capability. In 1987, the company went public on NASDAQ, but the crisis of the financial markets[7] and the following recession generated losses that were so serious that they caused the delisting of the company. In 1994, after an internal reorganization, the new company called Flextronics International, based in Singapore, went public again.

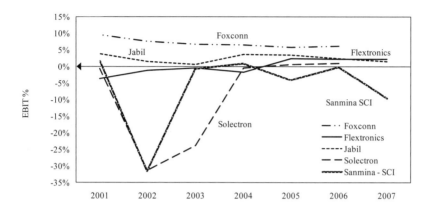

Source: Orbis.

Figure 7.8   Top Class EMSs' compared EBIT margin

Since the 1990s, the company has been growing thanks to its M&A operations; its larger size has forced the creation of a centralized infrastructure to support the purchase, production and distribution departments. A model for the industrial layout and process unification has been implemented at the global level, involving the suppliers, with the aim of reducing the related costs.

FLEXTRONICS STRATEGIC PATH

The early entrepreneurial idea was that of offering the service of electronic board assembly. In the 1980s, the company started a process to change its business model including its design service. Thanks to the opening of new production plants in Asia, it expanded its production capability. Since a crisis associated with the downturn in the US market at the end of the 1980s, Flextronics has been growing mainly through exogenous processes, expanding its business model along the electronics outsourcing supply chain, with services associated with design, manufacturing, logistics management and after-sales service.

The company, which owns production plants in 25 different countries and employs 116 thousand people (2007), reached a turnover of 19 billion US

dollars during the 2007 fiscal year, with a 23 per cent increase over the
previous year.

As early as 1998, the company started an exogenous growth process,
increasing the value of its assets by almost six times. Yet, despite these
investments, turnover did not grow proportionally, a sign of the difficulties in
short-term integration generated by the M&A transactions.

The chart in Figure 7.9 analyzes the company's performance, showing the
EBIT margin as a function of the asset turnover. As with many other EMSs,
the reduction of the economic result in the years 2000–2002 is evident. The
fast growth of the information technology industry in the previous years had,
in fact, brought an increase in outsourced production, persuading EMSs to
expand their production capability. The drop in demand emphasized the
excess in the assets and the plants' reduced saturation rate.

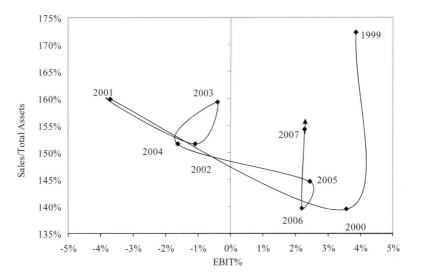

Source: Orbis.

Figure 7.9   Total assets turnover vs. EBIT margin of Flextronics

The excess in production capability cut the EMSs' bargaining power with
their clients, causing a decrease in the sales prices in order to keep operating
the factories, which were purchased only a few months before the economic
slow-down. It should also be noted that the economic situation was also
jeopardized by the costs of organizational restructuring of the acquired
companies and by the financial charges related to the same acquisitions.

Flextronics's next strategy has focused on flexibility by the reduction of development and production time; for this purpose it has moved towards verticalization through a complete range of services such as design, assembly, testing and quality control, as well as the management of logistics, distribution and after-sales services. Regarding the reduction of costs, the majority of the production capacity has been delocalized to low-labor-cost countries, while R&D divisions have been kept close to the client.

SOLECTRON

Solectron was founded in Milpitas (California) in 1977. During the 1980s, it experienced an expansion phase due to the significant growth of the electronics market. It was created with the aim of supporting OEMs with more production capability. Solectron defined its business model by also offering specialized services for design and production, thus orienting its strategy towards a growing differentiation.

The growth of the company in the EMS industry has benefited from its remarkable advantage in terms of acquired know-how, which allowed it to offer its clients the opportunity to use specific plants, and ability to manufacture any electronic board, without the client making any investment.

In 1989, the company went public on the New York Stock Exchange and in the 1990s it started an acquisition policy with the purpose of reinforcing its competitive position, especially in the Asian market. Solectron succeeded in implementing the same production and organizational model in all the new plants.

During the 2000–2002 downturn, Solectron was heavily affected by the crisis and underwent heavy losses. The duration of this situation, also throughout the market recovery phase, forced the company to implement a complex restructuring process in 2005. In 2006, Solectron held a market share of 6.8 per cent, with a turnover of 10.6 billion US dollars, exceeding the figure of the previous year by 1.1 per cent, with around 45 thousand employees. The reference market was the American one with a sales share of about 30 per cent.

As far as the company's economic performance is concerned, Figure 7.10 shows the relation between the EBIT margin and the assets turnover in the 1998–2006 period.

Until 2001 Solectron was the market leader but started to slowly decline until, in 2002, its losses were as high as 32 per cent and only in 2005 did it show positive margin figures. There are many reasons for this situation; first, the lack of diversification of the client base exposed the company to risks derived from a reduction in sales volumes and depreciation of the stock due to obsolescence if a client cancelled or reduced his orders.

Besides the heavy decrease in the production saturation rate, a situation also common to the other Top Class EMS, another criticality was the strong dependence on the information technology industry: workstations, personal computers and peripherals represented 50 per cent of its 2001 revenue.

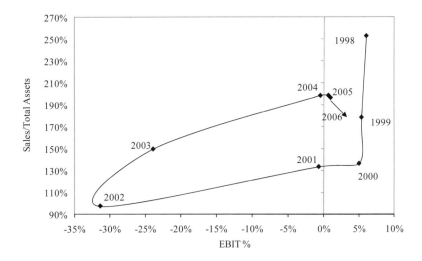

Source: Orbis.

Figure 7.10   Total assets turnover vs. EBIT margin of Solectron

The size of Solectron (Figure 7.11) on the one hand represented an advantage in terms of bargaining power, but on the other implied a limited flexibility, especially with regard to the possibility of reallocating its production sites in regions with a lower labor cost. In fact, in those years, more than 80 per cent of the plants were located in North America and Western Europe.

The 2000–2001 period was characterized by a strong exogenous expansion of the EMS companies, that carried out important acquisitions. Following the example of Sanmina–SCI merger completed in 2001, Solectron believed that growth was the way to remain at the top of the market. In 2000, the company announced the acquisition of NatSteel Electronics, valued at 2.4 billion US dollars; the acquisition was concluded at the beginning of the next year. Again, in 2001, it also concluded the acquisition of C-Mac Industries. The price of this operation was 2.7 billion

US dollars, an amount which corresponds to almost 50 per cent of the total M&A operations carried out by Solectron in the decade 1998–2007.

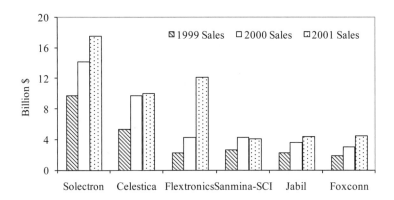

Source: Company reports.

Figure 7.11   Sales of the main EMSs (1999–2001)

The availability of a better production capacity obtained through acquisitions, however, turned out to be useless, due to the drop in the demand for electronic products. Heavy losses were caused by a drop in sales on the one hand, and by the high costs of restructuring the new subsidiaries, increased by the debts generated by the acquisitions, on the other hand.

Solectron decided to keep its design centers in the USA and Europe, while it delocalized the production facilities to low-labor-cost regions. Nevertheless, the company had some weak points; one problem was due to the fact that Solectron did not effectively widen its client base. The ten most important clients in 2001 still represented 60 per cent of the total turnover in 2006. As a consequence, the transfer of some orders from Solectron's clients to other EMSs further jeopardized its growth.

FLEXTRONICS AND SOLECTRON TO MERGE

After the 2002 crisis, Solectron faced a slow recovery that generated a decline in the company's global dimensions. During 2006 Solectron announced the forthcoming closing of plants in Western Europe and the USA. This scenario created all the conditions to project a merger in which Flextronics would acquire Solectron, for a total transaction value of about 3.6 billion US dollars, mainly through the exchange of shares.

Considering the dimensions of the companies involved, the Flextronics–Solectron merger affected the competitive area of the EMS industry, with a further increase in concentration. Flextronics pursued some objectives related to achieving economies of scale and an increase in production volume, to market share growth, and to a higher degree of product diversification. Regarding Solectron, the operation appeared to have been an attempt to exit from a complex situation – in terms of profitability – that had persisted since 2001, to return to representing a market leadership in many segments, exploiting its complementarities towards Flextronics in the different businesses.

In addition to all this, the company attempted to rapidly increase its turnover and market share in order to be able to compete, also on the basis of size, with the sector leader Foxconn, who had experienced an exponential development of its market share. Foxconn's success can be attributed to the particular strategy implemented, which involved the following key points:

- *Selection of a world-class client base*
  Unlike its competitors, and in contrast to the risk diversification principles, Foxconn has kept a highly concentrated client base; over the years it has been able to consolidate its position and to increase the clients' loyalty by developing increasingly specific competences and highly customized products.
- *Targeted M&A operations*
  Foxconn has chosen to limit its external growth through a few well targeted acquisitions, trying to find targets characterized by distinguished know-how competence.
- *Vertical integration*
  Another distinctive factor of Foxconn's strategy is its strong vertical integration, justified by the possibility of guaranteeing a major cost control and operating in areas characterized by better margins with respect to the EMS sector, thus increasing its profits.

The Flextronics-Solectron operation is oriented towards the creation of a company with a stronger competitive position, able to deliver performances comparable to Foxconn's. The goal is pursued along different strategic paths. The operation appears indeed to be an example of horizontal integration between companies operating in the same business area, and can be classified as EMS consolidation.

Upon the start of the merger operation, the potential synergies coming from the merger and involving several areas have been evaluated. An important feature to ensure the efficacy of the transaction concerns the diversification and widening of the products/services portfolio. Thanks to the complementarity of the competences (Solectron, on the one side, developed know-how, technology and innovation; Flextronics, on the other, was oriented towards the continuous search for high production volumes at low costs), the services offered will be broader. The new company offers services ranging from new product design with innovative solutions to after-sales service and maintenance. This should also ensure the opportunity to acquire a higher number of clients and above all increased volumes, which should then be followed by an increase in turnover and the achievement of economies of scale.

A more balanced product mix will contribute to limiting the demand volatility typical of the EMS industry. After the merger, the wider business area is the IT infrastructure sector (Figure 7.12); this growth will imply a lower rate on the sales coming from the mobile sector, since Solectron did not control this business area.

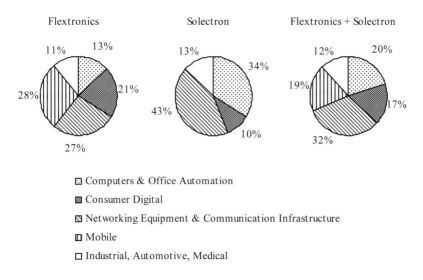

Source: Company reports.

Figure 7.12   Market segmentation after the merger of Flextronics and Solectron

Additional synergies come from the geographical complementarity of the markets. The merger of the two companies should ensure a better coverage of the world market. In fact, the high prevalence on Solectron's revenues from the US and Latin American markets should be balanced by that of Asia, which is the Flextronics reference market.

The operation should also positively affect the client portfolio, thanks to the consolidation of the relationships with the OEM clients that are common to both companies; they will therefore save on transaction and logistics costs.

RISK FACTORS

An M&A operation, along with the advantages derived from the synergies, also implies costs and risk factors that involve many technical and organizational aspects, including the management of human capital. The integration of two organization of such large sizes, like Flextronics and Solectron, might prove to be a complex and long-term process.

- *Integration time*
  The operation has the aim of competing with Foxconn in terms of growth, but considering the rapid expansion of the Taiwanese company, a delay in the integration time could cancel the advantage coming from the merger and put a stop to an efficient opposition to Foxconn's leadership.
- *Integration of human resources*
  The problems can be identified with the difficulties in cultural integration, affected also by the roles the management will play after the merger; for this purpose, the ability to keep key employees, both Flextronics' and Solectron's, will play a crucial role.
- *Product integration*
  Joining the products portfolio of two companies that have a different strategic approach might be a risky operation. Flextronics seems to be more oriented towards cost leadership, while Solectron has always aimed at high-quality products.
- *Cultural risks*
  The integration process between two companies affects their organizational culture; in particular, higher level risks appear when the two companies belong to countries with different cultures, as in the case being analyzed.
- *Access to credit*
  The costs of the transaction will cause an increase in the financial debt that could limit access to credit.
- *Integration costs*
  Integration and reorganization costs might have a negative influence on profitability, delaying the benefits generated by the synergies.
- *Information system*
  The newly integrated company will have to establish efficient

communication systems that allow the exchange of data and procedures; the most critical phase concerns the integration of the information systems.

A complete view of the benefits coming from the merger will be possible only after the effects of the synergies and reorganization are manifested, with the complete integration of the two organizations involved and the total inclusion of the costs in the new company. Moreover, the merger occurred not long before the 2008–2009 credit crunch, an unexpected event to the management.

The operation enables the new company to compete with Foxconn in both dimensional and market share terms. The effect of the operation might drive the market towards a duopoly; in fact, the turnover values, achieved in 2006 by the three main companies, represent 50 per cent of the market share.

One of the reasons that pushed Flextronics to acquire Solectron, and not another Top Class EMS, was probably also the low expenditure connected to the operation, since Solectron was estimated at about one third of its turnover. In comparison, the acquisition of Ambit by Foxconn had a transaction value of 1.5 times its turnover, which represents, in proportion, five times the value of the Flextronics–Solectron transaction.

It is surprising, though, that Flextronics, which has always oriented its strategy towards exogenous growth, did not turn to the acquisition of a company with better margins, albeit with turnover lower than Solectron's. As an alternative, in view of its vertical integration, the preference might have fallen on an ODM firm, whose segment has been characterized, over the last years, by a higher profitability level with respect to the EMS segment.

MERGER AND FINANCIAL MARKETS

It is interesting to analyze the stock performance of the shares of the companies' involved in the merger in the two periods before and after the announcement of the operation. Figure 7.13 represents the trend of the shares of the target company around the announcement date. On the day after the announcement of the agreement, the value of Solectron's shares soared by 15 per cent with respect to their opening value, and they remained almost stable until the date of the conclusion of the acquisition.

On the day of the announcement of the acquisition the total capitalization of the two companies was 12 per cent higher than the same value calculated three months before. Five months later, Flextronics–Solectron's total value decreased; in particular, on March 31, 2008 the company's capitalization deriving from the M&A operation had decreased by 24 per cent.

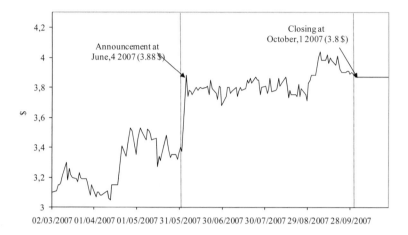

Source: Datastream.

Figure 7.13   Stock price performance of Solectron

NOTES

1.   The list includes only M&A operations closed within the period, excluding inter-group operations not aimed at the exogenous expansion of the head company. Also excluded were M&A operations carried out by subsidiaries, before they were in turn acquired by the object companies of this study; finally, for the same reasons, all buy-back operations were also excluded. Whenever Top Class firms acquired assets instead of company shares, the related operations were listed among M&A since they are consistent with the exogenous growth process.

2.   The analysis includes 194 M&A operations within the EMS industru. Yet, the M&A activity was limited to 178 operations, excluding six joint-venture operations, six operations of increased share participations with respect to subsidiaries and four minority stakes having EMS or ODM Top Class firms as opposite parties.

3.   The figures refer to M&A operations of Top Class EMS firms closed by October 31, 2007.

4.   The cumulated value of M&A operations and the average value of each transaction of the listed companies refer only to those operations whose values were disclosed to the market.

5.   Sanmina–SCI Corporation and Jabil Circuit closed their financial years on September 30 and on August 8: their five-year CAGR therefore refers to the period of 2002–2007.

6. The analysis includes 59 M&A operations within the ODM sector. Yet, M&A activity was limited to only 28 operations; from the initial 59, with the exclusion of five joint ventures, 15 operations of increased share participations with respect to subsidiaries, nine minority stakes Top Class EMSs or ODMs or target of the respective M&A operations, and two mergers joined in one single transaction.

7. On October 19, 1987, the Dow Jones index suffered a loss of 22.6 per cent in one day, while NASDAQ lost 11.4 per cent.

8. Industry Evolution and Strategic Positioning

INDUSTRY LIFE CYCLE

No market, although consolidated, can be considered static and unchanging. According to economic theories, a life cycle characterizes all economic sectors; it is composed of the initial birth stage, a next rapid growth, followed by a long maturity period and, often, by a decline stage. This is also true for the electronics outsourcing industry, whose structure depends on the interaction of external forces, such as change in demand, technological evolution, conjuncture, and forces within the sector, such as the intensity of competition and the evolution of the offering of new goods and services.

The change in the economic and technological context started in the early 1990s, when the process of electronics outsourcing took its first significant step. Economically, the opening and globalization of the markets changed the competition environment, moving the manufacture to low-labor-cost Asian countries. Technologically, the increased complexity of electronic devices, manufacturing processes and applications has encouraged external contracting and outsourcing to specialized companies.

While at the beginning of the 1990s the electronics outsourcing industry was starting, mainly through small and medium companies, the economic and technologic evolution triggered a rapid expansion process with a trend towards aggregation and consolidation of global companies. More recently, since the early 2000s, the growth has been characterized by a dimensional and functional segmentation (EMSs and ODMs), highlighting different strategic focuses as well as consolidations typical of industries that are approaching maturity.

The trends are still in progress and, by detecting the position of a sector in its life cycle, it is possible to define the best development and growth strategy; we can obtain some indications of the evolution criteria that support the growth of EMSs and ODMs. Although every sector shows its own particular traits, the scientific literature has shown that it is possible to discern regularities and repetitions that allow the identification of 'stages' or clearly distinguishable periods along the life of that sector. Among these are the initial period and creation of the sector, followed by a significant expansion phase and later by periods of consolidation and, sometimes, decline (Figure 8.1).

Every stage shows special traits highlighted by the trends of different parameters, such as the sector revenues, the number of existing businesses, and the average prices.

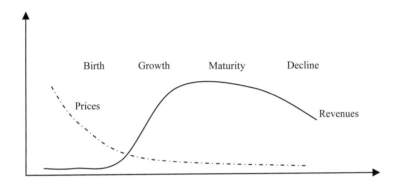

Figure 8.1   Industry life cycle

The automotive industry, for example, is a consolidated industrial sector studied by many experts in business strategy; the number of car industries grew significantly from the end of the 19th century until the 1930s. Later, and especially after the end of WWII, the sector experienced a concentration policy that brought a decrease in the number of car industries. In fact, after a fast expansion linked to the Western countries' mass motorization, a more moderate growth phase came, followed by a steady stage. The sector experienced the transition from an initial and balanced growth to an expansion phase, followed by a slowdown, until it entered a substantially steady period. The transition was also marked by an average price level that decreased progressively over time.

Among the different definitions of the sector, it is interesting to look at Andrews and Wilson's contributions on the supply side and Porter's contribution on the demand side.

From the supply-side point of view, Andrews and Wilson (1951) define a sector as a group of firms that, having analogous competence, use similar processes and the same set of knowledge.

> An industry consists of all businesses which operate processes of a sufficiently similar kind (implying the possession of substantially similar technical

resources) and possessing sufficiently similar backgrounds of experience and knowledge so that each of them could produce the particular product under consideration.

From the demand-side point of view, Porter (1980) refers to a sector as a group of competing companies that produce products or services in direct competition with one another, or groups of similar products and services that satisfy similar needs.

> An industry (whether product or service) [as] a group of competitors producing products or services that compete directly with each other.

In agreement with the seminal work of Abernathy and Utterback (1978), the initial phase of the formation of a sector is characterized by a level of instability that is caused by the different technological alternatives available and by the high innovation level of the product. The model is based on the understanding that a product life cycle is characterized by a dominant project emerging among the various proposals. When a product is put on the market, the level of uncertainty about the consumers' preference, as well as the necessary technologies that should be adopted, is very high. For this reason, every company suggests different versions, but in general, a standard will emerge, *de jure* or *de facto*, either through a regulator or through a widespread consensus among consumers and manufacturers.

A particular sales level related to the demand dynamics and the competition intensity corresponds to each of cycle stages. It is possible to relate the sales growth rate trend within a certain sector as a consequence of the interaction between the players within the sector and the competing businesses. The scientific literature suggests that the demand and the offerings show a typical trend, corresponding to certain behavior by both the clients (demand side) and the manufacturers (supply side).

As far as demand is concerned, during the initial stage (birth or introduction), sales appear to be of limited importance; potential customers are those who are particularly open to experimental innovations, with a value and use function that are to be defined. Later, during the growth stage, as a dominant project emerges, the product becomes more economically accessible and the level of sales increases rapidly as happens with mass products, for example. At the end of the expansion stage, that is in coincidence with the saturation of the reference market, sales are always more characterized by demand for replacement (i.e., replacement of old products with new ones), and of the turnover of new consumers who take the place of old ones. This is the typical maturity situation for a sector that marks every economic environment, followed by a decline phase, with a drop in sales, number of products and of companies competing in that industry.

Meanwhile, on the supply side, the initial stage of the life cycle is characterized by little-known technological innovations, by a limited production rate and a high fragmentation of businesses. In the growth phase, a better knowledge of the technology allows the companies to accumulate experience, to standardize the product and to reduce their prices; product innovation is replaced by process innovation (Figure 8.2).

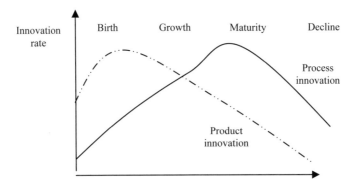

Figure 8.2   Product life cycle

During the maturity phase, the supply side shows a higher level of competition with a noticeable effect on price dynamics: the manufacturers compete to maintain their production rates, to ensure distribution to the end markets and to consolidate their brand. Competition becomes tough, the sector is consolidated and the strongest companies emerge. The intensity of the competition at the average price level depends on the ratio between the industry's capacity and demand and to the wider international competition. In the next decline stage, the price competition increases, with investments aimed at improving efficiency, reducing costs and at rationalizing the productive capacity; many companies abandon the sector.

Concerning success factors – those factors that together with demand and supply define the sector behavior along the life cycle – in the early stage interested pioneer consumers experiment with the new products; therefore, the diffusion of information by the user plays a fundamental role.

To ensure the transition to large-scale diffusion, companies need to invest in R&D and in marketing. In a first phase, the R&D activities allow them to improve the product standard while later, once the innovation effects have ended, they aim at modifying the process in order to increase its efficiency.

The speed at which the standards are presented to the market becomes a crucial factor to ensure a dominant design. Marketing and promotion investments also show their effects in two phases: building the product image and, later, establishing a widespread distribution network.

The maturity stage is characterized by a period of time when the weaker companies are obliged to abandon the sector; the potential market is affected by a limited number of new clients and by the entry of new companies attracted by the margins of that sector. The potential market share can be preserved through economies of scale, segmenting the market and launching new generations of products.

Decline is characterized by competition on the price level only, highly reduced margins, departure of several companies from the sector and by very few loyal customers; the proposal of a possible new product or service accelerates these dynamics, causing erosion of the market.

The studies of industry dynamics allow us to substantiate with precision the conceptual structure of life cycle, both for the economic implications of sector maturity and decline and also for the consequences in terms of management strategy. The leading traits of demand, products offered, success factors and the structure of the competition in each phase of the sector life cycle are summarized in Table 8.1, with special reference to the demand structure and to the technological level and characteristics of the product. The last lines of the table show a synthesis of the most important factors related to a company's competitive position.

The dynamics underlying a sector's trend can be gathered by measuring some key variables whose definition is consolidated in literature and classified in terms of exogenous source (demand side) and endogenous source (supply side).

The important demand-side variables take into account the evolution of the industry, which depends mainly on exogenous factors and their related trends. The demand-side factors and growth rates are the main drivers of the product life cycle:

- Sales value
- Sales volume
- Imports and exports
- Market segmentation

On the other hand, the supply-side determinant variables include factors that refer to companies; some factors can be under the control of the company itself, both individually and as a sector, and can identify their aptitude to respond to the market.

Table 8.1   Industry structure and life cycle

	Birth	Growth	Maturity	Decline
Demand	Limited to early adopters: high-income, avant-garde.	Rapidly increasing market penetration.	Mass market, replacement/repeat buying. Customer knowledgeable and price sensitive.	Obsolescence.
Technology	Competing technologies. Rapid product innovation.	Standardization around dominant technology. Rapid process innovation.	Well-diffused technical know-how; quest for technological improvements.	Little product or process innovation.
Products	Poor quality. Wide variety of features and technologies. Frequent design changes.	Design and quality improve. Emergence of dominant design.	Trend to commoditization. Attempts to differentiate by branding, quality, bundling.	Commodities the norm; differentiation difficult and unprofitable.
Manufacturing and distribution	Short production runs. High-skilled labor content. Specialized distribution channels.	Capacity shortages. Mass production. Competition for distribution.	Emergence of overcapacity. Deskilling of production. Long production runs. Distributors carry fewer lines.	Chronic overcapacity. Re-emergence of specialty channels.
Trade	Producers and consumers in advanced countries.	Exports from advanced countries to rest of the world.	Production shift to newly industrializing then developing countries.	Exports from countries with lower labor cost.
Competition	Few companies.	Entry, mergers and exits.	Shakeout. Price competition increases.	Price wars, exits.
Key success factors	Product innovation. Establishing credible image of firm and product.	Design for manufacture. Access to distribution. Brand building. Fast product development. Process innovation.	Cost efficiency through capital intensity, scale efficiency, and low input costs.	Low overheads. Buyer selection. Signaling commitment. Rationalizing capacity.

Source: Grant (2008).

- Number of operating companies in the sector and their concentration
- Output and productive capacity
- Number of employees
- Average overhead
- Profitability
- Invested capital
- Merger and acquisition activities
- Innovation (R&D investments, patents)

Any strategic hypothesis of sector growth must take into account the present position in its life cycle. The aforementioned indicators can help to detect such a position and, based on this, it is possible to define the competitive strategies for further growth. In particular, all the companies that belong to the electronics outsourcing industry contribute to the definition of the sector itself and are conditioned by the industry's global evolution. For this reason, perspective considerations on EMSs and ODMs can be supported by the analysis of the current position along the life cycle: is there still space for growth or is the expansion phase over, and are only the moderate increases typical of the maturity phase possible? Do different positions along the life cycle curve exist depending on dimensional and market aspects?

Table 8.2   Sample of Top Class EMSs

	Sales 2007 ($M)	EBIT (%) 2007	Employees 2007	Headquarters	Stock market
Foxconn	52 495	6.3	550 000	Taiwan	Taiwan SE
Flextronics	29 336	0.6	162 000	Singapore	NASDAQ
Jabil Circuit	12 291	1.5	61 000	Florida (USA)	NYSE
Sanmina–SCI	10 384	−9.2	45 610	California (USA)	NASDAQ
Celestica	8 684	0.9	42 000	Canada	Toronto SE
Elcoteq	5 911	−2.6	24 222	Finland	Helsinki SE
Benchmark	2 916	3.6	10 522	Texas (USA)	NYSE
Venture Manufact.	2 690	8.0	n.a.	Singapore	Singapore SE
USI	2 008	3.8	12 905	Taiwan	Taiwan SE

Source: Thomson One Banker.

Table 8.3   Sample of ODMs

	Sales 2007 ($M)	EBIT (%) 2007	Employees 2006	Headquarters	Stock market
Quanta Computer	23 969	3.4	67 291	Taiwan	Taiwan SE
Asustek Computer	23 289	5.2	8 885	Taiwan	Taiwan SE
Compal Electronics	15 362	4.1	38 656	Taiwan	Taiwan SE
Wistron	8 841	3.1	31 682	Taiwan	Taiwan SE
TPV Technology	8 459	3.0	27 320	Hong Kong	Hong Kong SE
Inventec	8 087	2.6	26 447	Taiwan	Taiwan SE
Lite-on Technology	8 074	5.3	68 127	Taiwan	Taiwan SE
Tatung	7 060	7.6	39 140	Taiwan	Taiwan SE
Innolux Display	4 846	11.6	29 300	Taiwan	Taiwan SE

Source: Thomson One Banker.

The following considerations are intentionally referred to Top Class EMS and ODM companies. In particular, companies who show an operational continuity in the previous decade are selected in order to examine a time basis that is sufficiently indicative. The companies listed in Table 8.2 (EMSs) and in Table 8.3 (ODMs) match the criteria and represent about 68 per cent of EMSs' overall revenues and the 89 per cent of ODMs' revenues.

TREND OF SALES

Figure 8.3 represents the sales trend of the EMS sample selected from 1998 to 2007, both as value and change, along with an elaboration to isolate the effect of Foxconn's presence, as has been done in previous chapters.

We can observe intense growth of the sector in the reference period, with the exception of a steady stage in the 2000–2002 time period. Between 1998 and 2007, the total turnover of the sample of EMS businesses grew from 20 to 125 billion US dollars, and the 2006–2007 growth rate was about 13 per cent per year. It should be highlighted that this analysis could provide misleading indications if one did not consider separately the contribution of Foxconn, whose dimensions and growth significantly affect the entire sector. Yet, even without Foxconn, the sector appears to be growing albeit at more limited rates. Between 1998 and 2007, the overall turnover passed from 20 to

74 billion US dollars, and the percentage growth settled in 2007 at 4 per cent, after a moderate growth period and even a reduction during the 2000–2002 downturn.

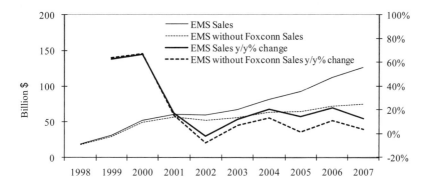

Source: Orbis, Lexis Nexis.

Figure 8.3   Sales of the Top Class EMS sample

Also in the ODM sector, which consolidated in recent years and was thus free from the influence of the downturn period, we can notice that the expansion phase is still in progress (Figure 8.4) and that it has allowed the selected sample to achieve a turnover of 25 billion US dollars in 2002, which grew beyond 107 billion US dollars in 2007. The 2007 growth rate was equal to more than 29 per cent, much higher than the world economy growth rate.

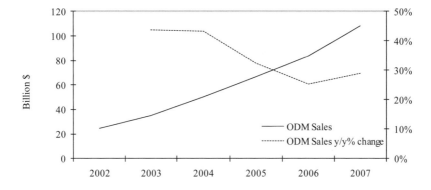

Source: Orbis, Lexis Nexis.

Figure 8.4   Sales of the ODM sample

PROFITABILITY

The ability, flexibility and readiness to respond to the new needs that the
market increasingly demands can be described by the supply-side factors and
the company's aptitude to keep such factors under control, profitability
among them. The analysis of the economic results of the reference sample
highlights and amplifies the effects of the 2000–2002 downturn in the EMS
industry, as well as the subsequent recovery.

 During the recession period the EBIT was strongly negative in turnover
percent terms (Figure 8.5). Even Foxconn's presence was not able to yield a
significantly positive contribution. After negative values as high as 10 per
cent in 2002, the EBIT margin increased again up to 2 per cent in 2006, to
drop close to zero the following year.

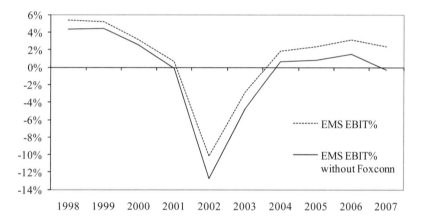

Source: Orbis, Lexis Nexis.

Figure 8.5   EBIT margin of the Top Class EMS sample

 The above indicator, through the relation between EBIT and revenues,
allows making considerations on the part of the industrial margin that are
incorporated in every monetary unit of goods sold. This examination
highlights the fact that an increase in the economic profit as an absolute value
cannot be attributed mainly to an increase in sales price or to a cost reduction,
with subsequent improvement in the efficiency, but rather to the turnover
increase of 2004–2007.

 The trend of ODMs' profitability appears to be different from that of
EMSs', in that it has been characterized by a moderately changing behavior;
the margins seem to have been, at least, preserved (Figure 8.6).

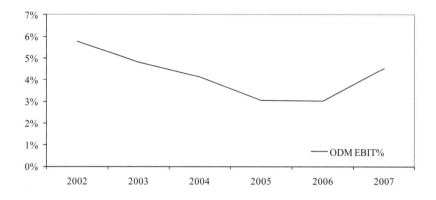

Source: Orbis, Lexis Nexis.

Figure 8.6   EBIT margin of the ODM sample

TOTAL ASSETS

EMS and ODM activity requires large investments to ensure proper operations. During observation periods, the level of investment increased remarkably by approximately the same value for the EMS sample (Figure 8.7) and the ODM sample (Figure 8.8).

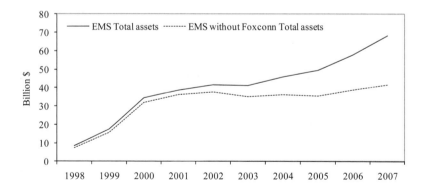

Source: Orbis, Lexis Nexis.

Figure 8.7   Total assets of the Top Class EMS sample

Foxconn's presence accounts for the real increase in the capital invested in the industry, which would otherwise have been almost steady. Efficiency and cost control seem to be achieved by increasing capital intensity in production processes. Economies of scale require large investments and their increase in absolute value appears to be normal in the industrial sectors that are typical of mass-market products.

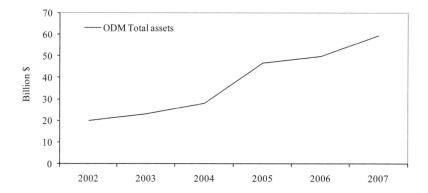

Source: Orbis, Lexis Nexis.

Figure 8.8   Total assets of the ODM sample

The working capital has an important role in the financial structure of the EMS/ODM companies and is a significant share of the allocation of the capital employed. In fact, the strong need for cash is one of the structural problems of electronics outsourcing companies, and is caused by many factors.

• The extent of the production cycle goes from the first purchase of single components to the beginning of manufacturing, which is possible only when all the components are available, to the assembly and the preparation of the end-product to be sold. A large amount of electronic components remain in stock for so long.
• The need to maintain a strategic stock of electronic components to prevent a production stop caused by recurrent component shortages due to the cycles of supply and demand.
• The frequent critical disparity for EMSs/ODMs between the payment conditions in purchasing and the sales conditions, with consequent cash burning.

EMSs AND ODMs BETWEEN GROWTH AND MATURITY

The EMS and ODM segments show trends and values of the analyzed indicators that suggest a position which is still growing, but not far from the consolidation and maturity phase.

- *Trend of sales*
  The revenues of both the EMS and ODM sectors grew with an intensity that was consistently high, though lower than in the previous period. The end of the growth trend, typical of the expansion stage of a sector, appears to be approaching, although the potential market of electronic components is all but saturated. The ODM sector seems more dynamic than the EMS sector and placed in a less advanced position in the curve of the cycle of life.
- *Profitability*
  The margins are limited consistently with the sales increase and price competition. Regarding EMSs, despite their more modest value, they show certain stability, while the margins of ODM companies are higher, but declining. This situation confirms the positioning suggested by the trend of sales: EMS and ODM sectors are growing, but not far from maturity; EMS companies are a bit farther along the life cycle curve.
- *M&A Activity*
  As discussed in the previous chapter, the M&A activity is strong with regard to the EMS industry. Recently the ODM sector also showed evidence of growth through acquisition.

The results of the variables analyzed seem to consistently confirm, for the Top Class EMS sector, the closeness of the transition between the growth stage and the maturity one. With reference to the more recent ODM sector, some indicators enable identification of the position in a stage of advanced growth (Figure 8.9).

The above considerations are based on quantitative elements attributed to larger EMS and ODM businesses. Yet, the EMS sector is actually made by companies with much broader dimensional dynamics; for this reason, the positioning of smaller EMSs on the life cycle curve might not coincide with that of Top Class EMSs. In the absence of a significant number of listed Global Class EMSs, the evaluation of position indicators, used in the previous paragraphs, are not immediately replicated for this segment; some preliminary considerations, however, seem to provide evidence of a still significant growth potential, in terms of both revenues and margins, thus suggesting that Global Class EMSs are in a position that is antecedent to the growth phase along the life cycle curve.

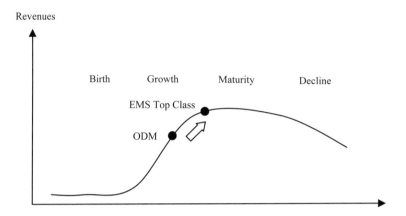

Figure 8.9   Top Class EMS and ODM industries along the life cycle curve

Another consideration involves the heterogeneity of Top Class EMSs as a consequence of Foxconn's presence, whose dimensions and performance are such as to significantly affect the behavior of the sector. If the Top Class EMS segment is positioned between the growth and the maturity stages, Foxconn, instead, has the characteristics of a business in its full expansion phase.

In some studies dedicated to the analysis of maturity of industrial sectors (Cassia et al., 2006), it has been highlighted that in many sectors defined as mature, where the opportunities for new businesses appear to be limited, there are some 'emerging' organizations – that is, businesses that stand out from the average ones for their growth capacity and ability to generate value. Indeed also in traditional industries there are firms that deviate from the general trend and are able to open new paths of growth. Those businesses can achieve profitability levels significantly higher than other companies within the same industry: pushed by the increasing competitive pressure, they move to counter to their industrial domain.

They often experience a new entrepreneurial phase, where the consolidated business management methods are discussed to create new ideas for the repositioning of the company along the production chain and for the detection of the highest added value activities within the value chain.

GROWTH AND DEVELOPMENT PATTERNS

The growth of EMSs and ODMs follows the same pattern previously studied in literature for the best part of industrial companies. Table 8.4 shows some noted authors and growth models; in particular, it lists a recent model specifically studied for the development of electronics outsourcing companies (Zhai et al., 2007).

Table 8.4   Company life cycle patterns

	Description
Ansoff (1965)	Long-term planning process aimed at market development
Greiner (1972)	Growth model based on the company's life cycle
Kazanjian and Drazin (1989)	Company development model related to the development of company products and functions
Hanks (1990)	Company life cycle described by the variables crucial for the organization
Peng and Tan (2004)	Some organizational steps, where the organization implements different transformation and diversification strategies
Zhai et al. (2007)	Specific for EMS/ODM companies and based on the development of the company's capabilities. Four growth stages: penetration, accumulation, evolution and adjustment.

According to Zhai et al. (2007) analysis, a development model for the companies involved in electronics outsourcing includes four stages (penetration, accumulation, evolution and adjustment), characterized by their own particular traits in the development of the company functions. Each stage follows the previous in a temporal sequence.

- *Penetration*
  A company that wants to enter the electronics outsourcing industry starts to leverage its available resources, such as low-cost labor, know-how, and the founder's network of contacts.
- *Accumulation*
  The company gathers the resources for future development and learns from the external environment. There is an imitation process of competitors on the use of available resources. In this stage, the company moves along the supply chain towards high intensity labor services and, in general, the diversification level is quite limited.
- *Evolution*
  New organizational procedures are developed; they are based on a better understanding of production and provisioning logics. A continuous process improvement is implemented, together with the reconfiguration

of production lines and the expansion of the production capacity. In this stage, characterized by independent innovation and by the growth of the company's capacity, the production volumes grow rapidly thanks to geographical expansion.

- *Adjustment*
  Thanks to an accumulation of knowledge and competence, the new goal is restructuring the whole production system aimed at increasing the efficiency and reducing operating costs. Typical activities in this stage are integration of the supply chain and reorganization of the logistics-production flow. Furthermore, the knowledge that was acquired through the expansion of the services offered to clients is exploited successfully, such as, for example, design and after-sales. The following evolution can cause the transformation of EMS firms according to the ODM model.

Table 8.5 summarizes the growth stages according to the model of development capacities. According to Zhai et al. (2007) EMSs grow along three different dimensions: product, service and capability.

- *Product*
  This dimension is related to the development trend of those products requiring ever more complex technologies. Initially, EMSs are not able to build technological barriers. As EMSs develop new abilities along the supply chain, they create more and more complex products. Observing the development curve of electronic products as a function of added value (Figure 8.10), as originally proposed by Stan Shih, the founder of Acer, the company moves towards the top left part of the curve.
- *Service*
  EMS companies try to integrate along the supply chain to increase the added value offered. Many of them, in fact, start with high-intensity labor services, such as production or distribution, and then integrate upstream with higher-added-value services based on technological development, such as design.
- *Capability*
  The main aspect in the development of EMS companies is evolution of company competence and organizational procedures. EMS firms start the development by using consolidated technologies. As they accumulate resources and knowledge, innovation and organizational capabilities are introduced in order to continue to compete in the market. After this phase, they require an adjustment stage to optimize the entire system, to follow the market trend and to prepare for further growth.

Table 8.5   *Capability development in EMSs*

	Penetration	Accumulation	Evolution	Adjustment
Products (complexity of manufacturing processes and technologies)	Start production from labor-intensive component/ products Leverage existing resources for production, e.g. founder's educational background, local economic policy and low-cost labor Choose a product/ component as core product/ component for long-term capability development	Production knowledge accumulation through duplicate processes from customers Diversify customers to learn from different production practices Utilize existing production capability to access other products Codify manufacturing knowledge Improve production system; expand capacity incrementally Follow universal manufacturing technology trend	Deliberately build continuous improvement system Develop process design and redesign capabilities Codify knowledge of process design Continuously develop new organizational routines to enhance production services (volume ramp-up, co-design production system with OEM customers)	Integrate components production capabilities to manage full system manufacturing Adapt production knowledge to address more complex components/ products Utilize production to enter new sector/industry
Services (servicing processes along the supply chain)	Selectively position in the lower stream of supply chain with high-labor and low technology contents Leverage existing local resources such as low-cost labor, personal networks, and privileged local economic policies	Expand along the supply chain by providing more value-added services (mainly contain labor-intensive contents) Adopt multiple methods (alliances, geographical expansion) to enrich service provision	Continuously improve existing services Utilize existing process knowledge to support tech intensive projects Continuously develop new organizational routines to support new services	Restructure organization to address new services Services (production network/supply chain/global design network) restructuring Integrate services to provide comprehensive services

Source: Zhai (2007).

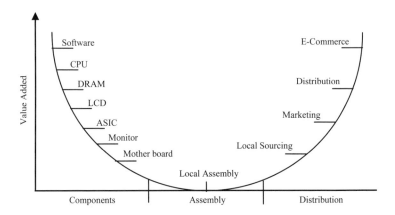

Source: Zhai (2007).

Figure 8.10   Added value along the electronics outsourcing value chain

COMPETITION STRUCTURE

Competition in the electronics outsourcing industry takes on a dynamic dimension as a consequence of the fast evolution of economic and technological aspects. Macro trends, such as globalization and the opening of markets, merger of different players in the sector, dimensional segmentation, technological development that moves intellectual property along the chain, are modifying the competitive scenarios.

To understand the competition of the electronics outsourcing industry it is useful to concentrate the study on the market dynamics and on the relationships between the players within the supply chain, following Porter's (1980) framework. The five forces model takes into account not only the direct competition among EMS companies, but also the competition aimed at capturing the supply chain profits considering customers, suppliers and outsider firms that could potentially enter the sector, as well as companies that could meet the customers' needs with different products or services.

The competitive scenario shows the need to take into account the size of the ODM and the EMS and the existence of sub-industries where Top Class EMSs, Global Class EMSs and Local Class EMSs compete separately. Obviously, border interferences between the single sub-sectors exist, but the scenario appears to be differently favorable to the various dimensional classes.

- *Internal competition*

  Top Class EMSs are limited in number, characterized by large dimensions and by great experience in the mass production business. A favorable press on oligopolistic marginality is countered by an excess in production capacity and the consequent rigidity in the cost structure that leads to a high level of competition, especially during demand decrease. Similar considerations apply to ODMs.

  The situation of Global Class EMSs is different: although they are more numerous, they are characterized by a more flexible organizational structure that allows them to adjust more easily to demand variations. Additionally, Global Class EMSs are not normally involved in very high-volume and highly variable productions (ICT, commodity, etc.), but rather deal with industrial, or more specific applications that are less subject to the frequent instabilities of the market. The intensity of internal competition is less strong than that occurring between Top Class EMSs, also because of their more niche-related specialization level, with minor market fluctuations and smaller volumes.

  Local Class EMSs, also, are not affected by a high level of internal competition thanks to the privileged relationship they establish with their clients, with whom they maintain habitual practices.

- *Suppliers*

  EMSs/ODMs' reference suppliers operate in the area of electronic components as component suppliers or distributors. In the initial phases of the outsourcing process, component suppliers had the OEMs as their partners; it was only later that EMSs developed a purchasing department, and this was because, thanks to total volumes, it allowed them to take part of the profits (Barnes et al., 2000). In any case, the suppliers hold a high bargaining power over the EMSs/ODMs: the smaller the clients the more power they have. This is an important criticality for Local Class EMSs, but it should not be ignored by Top Class and Global Class EMSs either, not only concerning the cost, but also with regard to the availability and delivery time of electronic devices. Due to the market structure of electronic components, and semiconductors in particular, there are tangible cyclical phases in the demand and supply, with frequent shortage problems and fast price variations.

  While larger ODMs and EMSs have a well tested sourcing and logistics organization that reduce the problems also by means of a prudential stock policy and of structured contracts with their suppliers, the Local Class EMSs are more frequently likely to find themselves in a stockout situation, with consequent halts in the production.

- *Clients*

  Whatever the size of the EMSs, the bargaining power of their clients is usually high, and it is higher if there is a dimensional disparity: in fact, the cost structure sometimes persuades the EMS to accept production orders with low margins.

Normally the Local Class EMSs are characterized by a lower bargaining power, because they usually do not add any intellectual property to their production and they are a sort of external department of clients.

Even Top Class EMSs and ODMs, due to excessive production capacity, are tempted to reach an agreement with their clients, even when not advantageous. The situation might change with time, as the demand for EMS services grows, with a subsequent increase in the plant saturation level.

- *New entries*

  The limited margins and the high production capacity discourage the establishment of new businesses within the EMS and ODM sectors. This is consistent with the relevant barriers of entry, related to the growing sizes of EMSs/ODMs as a consequence of acquisition operations, as well as of the new technological skills needed to deal with the current electronic technologies.

  A possible internal threat between the two Top Class EMS and ODM segments is represented by the dimensional growth of the latter, which in some specific situations characterized by high volumes and product standardization can compete especially with Top Class EMSs. The border between the two sectors is increasingly blurred and there are overlaps that increase competition in some product lines.

- *Substitute products*

  At the moment, the introduction to the market of electronic components so innovative that they do not allow the EMSs to rapidly convert their plants is not expected to occur.

  It is instead possible that new end products, that incorporate electronic parts previously supplied by EMSs, become available, thus reducing the latter's market while widening the ODMs' sales.

The competition structure can be drawn with reference to the different EMSs' dimensional classes. Table 8.6 highlights a rather intense competitive situation, positive for the clients, partly due to their control and visibility in the end market.

Table 8.6   Porter's competitive framework for EMSs

	Top Class EMSs	Global Class EMSs	Local Class EMSs
Internal competition	High	Medium	Low
Clients' bargaining power	High	Medium	Very high
Suppliers' bargaining power	Medium	Medium	Very high
Entry of new competitors (ODMs)	Medium	Low	Very low
Substitute businesses (ODMs)	Medium	Low	Very low

Some differences emerge, mainly associated with the EMSs' dimensional characteristics and to the consequent positioning that validate the segmentation of the industry. In particular there are some characteristic features for each segment.

- Top Class EMSs belong to a segment that is affected, with the exception of outliers such as Foxconn, by an unfavorable competitive condition, mainly associated with the rigid cost structure and to overproduction that leads them to achieve large volumes paying less attention to the margins. In addition Top Class EMSs serve the mass markets that are very sensitive to downturn and volatility problems, as well as to the possibility that substitute products, made available by technological improvements, are introduced.
- Global Class EMSs operate in a segment that is characterized by high volumes, but is usually more stable and not a mass market. Furthermore, the business model implemented and the type of relationship with the clients assign value more to innovation than on volumes. For this reason, in spite of operating in a highly competitive sector, the margins of Global Class EMSs are, on average, higher.
- Local Class EMSs are normally subject to very high competitive pressure, not so much from their direct competitors, but due to the significant bargaining power of the clients, who directly modulate both their sales and profits. Considering the small dimension and the high risk associated with a limited number of clients, the attractiveness of this segment is moderate.

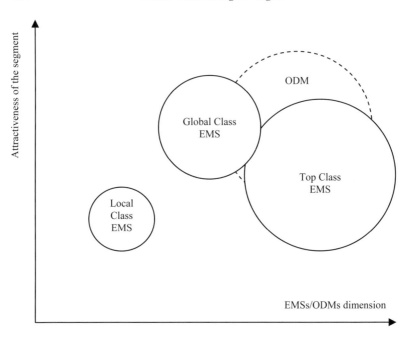

Figure 8.11   EMSs/ODMs dimension vs. attractiveness of the industry

Discussing the strategic positioning of an EMS firm could therefore be misleading, since the dimensional segmentation generates a different attractiveness for each individual segment.

The Top Class EMS segment is characterized by a high level of internal competition, aimed at capturing the clients that bring large production orders of consumer products. Moreover, the same products are also the primary target of ODM firms. The profit level, then, cannot but settle on limited values.

At the opposite end, the Local Class EMSs do not suffer from a high level of internal competition, but compete without success with clients and suppliers to hold part of the supply chain margins. The absence of an added value in terms of intellectual property places this segment in an extremely uncertain situation.

The Global Class EMS segment seems to reach a satisfactory level of attractiveness more than the others, according to Porter. They hit a balance between sufficiently high production volumes – so much so as to make it possible to keep dimensions that are adequate to global competition – with resources dedicated to research, development and innovation. They usually have an organizational flexibility that allows a fast response to clients' needs and a strategic positioning in sectors that are less subject to high market variability.

INTERNAL AND EXTERNAL FACTORS

For the purpose of evaluating growth paths, it is interesting to list the main strengths and weaknesses within electronics manufacturing services, as well as the threats and opportunities that could arise externally. The internal and external factors contribute to a description of the competitive advantages and the strategic framework.

Strength factors
- Technology and process know-how
- Interdependence with clients for service
- Service management during the entire life cycle of the product
- Customization and flexibility skills
- Diversification of the client base by industry
- Diversification by product range

Weakness factors
- High fixed costs
- Excess of production capacity
- Limited profitability
- High financial costs
- High start-up costs for new production lines
- Shipment costs
- Human resources management due to different cultures

Opportunities
- Growth of the outsourcing market
- Increase in production efficiency through technology
- Improvement in global communication among production sites
- Global sourcing

Threats
- High competition pressure over prices
- Complexity of global logistics and increase in shipment costs
- Very fast technological changes in production processes
- Costs related to compliance with environmental regulations
- Risks connected to exchange rates
- Political instability in emerging markets

OUTSOURCING MODELS COMPARISON

In mature high-volume markets, where the dominant design and technological standards are definite and stable, the ODMs' business model seems to be superior. They manufacture the same products as EMSs but at lower costs, thanks to their specialization, pursuing efficiency more than the others and paying great attention to the design phase. The evolution of the business model shows that the change from contract manufacturing to EMS took place precisely because of this higher production efficiency and that, at present, the situation is again evolving supporting ODMs in some sectors.

The logic behind the production and organization of different business models developed successively leads us to assume that the costs borne by OEMs vary depending upon the type of supplier on which they have chosen to rely.

Table 8.7 shows a description of the costs for the OEMs following the electronic technology outsourcing model and lists the advantages acquired with a more extended use of outsourcing for the main cost items.

It can be observed that, by using contract manufacturing services, OEMs also have to bear the costs generated by procurement and R&D, activities that do not lie within the core business of those firms and on which it is neither possible to take advantage of volume discounts nor of the accumulation of competence that could be applied to develop new solutions.

Furthermore, the lack of integration in the supply chain implies an increase in the fixed costs that makes it even less convenient for an OEM to give supply contracts to a contract manufacturer. Similar considerations can also be made for business models involving EMSs and ODMs, with different levels of extension of the supplied services and of the associated intellectual property. With regard to this issue, it can be observed that resorting to outsourcing in different stages of the supply chain allows a major cost reduction; furthermore, paying more attention to the design stage allows the expenses in both the purchase of components and in the production stage to be reduced (Design for Manufacturability).

In Table 8.7, the EMS segment has been intentionally divided by adding a sub-segmentation characterized by greater intellectual property (EMS+Intellectual Property). The segment is very heterogeneous and includes companies whose services start downstream of the design stage and others which, instead, include it in their offered services. The cost structure sustained by the OEM client is different in the two cases because the final cost can be lower when the design is carried out with competence in both product engineering and in production.

Table 8.7   Cost structure in outsourcing models

	Contract Manufacturing (CM)	EMS	EMS + Intellectual Property	ODM
Cost of the components (bill of material)	No cost reduction for OEMs (they are responsible for the purchase of materials).	EMS reduces the components costs by purchasing by volumes for several OEMs.	EMS optimizes project through re-engineering to reduce costs.	ODM designs aimed at the lowest possible cost of materials.
Transformation costs	Reduction in assembly costs. CM develops process improvements.	EMS minimizes costs of stock and logistics.	EMS modifies project parameters to achieve the lowest possible process cost (Design for Manufacturing).	ODM designs aimed at the lowest possible process cost (Design for Manufacturing).
Fixed costs	OEM does not carry out any upstream integration with CM.	Integration of the supply chain to reduce costs.	Integration of the supply chain to reduce costs.	No downstream integration with OEMs.
Product R&D costs	OEM bears all costs and maintains the IP.	OEM bears all costs and maintains the IP.	EMS/OEM share R&D costs.	ODM bears all R&D related costs and maintains the IP.

Source: Report PriceWaterhouseCoopers.

Through all of these arguments, we can imagine an expected growth of the ODMs in the coming years, especially considering which products will be subject to the greatest development and the trend towards quick success in the market. In many new product categories, in fact, the need and advantage of outsourcing to ODMs will be perceived by the OEMs from the very first stage of the product life cycle, because the product standards will be characterized by shorter definition times and by an easier standardization of the components. This trend puts a limit on OEMs in the differentiation of the product to better meet the non-expressed needs of the customers. In spite of this, in many sectors the development dynamics have led to the immediate entrusting of the supply to ODMs. Recent examples are provided by Blue-Ray/DVD players, PDAs and MP3 devices, as well as the case represented by LED/LCD television sets, where the ODMs were involved in the value chain optimization from the time the product was developed.

In response to this threat, Top Class EMS manufacturers, having a higher bias for greater volumes and low mix, should focus mainly on the design stages that might represent an important competitive advantage in opposition to the standardization of ODMs. In such markets, where competition mainly takes place in price, branding and the range of services offered to the client, the commodity nature of the products increases the pressure on profits, generating serious problems in finding financing sources for R&D activity. This situation might represent a strong incentive for OEMs to search for partners along the production chain who have the necessary competence to develop the design and who are committed to product and process innovation. In return, the EMSs would obtain valuable conditions, both for the prices of transferring the products along the value chain as well as for market stability and the opportunity to optimize the demand forecasts. In the past, the minimization of stock and the risks related to inaccurate estimates gave rise to major problems of oversizing the production plants and the value of the working capital.

The EMSs that will meet the OEMs' needs will have to choose between offering a co-design service – which implies a collaboration with the client – or a totally autonomous design acquiring traits and behaviors similar to those of ODMs. In this regard, the convergence trend between Top Class EMSs and ODMs appears to be confirmed.

ELECTRONICS OUTSOURCING TRENDS

With reference to the discussion about the positioning along the life cycle and the related competitive scenario, some prospective data on the importance of electronics outsourcing appear to be interesting, notwithstanding the remarkable uncertainty due to the 2008–2009 financial crisis. Consistent with the described transition between the growth and the maturity stage, a substantial stability of industry sales is expected.

The estimates of trade associations and research institutes highlight a progressive decrease in the growth rate of EMS and ODM revenues in the 2004–2012 time period (Table 8.8). In fact, the slowing growth and the consolidation towards sector maturity have been confirmed.

The ODM sector achieved a sales volume close to 50 billion US dollars in the years 2002–2003, five years later than the EMS sector, pushed by the growing trend of globalization of the markets. This opening in the competitive arena has encouraged the development of the typical business pattern of the ODMs who, by designing and completely manufacturing their own products, base their production activity in low-labor-cost countries and supply the goods outsourced by western companies at lower prices. Despite the time shift in the achievement of the 50 billion dollar threshold, the ODM sector had a significant and continuous dimensional development in the period between 2002 and 2008. Nevertheless the effects of the downturn upon ODMs are visible in the forecasts of the future years.

Table 8.8   *Sales and sales estimates of the EMS and ODM industries (2004–2012)*

Sales (Billion $)		2004	2005	2006	2007	2008	2009E	2010E	2011E	2012E
EMSs	Sales	122.4	137.1	161.3	186.5	177.4	156.1	157.7	156.1	160.8
	Growth		12.0	17.7	15.6	−4.9	−12.0	1.0	−1.0	3.0
ODMs	Sales	70.0	85.1	102.7	121.6	123.3	114.7	120.4	119.2	125.1
	Growth		21.6	20.7	18.4	1.4	−7.0	5.0	−1.0	4.9
Total	Sales	192.4	222.2	264.0	308.1	300.7	270.8	278.1	275.3	285.9
	Growth		15.5	18.8	16.7	−2.4	−9.9	2.7	−1.0	3.9

Source: iSuppli, Technology Forecasters (2009).

9. Design Outsourcing

There is a growing interest in the development of business models that aim at offering high-added-value services. Companies along the electronic sector chain are primarily focusing on design services, pursuing the profits associated with differentiation strategies, aware that the basis of the future competitiveness of their product is created at this stage of the value chain.

Among all possible strategic solutions to hit the target, the diffusion of joint design manufacturing (JDM) is of great interest. JDM is one of the business models of the wider category of design outsourcing services. In JDM shared projects are carried out where the generation and the ownership of the intellectual property are shared by the client (usually an OEM) and the supplier (typically an EMS). This ensures EMSs the creation of stable collaborations with their clients, a significant differentiation of the offered solutions, an increase in their bargaining power thanks to the development of high-added-value activities, and a reduction in market risk.

Design outsourcing refers to the decision made by companies to resort to outsourcing for the design of their products. Unlike other outsourced activities, design outsourcing does not normally involve benefits in terms of reductions in cost and time-to-market. Yet, the design and development of a new product means, above all, innovation; really, design outsourcing is a synonym of 'innovation outsourcing' and acquires an important strategic value for the company business model. As a matter of fact, the outsourcing of R&D activities is often linked with the growth of the research competence inside the company that resorts to outsourcing; this is due to the need to keep some skills inside, also for reasons of confidentiality, trust and appropriability. The term 'R&D' encompasses not only design activities, but also product engineering and the making of prototypes. Furthermore, innovation involves not only the idea of a new process/product, but also the steps that lead to the marketing and sale.

The outsourcing of innovation and design activities is present in several sectors, such as high-tech electronics, chemical, pharmaceutical, automotive industries, and acquires different connotations. Along with a horizontal cooperation between companies belonging to the same production sector (sometimes even between direct competitors), a vertical collaboration is tied in within the supply chain, between suppliers and clients.

DETERMINANTS OF DESIGN OUTSOURCING

The scientific literature describes the typologies of partnerships and the motivations that encourage companies to search for alliances to share R&D activities.

- *Partnerships aimed at a general technological research*
  These partnerships involve the sharing of resources and the opportunity to make use of scientific and technological knowledge that is not available inside the company. Related to this need is the growing complexity of technology within the sectors and the cross-fertilization trend among scientific disciplines. The resort to strategic alliances and to the sharing of R&D allows a company to monitor the evolution of more technological sectors, so that it can take advantage of possible synergies resulting from new discoveries, thus ensuring a future competitive advantage.
- *Alliances for the joint development of a specific project*
  Firms may be motivated by the will to capture and acquire the specific skills and technological knowledge of the partner. Additionally, jointly developing new products could reduce time-to-market.
- *Alliances for the creation of a new market or to gain access to an already existing market which is unknown to the company*
  In this case, both companies involved in the design outsourcing relationship can achieve a broader product range.

Fine and Whitney (1996) have identified the use of design outsourcing as an answer to internal dependency problems within a company:

- *Resource dependency*
  The company has the knowledge and skills to design the product, but chooses outsourcing to bypass its lack of in-house resources (economic resources, plants, facilities, time, management focusing). This need is at the base of the origins of electronics outsourcing, when OEMs resorted to the production capacity of other companies to face peak demand periods.
- *Knowledge dependency*
  The company does not have the necessary knowledge and skills to design a product; if it tried to develop those new abilities it would have

to bear high costs and an extremely long development time. Instead resorting to outsourcing could exploit the knowledge of the supplier.

Even with resorting to outsourcing, companies do not give up maintaining and developing some key skills within the company (Table 9.1), including the ability to define the component specifications, to find the suppliers and develop relationships with them, and to ensure the specifications are met.

Table 9.1   Knowledge dependency and use of design outsourcing

Ability to identify qualified suppliers

Ability to define component specifications

Ability to evaluate offers

Ability to verify that the product meets the specifications

Improve the offer

Ability to cooperate with the suppliers in technical matters

Ability to cooperate with the suppliers in the operations

Improve the product

Internal design skill

Growing dependency on knowledge

Authors like Levin et al. (1987) as well as Hamel and Prahald (1990) point out that companies have assets and expertise resulting from investments made in the past and experience, that they try to develop in order to get a competitive advantage.

They decide upon the outsourcing of R&D activities when their internal competences are too weak or because they want to keep only a few key skills internally, on which they can concentrate their investments within the company.

INNOVATION THROUGH OUTSOURCING

Companies search for innovation outside their organization through many channels and methods.

- *Buying innovations on the market*
  Companies can apply to universities, consulting firms and private research labs.
- *Investments in innovators*
  Companies acquiring shares of innovators to benefit from their discoveries is a common activity among electronic firms.
- *Co-sourcing*
  Innovation shared through consortia, partnerships and joint ventures. Since innovation can become very expensive, some companies join to share the costs. In chemical and oil industries, these proposals are often started by direct competitors. Businesses in the car industry use co-sourcing to achieve compliance to the regulations, such as gas emission standards.
- *Community sourcing*
  This approach to innovation consists of taking advantage of the knowledge and know-how that can be generated by the community of users who are experts in the company's products. This is distinctive of the software industry.
- *Resourcing*
  The companies support their internal staff by searching for advanced instruments and equipments, as well as personnel, from external suppliers.

Each innovation channel is characterized by specific traits and opportunities in terms of costs, integration among the partners, achievement of differentiated products, opportunity to maintain the exclusive ownership of the innovations, direct control of the client over the results and simplicity in the partnership management.

Different strategies can be identified in order to outsource design and intellectual property. A first level involves the products independently designed by the client, who therefore remains the sole owner of the intellectual property, or by the supplier with contractual transfer of the intellectual property. This is the situation that occurs when an OEM resorts to the services offered by an EMS for the design and production of products that are completely defined by the client company.

On a different level, JDM can be tied in. The client shares his/her knowledge on the market and the requests concerning the product, while the supplier offers support during the design phase and the services needed to introduce the new product. The intellectual property of the new products is shared with the client.

Lastly, we find the ODM strategy. ODMs develop and own the property of a product, sold to a number of OEMs with a very low level of customization.

Table 9.2   External innovation outsourcing

Channel types	The Innovation Chain		
	Discovery	Development	Commercialization
Buying innovation on the market	Sponsored research	Innovation-for-hire	Strategic procurement
Investing in innovators	Early-stage venture capital	Late-stage venture capital	Equity plays
Co-sourcing	Discovery partnership	Development partnership	Commercialization partnership
Community sourcing	Open problem solving	Enabled development	Standing customer panel
Resourcing	Contracting for outside tools and talent	Contracting for outside tools and talent	Contracting for outside tools and talent
Investing in innovators	Early-stage venture capital	Late-stage venture capital	Equity plays

Source: Linder et al. (2003).

Table 9.3 summarizes the main differences between the different levels of design outsourcing.

Table 9.3   Design outsourcing partners

Design outsourcing partner	Intellectual property ownership	Customization level	Stage where the cooperation starts	Communication of the design specifications
EMS	Client	High	Middle	Mono-directional
JDM	Shared	High	Beginning	Bi-directional
ODM	Supplier	Limited	Advanced	Bi-directional

DESIGN OUTSOURCING STRATEGY

The decision to adopt the design outsourcing is a complex and strategically important process. Many contributions in the scientific literature explain this trend.

- Quinn and Hilmer's model (1994) analyzes two dimensions: the competitive advantage and the level of strategic risk related to outsourcing. The model suggests that activities with a high competitive potential and high strategic vulnerability should be carried out internally. A moderate strategic risk and a moderate competitive potential characterize the activities that can be handled through different types of relationships, such as short-term contracts or joint development, with a partial or total control by the supplier. Finally, low-risk and low competitive potential activities can be handled with ample autonomy and control from the supplier.
- Venkatesan's model (1992) identifies two types of activities: core activities that are critical for the performance of the final product and are carried out exclusively inside the company; non-core activities, that are outsourced.
- Olsen and Ellram's model (1997) focuses on a stage that comes after the choices on outsourcing have been made, concentrating on the activities and products for which the decision to resort to outsourcing has already been made, and analyzing the types of relationships that can be established between client and supplier.

The models are synthesized in Table 9.4, where we notice an existing correspondence between the categories to classify the different activities.

Table 9.4   Decision-making models for design outsourcing

Make or buy	Design Outsourcing Models		
	Quinn and Hilmer	Venkatesan	Olsen and Ellram
Vertical integration	Strategic control	Core	—
Cooperation	Moderate control	—	Strategic
Buy	Low control	Non-core	Non-core

It is necessary to take place an assessment of possible partners in order to make a decision concerning the use of outsourcing (Kamath and Liker,

1994).

- *Partners*
  They process activities and products independently and submit them to OEMs at the end of the process in order to integrate them in their finished products. They take the responsibility to develop complex sub-systems and are partially involved in the definition of specifications from the initial phases of a product development; this is the case for JDM.
- *Mature suppliers*
  They start to develop the products without waiting for the client's request. This is the case for ODMs.
- *Young suppliers*
  They can produce only if the OEM gives them detailed specifications or, in the case of EMSs, they manufacture products upon a specific request from the client.
- *Contract suppliers*
  They offer standard parts, available from their catalogue. This is the case for ODMs.

The decision concerning design outsourcing is not limited to the choice between resorting to outsourcing versus internal production, but rather the choice of a type of relationship among a wide range of possible partnerships with suppliers, where total outsourcing and in-house production are the extremes.

In the case of activities/products with low strategic value and limited competitive potential, the relationships with the suppliers can be regulated by spot contracts. Products with low strategic importance are usually supplied by young suppliers.

Instead, mature suppliers are involved in the case of medium strategic risk. If the competitive advantage is low, the suppliers work with long-term contracts; when the competitive advantage increases, the company turns to joint development of the product.

In the case of high strategic exposure, the suppliers are involved and act as partners. If the competitive advantage is low, the company chooses joint development, because the OEM intends to exert a certain level of control. If the competitive potential increases, the company chooses a relationship where only some components or some steps of the production are developed jointly, while the others are developed in-house by the OEM.

The aspects related to innovation are tightly connected to the wider problem of a company's strategic approach. The decisions to outsource part of the product design depend on several factors, among them clients' preference, the technology involved, competitive positioning, the suppliers' ability and the architecture of the product to be manufactured.

From this viewpoint, in-house production brings more benefits when the clients' preference affects the product characteristics (customized products), the technological changes are fast, the necessary competences do not exist along the supply chain and the product has an integrated and non-modular structure.

Conversely, outsourcing can bring important advantages in a company that manufactures highly standardized products, in a context characterized by slow technological changes, where the supply chain has developed the necessary competence and the product architecture is modular.

Among these scenarios various intermediate levels can be identified. For those products where the consumers' preferences are important and which have a high rate of technological growth, if the capability and know-how of the suppliers is high and the architecture of the product is modular, joint design can represent an appropriate solution.

In the case of modular products and suppliers with a limited know-how, OEMs can outsource the least complex parts of the product and keep the ones with higher added value internal.

A determinant dimension in the choice to 'make' or 'buy' is the economic value: elements with a high strategic and economic value are better candidates for insourcing, while those characterized by a low strategic and economic value are more suitable for outsourcing. The strategic and economic elements that determine the strategy to be adopted are listed in Table 9.5.

Table 9.5   Design outsourcing reference models

Design outsourcing model	Fully outsourcing design	Joint Design Manufacturing	In-house design
Importance of the client	Medium	High	High
Technology growth rate	Low	Medium	High
Competitive position	Disadvantaged	Medium	Advantaged
Suppliers' capacity	High	Medium	Low
Product architecture	Highly modular	Partially modular	Not modular
Added value	Low	Medium	High

The fully outsourcing strategy is used for commodity products with a low differentiation and where the price is the market competitive variable. It is also used when OEMs depend on the supplier for the knowledge needed to develop the product and could involve different types of cooperation between the supplier and customer with different costs and time-to-market.

- *Existing project*
  The ODM supplies a product that has already been fully developed; the OEM buys the 'black box' product labeled with its own brand.
- *Restyling*
  The OEM carries out a marginal restyling of the supplier's project, according to its own marketing strategies. For example, some desktop PC suppliers evaluate the LCD monitors made by different ODMs, select one of them and customize its look, labeling it with their own brand.
- *Design of the product starting from the general characteristics requested*
  The OEM specifies the product's characteristics, its performance and shape and delegates the management of the entire design process to the supplier.
- *Design starting from the product specifications*
  The OEM supplies precise specifications that the final product must meet, including details on the selection of the suppliers, of the components and of the compatibility requisites.

In the case of fully outsourcing design, the complete ownership of the product intellectual property remains with the supplier, which means there is no IP sharing.

JOINT DESIGN MANUFACTURING

The JDM business model is the implementation of participative projects where the generation and, therefore, the ownership of the intellectual property is shared between the client, usually an OEM, and the supplier, which in the electronic sector is typically an EMS; the firms that offer JDM services are known as joint design manufacturers. In this kind of cooperation the design teams of the partner companies collaborate in the product design process: each partner must design specific modules that will then be integrated in the final product and placed on the market by the OEM.

The management of the intellectual property and the sharing between the partners are the most distinctive and characteristic elements of the JDM strategy with respect to other kinds of design outsourcing. Yet, the aspects related to the control of the product components and to the management of the supply chain are not of secondary importance.

The joint design strategy is used for those products for which the client company has been shown to possess a strategic advantage associated with the design of some of the product modules; the company can outline the characteristics that the parts, whose design is assigned to the supplier, must meet. The decision to use joint designing is easier for high-profit products and whose competitive advantage is the product differentiation and not the price. The OEM could include restrictive clauses in the contract, concerning the possible transfer of knowledge and technology, with the aim of obtaining a high level of control.

ADVANTAGES OF JDM

Adopting JDM has some advantages with respect to fully outsourcing and to in-house design.

- *Product differentiation*
  OEMs can differentiate their products and design them according to the special requests of the end-user, unlike ODMs who offer standardized solutions. JDM offers the opportunity to outsource the design of the non-critical components of a product and to keep control of the product differentiation associated with the design of the key elements handled directly by the OEM.
- *Control and visibility*
  The OEM can specify the characteristics, the performance, and the shape that the product must have and the guidelines on the selection of the suppliers and on prices. This allows OEMs to maintain their existing relationships with component suppliers and to keep their control over the supply chain by directly negotiating the prices, terms and conditions of the critical components.
- *Decision making*
  The OEM holds a strong bargaining power and can obtain a design that responds to its strategic objectives rather than to those of the supplier's, because decisions are not completely entrusted to the supplier.
- *Knowledge transfer and benchmarking*
  Since the companies offering JDM services cooperate with several OEMs, they are more updated about the sector's most recent innovations. JDM allows the in-house product development team of the client to cooperate with those companies and increase their knowledge. This bilateral transfer of knowledge represents one of the most significant advantages for many companies. Joint design represents the opportunity to create a benchmark with the competitors within the same industry and in turn contribute to the OEM's continuous evolution.

The main motivation that leads to the JDM model is the opportunity to create long-term and binding relationships. With JDM the supplier designs a specific module for the client's product and shares the related intellectual property; from the supplier's point of view, the client is bound because its modules act as barriers to the entry of possible competitors.

DISADVANTAGES OF JDM

Although JDM solves some problems related to the fully outsourcing model, it does represent a risky strategy because, especially in the long term, the OEM could lose its competitive advantage if the characteristics of the product should lose their uniqueness, turning it into a commodity. There are a few problems associated with the implementation of a JDM strategy.

- *Costs and Investments*
  In a short-term perspective, JDM is more expensive than fully outsourcing because the OEMs, besides keeping their internal team, must also face external relationships and coordination activities.
- *Coordination*
  Coordination problems may arise among the OEM's and supplier's design teams.
- *Time-to-market*
  The product's time-to-market can be longer than the one achieved with a fully outsourcing strategy. In fact, the product must be developed in collaboration, and this process requires good coordination between the two design teams.
- *Knowledge spillover*
  In the JDM model, there is the risk of an undesired transfer of knowledge and information because the design teams of the two companies work closely with each other.
- *Competition with the supplier*
  JDM implies the risk of turning the supplier into a possible competitor, due to the transfer of information and experience. The supplier works with different clients and therefore accumulates a level of knowledge that enables it to autonomously design and develop the OEM's products within its own organization. This can reduce the OEM's competitive advantage and transform the relationship into complete outsourcing of the design activity.

Global Outsourcing Strategies

JDM AND THE SUPPLY CHAIN MANAGEMENT

The design of a product affects all stages of the product life cycle, such as the provisioning of components, the actual production, and after-sales services. In the designing, it is therefore necessary to take into account the complete supply chain (design for supply chain or DFSC).

> There is no shortage of business or operational challenges that high tech product companies face in current market conditions. Short product lifecycles, competition, product variety, availability, global markets, fluctuating demand, steadily declining prices, increasing cost of components, component availability are just a few that make the short list. It comes as no surprise that so many high tech product companies face difficulty turning profits consistently. While product innovation may help in the short term it does not guarantee long term viability and growth. The only safeguard that high tech companies can build in such an environment is exceptional operational performance [...]. The current method that most high tech product companies choose for improving supply chain performance is to implement sophisticated advanced planning systems, operations management software and real time inventory management processes. These processes and systems have improved inventory management practices and clearly reduced the cost structure. But the focus of these processes and systems is operational and does not quite influence the design, manufacturing and supply chain decisions that set basic targets for supply chain performance of a product line. On the other hand the product development phase of the product line offers a large opportunity to design superior supply chain performance. The product development phase offers wide latitude in terms of product design, components, manufacturing and supply chain strategies that can be used to achieve superior supply chain performance [...]. The business process and analysis approach for 'Design for Supply Chain' can be used during the product development phase to design superior supply chain performance into products.
> *Source*: Samsung Data Systems (2007)

Resorting to design outsourcing makes it more difficult to define and apply a supply chain management system because it significantly increases the number of players involved. In the specific case of JDM, some key aspects should be considered.

The suppliers of high-tech components play an important role within the supply chain. They behave more like collaborators rather than suppliers, because many high-tech products are modular and innovation is integrated in the products especially through the development of the single components. During the supplier evaluation stage, it is therefore necessary to take into account not only the economic facts but also the strategic importance of the supplier, his past performance, his lead time and his ability for innovation. In a fully outsourcing model the OEM depends on the ODM for the entire design phase of a product and its level of involvement is minimal; it has neither control nor visibility of the selection of the suppliers of the various components. Conversely, in a JDM collaboration, the OEM practices a modest level of control over the process of selecting a supplier: the cooperation between the partner companies makes information exchange easy and sets precise priorities on the selection of suppliers.

Ragatz et al. (2003) have highlighted the existence of several benefits arising from the involvement of the suppliers from the first phases of design. Some of these benefits are the production of better and more numerous ideas, the development and distribution of new technologies, a time reduction of the entire development cycle of the product, an improvement in product quality, and cost reduction of purchasing the materials, thus generating a global competitive advantage. In a design outsourcing relationship, there is usually an information asymmetry between the partners involved: the OEM generally has more knowledge of the end market, unlike the supplier who knows in detail the technological developments along the whole chain. In JDM, the tight cooperation between the two companies' design teams reduces this information asymmetry.

The fewer suppliers that are available to deal with each element in outsourcing, the stronger the negotiating power those suppliers have against the OEM. Another risk related to single sourcing lies in the lack of redundancy along the supply chain, making it stiff and vulnerable to any change. It seems therefore more cautious to choose a strategy that implies the use of more suppliers of strategic components, with the opportunity to take advantage of the product interchangeability to face any arising perturbation. In the case of commodity products, the pressure for cost reduction is very high and multiple sourcing offers the possibility to increase competition between suppliers and to reduce prices. Actually, we should face the problem considering all cost sources that are affected by the choice between single or multiple sourcing. The re-design costs of a product, for instance, are higher in the case of multiple sourcing and make this option less attractive. In a fully outsourcing strategy, the OEM is not able to influence decisions of sourcing during the product design phase. Meanwhile in JDM, since the OEM takes care of the design of higher-added-value parts, it has better control over the choice between single and multiple sourcing.

The range of electronic components is reduced by using components that are common to more products. The reduction also allows the company to take advantage of a higher aggregation of demand and encourages purchase planning. In a fully outsourcing partnership, the supplier is encouraged to implement the sharing of components whenever this can simplify the project of future products, reducing the time and costs of the design. In JDM the OEM controls the design process and can request that the partner works on projects with strong component sharing. Non-recurring expenses, such as the fixed costs of re-designing activities, are incurred by the partner who has the weaker bargaining power.

Modular products ensure a lower time-to-market and a good product variety. Designing modular products, though, requires an intense and constant teamwork between the partners. Most of the products of the high-tech industry are characterized by modular architecture and this makes the resort to outsourcing easier. Therefore, products that have a modular architecture make the implementation of JDM partnerships easier.

The strategy of designing products so that customization occurs only in the final stages of the production cycle is called postponement. The advantage is easier management of the uncertainties relating to the demand for each single product, reducing stock and increasing flexibility. In a fully outsourcing partnership, the benefits offered by postponement are perceived by the OEM, but the ability to put it into practice and the management of the increased complexity is exclusively the responsibility of the supplier. The benefits of postponement, therefore, are not equally divided between the partners, but there is a significant advantage for the OEM; implementation costs fall entirely on the supplier who is, therefore, not motivated to implement this strategy. With the JDM model the OEM might instead have, during the design phase, control over those product characteristics that favor its postponement.

ELECTRONICS OUTSOURCING AND JDM

According to their own dimensional and structural characteristics, the players involved in the electronics outsourcing supply chain (Top Class, Global Class, Local Class EMSs, ODMs) follow different strategies of growth and compete in contrasting competitive scenarios. JDM is one of the possible strategic actions carried out by companies in the electronic sector.

Top Class EMSs are positioned in highly competitive markets and whenever possible, in an attempt to reduce competitive pressure, they resort to differentiation, offering added-value services and paying special attention to design services. Yet, the characteristics of the market that they address, such as high volumes and commodity products, the large size and generally inflexible structure, make the implementation of the JDM model rather problematic.

Global Class EMSs operate in an environment where the competition level is less extreme than that for Top Class EMSs, above all because of the specific traits of the reference market and of the higher attention given to high-added-value activities rather than on the sales volumes. Therefore in this sector JDM relationships are encouraged and they ensure the EMSs, who are capable of implementing this strategy, a more loyal client base, a bigger market segmentation and, in turn, a reduction in competitive pressure, also erecting barriers that discourage the entry of new competitors. In this way, Global Class EMSs achieve higher margins than Top Class EMSs.

The context in which Local Class EMSs operate appears to be characterized by an intense competitive pressure, above all because of the high bargaining power of suppliers and clients: the first is due to the disparity in size of component suppliers with respect to small EMSs, and the second is due, mostly, to the lack of generation of intellectual property by smaller EMSs. Local Class EMSs are now focusing on a strategy pointing towards a high specialization of the solutions offered and to customer retention. The implementation of the JDM strategy could be promising in reaching these objectives, but this appears to be difficult because the businesses are small, with limited resources to support intense R&D activity.

The electronic outsourcing companies show different traits and response methods in the specific competitive arena that they are in. The strategies implemented to face these situations also differ, but they share the need to offer higher-added-value services to achieve better margins and to limit the clients' bargaining power (Table 9.6).

The electronics outsourcing industry has followed different growth phases, from R&D to manufacturing or from engineering to EMS services. They are characterized by different focuses on the outsourced activities as represented in Figure 9.1:

- R&D and design activities
- Engineering services
- Manufacturing
- EMS services (design, engineering, manufacturing, provisioning, logistics, distribution, and after-sales services)

The trend seems to point towards the request for integrated solutions with higher added value and, where possible, developed jointly with the client (JDM).

The development of JDM strategies seems to be mostly encouraged in sectors with a massive presence of Global Class EMSs, that is, in areas such as the aerospace and defense industries, as well as industrial electronics and electro-medical. In general, the JDM model is suitable in application fields characterized by non-mass and medium volumes.

Table 9.6   JDM and growth strategies in electronics outsourcing

	Reference market	Competition intensity	Implemented strategy	Objectives
Top Class EMS	High volumes, standardized products	High	M&A Convergence with ODM	Increase in production volumes, economies of scale, worldwide presence, wide products/services portfolio, widening of the client base, higher margins
Global Class EMS	Medium volumes, complex products	Medium	JDM	Development of specific skill, creation of stable cooperation with clients, increase in the bargaining power due to the development of high-added-value activities
Local Class EMS	Limited volumes, local market (often one single client company)	High	Development of intellectual property and high specialization	High client retention and offer of higher-added-value solutions to prevent from being excluded from the market
ODM	High volumes, standardized products	High	Development of standardized products sold to different clients, keeping the intellectual property	Achievement of higher margins thanks to intellectual property ownership

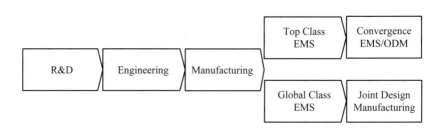

Figure 9.1   Evolution trends towards joint design manufacturing

JDM IN THE AEROSPACE AND DEFENSE SECTORS

In the aerospace and defense sectors, application of the ODM model is difficult due to the uniqueness of the sector and matters associated with the confidentiality of the products. The JDM model, instead, seems to be more appropriate. In fact, outsourcing is also increasingly practiced by the OEMs of these sectors; EMSs must therefore develop the necessary competence to respond to the new demand as well as providing JDM services.

There are some additional problems related to the application of outsourcing in the aerospace/defense sectors, due not only to the high technological level of the product, but, above all, to the matter of security and protection of the technology developed, with less opportunities for cross-fertilization effects. An example of collaboration in the military sector is the Sanmina–SCI/Sikorsky partnership that started in 2007 for the design of a third-generation communication system to integrate in large transport helicopters, for the US Navy. The system will offer advanced digital audio and data processing functions and transmission reliability of the audio signal.

JDM FOR MEDICAL SYSTEMS

The diffusion of electronics has also involved medical and life support systems: many devices, from the most sophisticated ones used in hospitals and specialized centers to the less complex, sold in pharmacies to individuals, are based on electronic systems. Some electronic applications for medical use concern sensors, diagnostic systems, real-time monitoring systems, non-invasive micro-surgery and image processing.

The production volumes of these items are often small, but these products require specific knowledge, similar to what happens in the aerospace and defense sectors. Global Class EMSs can often benefit from their knowledge and in particular from the advantage generated by cross-fertilization to offer suitable solutions to these applications.

Moreover, technology in the medical sector has become complex not only in relation to new products, but also to more sophisticated new production processes that require extended knowledge. The medical market offers better margins with respect to other segments and the demand for these products is more stable and predictable than in other industrial, military and aerospace segments. Yet, this market is characterized by high mixes and low volumes, where extended knowledge is required to meet the many standards and controls related to medical products; not all EMSs own the skills to take on this market.

An example of JDM cooperation is given by Sanmina–SCI and Innovia Medical, which has led to the development of a device to detect infections in children's ears. In this partnership, Sanmina entered the partner's supply chain during product design and development in order to ensure a shorter time-to-market and competitive prices.

10. Strategic Competitive Dynamics

Some trends in the global market for electronics outsourcing have been in operation to modify the traits of this industry for some time. Other trends are more recent, and their short-term effects on companies are already clear. As a result of many forces, some macro-trends are putting the industry under evolutionary pressure and selection effects, associated with the development strategies chosen by the companies.

- Continuous expansion of the electronics outsourcing industry
- Convergence between Top Class EMSs' and ODMs' paths
- Migration of intellectual properties from the system to the components
- Segmentation of the EMS sector

GROWTH OF THE ELECTRONICS OUTSOURCING INDUSTRY

Despite being in a life cycle position that is nearing the end of a rapid expansion, the sector may still be expanding and driven by some key factors.

The diffusion of electronic technologies in everyday life is still in progress. A growing amount of electronics can be found in devices, equipment and plants (cars, phones, entertainment, etc.). Thanks to modern micro-electronic technologies, the amount of 'intelligence' in the electronic items available in the market is increasing. Production, and often design activities, are outsourced.

Many OEMs have transferred all of the intellectual properties associated with electronic innovation, sometimes beyond the production domain, reaching a point of no return which hampers the re-appropriation of the skills required to carry out insourcing activities. Often, the assets have been given to Top Class EMSs and the core competency is no longer available internally.

There is still considerable room for growth in electronics outsourcing. The potential outsourcing market for each action area of EMS and ODM companies is represented in Figure 10.1.

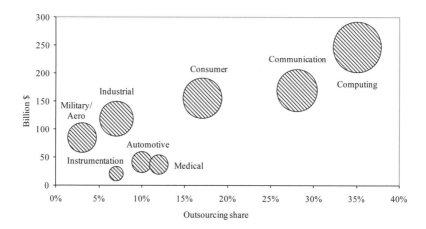

Source: Technology Forecasters (2006).

Figure 10.1   EMSs' and ODMs' potential market and current share

Computing and communication, two segments that yield the highest revenues to electronics outsourcing companies, are business areas where outsourcing is mostly used. Yet, the saturation rate appears to still be quite modest; in fact, only 35 per cent and 28 per cent of the opportunities, respectively, are seized.

As far as the other areas are concerned, there seem to be major growth possibilities in industrial electronics applications, where only 7 per cent of this market is outsourced. Due to security problems, the defense industry outsources only 3 per cent of the electronics they need.

It can be assumed that Global Class EMSs, more than Top Class EMSs/ODMs, take charge of the action areas providing the widest growth opportunities (for example, industrial systems, electro-medical equipment and electronic instruments).

EMS AND ODM CONVERGENCE

The two typical electronics outsourcing models, with special reference to larger companies, originated in different periods and historical moments. EMSs started to develop in the 1990s with Western companies that later became globalized through a policy of acquisitions and production de-localization in a range of market segments. The more recent ODM model is characterized by Asian origins and a growth that is directed towards specific segments with high intellectual property content.

As far as the business model is concerned, the strategic differences between EMSs and ODMs are significant; some of them are summarized in Table 10.1 and it is clear that the ODM model is valued because of intellectual property and the focus on specific products; higher product risk and costs of an R&D structure are associated with this model.

Table 10.1   EMSs and ODMs: strategic models compared

	EMS	ODM
Market segment	Wide range (communications, consumer, automotive, military, industrial, medical)	Mostly data processing, PC and notebooks. Moving into cell phones and PDAs.
Product mix	Various (from high volume/high mix to low volume/low mix)	Mostly high volume/low mix
Product maturity	Work with OEMs on emerging products and technology, products at any part of life-cycle	Mostly mature products with well-defined standards
Design	Some offer design services working closely with OEMs (cost reduction, DFM and time to market)	Skilled in providing low-cost design for limited set of products
Footprint	Top-tier EMS providers have global footprint	Mostly in Asia/Pacific region
Product branding	None	Several sell products under their own brand
Intellectual property	Customer owns intellectual property	ODM has own intellectual property
Other services	Direct order fulfillment to end customer, return and repair, other services to address OEM's needs	Only some provide additional services such as direct shipment to end-user

Source: Delattre et al. (2003).

Notwithstanding the initial differences, the two models seem to have started a process of converge that makes the differences between Top Class EMSs and ODMs more subtle. They compete in increasingly overlapping markets because the OEMs that are aimed at outsourcing design and production increasingly often need to choose between the two models.

The birth and expansion of the ODM model is, in fact, the most severe threat to the growth of the Top Class EMS segment. ODMs are directed towards sectors characterized by very high production volumes, with subsequently lower margins, and offer a substantial role in terms of intellectual property; this is a possibility that questions the EMS–OEM partnerships based on cost competition and time-to-market.

Still more important are the different types of contracts: OEMs purchase products from ODMs, not services. This has allowed the ODMs to catch the margins created by an increase in product engineering or production process optimization. In the case of EMSs, however, the profit produced by better efficiency is often transferred, almost completely, to the OEM client.

Geographic aspects increase the possibility for overlap between the two models. The ODM model, initially confined to low-cost Asian regions in terms of production plant location, has started to expand its production in the USA and Europe, thus disclosing its aim to compete with EMSs on the grounds of the latter's main value proposition: global presence and efficient logistics.

Through acquisition operations, some ODMs are occupying market positions that used to be typical of the EMSs; vice versa, and more intensely, some EMSs are moving their attention to design tasks that used to be typical of the ODMs. Over the last decade, Top Class EMSs have carried out intense M&A activity, originated by the need to increase their production volumes rapidly. Within a sector that, excluding the contribution of Foxconn, is steady in sales and has low profits, the growth through aggregation processes does not expand the overall dimension of the industry and increase the market share of the acquirer in an attempt to slowly achieve an oligopolistic situation, more profitable in terms of margins.

On the contrary, the ODMs' business model allows the companies to keep the intellectual property of the products they design, manufacture and sell to OEMs. The added value associated with IP increases the ODM companies' profit. Furthermore, despite a limited number of M&A operations, the industry has increased its total revenues with a significant annual growth rate, taking advantage of the market globalization trend and of the opportunity to use low-cost labor to meet the large OEM companies' request for low-price products. Companies with higher profits are the most attractive targets to be acquired. Some important M&A operations carried out by Top Class EMS companies over the last five years follow the described strategy: in 2003, Sanmina–SCI acquired Newisys, an ODM of data storage systems, while the following year Flextronics acquired the control of Microcell, an ODM operating in the sector of mobile phones. In particular, the strategy through which Foxconn carried out its remarkable growth process, although it is characterized by a limited resort to M&A activities, appears to be directed towards the acquisition of ODM targets, in order to implement some traits of its business model.

original design manufacturers (ODMs), which have dominated the market for outsourced production of mobile handsets, are facing rising competition from their contract-manufacturing cousins in the electronics manufacturing services (EMS) business. ODMs encountered fierce competitive threats from EMS providers in 2007. EMS companies such as Foxconn and Flextronics have extended their capabilities to include ODM offerings during the last few years through strategic acquisitions. These companies now are winning programs from ODMs by leveraging the benefits of these EMS providers' extensive global footprints and vertically-integrated supply chains.
Jeffrey Wu – iSuppli (2008).

Also due to the effect of M&A activities, the annual revenue growth rates of these two segments, although distinguished by a different position on the life cycle timeline, appear to be convergent in terms of both historical and perspective data, even if the ODM segment still holds a positive differential in terms of growth with respect to the EMS segment. Figure 10.2 highlights the difference.

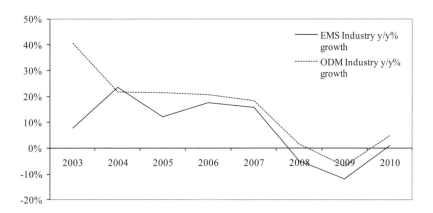

Source: Orbis, iSuppli.

Figure 10.2   Growth trend estimation of the EMS and ODM industries

There is an ongoing approach of the two market segments that seem to blur into one another, highlighting a convergence expressed also in the profit trend.

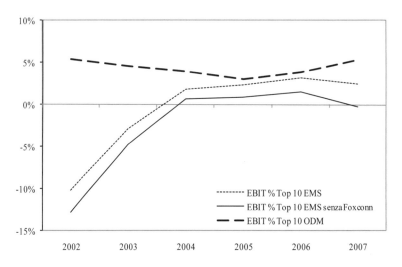

Source: Orbis.

Figure 10.3   Cumulated EBIT margin of Top Class EMSs and ODMs

Figure 10.3 shows analyses of the EMS and ODM profitability trend expressed in terms of cumulated EBIT margin of the first ten companies by turnover. The sales reduction that occurred in 2000–2002 drew the EBIT of the main EMSs to negative values. The situation became profitable again in 2004; then a growth path characterized the subsequent two years until an operating margin of 2 per cent of the turnover was achieved, with Foxconn's significant contribution. The 2008–2009 crisis, then, brought down the prospective data on profits again.

Meanwhile, over the last five years, ODM margins have followed an opposite trend with respect to that of the EMSs'. The ODM business model experienced a period of dimensional development, characterized by higher margins (in 2002, the EBIT margin was around 5 per cent), but later the segment profitability decreased progressively, consistent with what has been previously observed concerning its position in the life cycle.

The difference in terms of profitability derives, above all, from the differing levels of intellectual property in the EMS and ODM products, which in turn originate in the different innovation intensity of the two electronics outsourcing segments. Figure 10.4, which summarizes the importance of R&D investments in the EMS and ODM sectors, highlights the existing distinction. The R&D activity in the EMS industry changed from a value of 0.4 per cent in 2002 to 1.0 per cent in 2006, while R&D activity in the ODM industry was as high as 1.1 per cent of the 2002 turnover, growing to a peak of 1.5 per cent. These figures are consistent with the characteristics of the two markets. In fact, EMSs do not invest in product innovations, but rather invest mainly in process innovations with the potential to increase their efficiency and competitiveness.

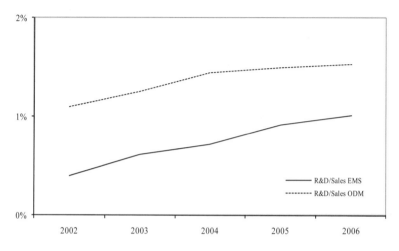

Source: Orbis.

Figure 10.4 R&D/sales of the EMS and ODM industries

It is reasonable to assume that EMSs are attracted to the ODM's higher-added-value activities and therefore they increase their investments in R&D to achieve a greater amount of intellectual property. The effect of this trend is to reinforce the convergence in terms of margins. The EMS industry is close to maturity and its margins can grow only moderately because of both the effect of efficiency parameters and the market concentration. The ODM industry, which is close to the end of the growth phase, is experiencing a reduction of profits, while maintaining a more favorable position than the EMSs, owing to the higher content of IP in its products. At the same time, EMSs are trying to recover their margins through a renewed attention to R&D.

The major contribution to the convergence scenario expressed by the growth trends, margins and R&D investments, comes from the leader EMS company, Foxconn, more than once said to be close to acquiring Quanta Computer, the world's second largest company in terms of turnover. Should this occur, the first contract design manufacturer company would be established; such a hybrid business model (EMS/ODM) would be the result of the real convergence of the two distinct models.

INTELLECTUAL PROPERTY MIGRATION

The current technological trend shows that innovation and IP content is migrating from the system level to the level of the single component. The beginning of intellectual property migration is conventionally attributed to the introduction of microprocessors by Intel in 1971; this event meant that electronic designers were no longer obliged to design a processing unit based on different components and electronic boards *de novo*, but could use an integrated device, ready for use. Since then, the trend has continued, as shown by the increasing availability of standard electronic devices that integrate systemic functions, previously carried out by complex dedicated electronic circuits (high resolution graphics devices, communication chips, analog to digital converter circuits, etc.). Entrusting third parties with the job of supplying some base elements of its first PC, the IBM led to the migration of the intellectual property from their own system to third parties' components, such as the microprocessor of Intel.

The migration of intellectual property brings about a shift of the profits along the electronics supply chain. The segments with higher IP content, mainly electronic component manufacturers, have benefits to the disadvantage of OEMs. For example, the main manufacturer of personal computer CPUs, Intel, had a net operating margin (EBIT margin) as high as 24 per cent of its turnover (2007), while the profitability for Hewlett-Packard and Dell, who use Intel CPUs, was only 8 per cent and 6 per cent, respectively, in 2007.

The increased availability of component IP also brings about an increase in the standardization of electronic products and a progressive reduction of specialization in mass markets. With reference to electronics outsourcing, the trend towards commodity devices benefits the ODM model more than the Top Class EMS model and the OEM clients. Again, the market of personal computers, characterized by an intense migration of IP from the system to the components, is extremely favorable to the ODM model. It appears, therefore, to be normal that 80 per cent of the portable PCs sold globally are manufactured by only a few large Asian ODMs who design and manufacture them for the whole world.

Two factors seem to be poised to contribute to the migration trend in the near future. Firstly, electronic component manufacturers want to sell their products to any client who is ready to pay the requested price, without distinction between OEM, EMS or ODMs; this situation encourages the development of the ODM segment because most of the IP is available on the market embedded into the components so that the quantity of R&D needed to obtain the end product is very low. Secondly, electronic component manufacturers compete within a market that is likely to increase the integration of functionality in electronic devices, often removing the same functionality from the contribution of OEMs; this suggests that many commodity products that are not yet ideal for the ODM segment will become so in the near future.

INDUSTRY SEGMENTATION

The above considerations highlight a net segmentation of the electronics outsourcing industry, both in terms of dimensions and applications. It seems reasonable to assume a superior specialization in some areas of the different dimensional classes, with a competitive scenario in which there are three operating segments: Top Class EMSs /ODMs, Global Class EMSs and Local Class EMSs.

It is unlikely that companies belonging to different segments will compete within the same market. Both from demand side, in terms of potential customers, and supply side, in terms of capability to propose products and services, the differences are significant. It is evident that Top Class companies should not be considered to be 'big Global Class companies'; they are, in fact, different 'agents' of electronics outsourcing, not associated or interchangeable. Where the first class comes in, the second normally does not, and vice versa. As a consequence, competition strategies will develop in different directions, though they are all pursuing a common goal, namely the highest possible return for their shareholders.

TOP CLASS EMSs' AND ODMs' STRATEGY

Large EMSs and ODMs will move towards a converging path that will make the two models interchangeable due to M&A operations among the large EMSs and the most important ODMs. Focusing on production will support high-volume sectors, thanks in part to the migration of IP from systems to components. The majority of production plants will be based in low-labor cost countries, though manufacturing facilities will be kept in Western countries.

Sales growth will be ensured by the widespread use of electronics in commodity devices, although to a lesser extent than the increases of the last years. Margins will undergo a compression, aligned with volume increases, but the potential decreases can be compensated for by technological actions in product and process engineering. The products will be configured mainly as commodities that will reach the final customer directly through the OEMs who, labeling them with their own brand, will guarantee their quality and performance. The role of the OEMs, then, will be determined by the defense of brand recognition, product innovation perceived by the client, management or ownership of sales channels, and the relationship with the end customer.

It is likely that the relationships between Top Class EMSs/ODMs and OEMs will experience conflicts in the management of sales channels and of the end customers. In fact, outsourcing companies might claim that better customer service can only be ensured by a direct relationship with the customers themselves.

Yet, the enormous dimensional growth of Top Class EMSs/ODMs could jeopardize one of the original competitive advantages of electronics outsourcing, namely, efficiency in operations. The occupation of segments of increasing importance in the value chain might highlight an identification similar to that of their customers (from the idea of the product to its design and production), but with a lack of a familiar brand. The distinction between clients and suppliers could gradually blur to the disadvantage of Top Class EMSs/ODMs that by their nature do not have control over the final section of the value chain, as OEMs do.

The Top Class EMS/ODM segment will set priorities for the search for efficiency in production. It will keep moving towards exogenous growth strategies through merger operations, attempting to take a larger part of the chain margins of the production and distribution of electronic components.

GLOBAL CLASS EMSs' STRATEGY

Global Class EMSs should follow a different path from Top Class EMSs in their attempt to serve clients who have different needs than those of Top Class EMSs' clients. In particular, they will control the sectors characterized by higher specialization, higher intensity of intellectual property shared with OEMs and middle production volumes. In their search for a higher level of differentiation, Global Class EMSs will have a propensity to work in the technological innovative sector.

Closer by nature to industrial sectors, they will set up an organization that will support more complex and customized products. Consistently, production plants will be located in Western countries for high-automated productions, but also in low-labor-cost countries for certain parts of the products and processes, with the aim of maintaining cost competitiveness.

Sales expansion can be achieved through diversification of industries that are characterized by intermediate volumes and specialization or through an increase in product IP, in which it is reasonable to expect some major investments.

Global Class EMSs will have to develop IP and supply design activities in alliance with their clients with the aim of finalizing shared projects with a common IP foundation. A migration from the model where the design is paid by the client towards a model where the production of intellectual property is co-financed, and therefore shared, by EMSs and OEMs, could contribute to stable relationships. The increased competition coming from the decrease of costs related to low labor costs in Asia will be over within a medium-term period as a consequence of mechanisms that are similar to those which generated it – that is the globalization processes that are leading to a reduction in existing economic gaps.

A competitive differentiation of Global Class EMSs from the large Top Class EMSs/ODMs lies also in their smaller size that allows them to implement more flexible and easily scaled models to respond more clearly to rapid changes in the demand from the market. In relation to exogenous growth mechanisms, aggregations between Global Class EMSs involving different regions and/or industries will be privileged. Unlike the Top Class environment, where no preference is given to a differentiation strategy to favor the high level of product standardization, the Global Class segment requires significant investments in the creation of the technological relationship with the client. The acquisition of small EMSs located in different areas and sectors could ensure more rapid expansion than the green-field growth processes.

LOCAL CLASS EMS STRATEGY

There are few opportunities for growth for the smaller EMSs, both because they cannot take advantage of the delocalization processes and because they are often not equipped in terms of specific intellectual property, which usually remains under the OEMs' ownership.

The opportunity to expand, although limited, might be encouraged in the case of high specialization for OEM clients that belong to the same sector. Yet, this requires investments in innovation by EMSs in order that they can keep the intellectual property generated, without transfer it to the OEM. The absence of IP generation by Local Class EMSs might persuade some traditional OEM clients to turn to the higher segment of Global Class EMSs, provided that the dimensional aspects in terms of production rate are consistent with the organization. For this reason, a selective reduction in the lower segment can be expected, counteracted only by the highly specialized Local Class EMSs, which will have invested in intellectual property with well remunerated applications even with low production volumes.

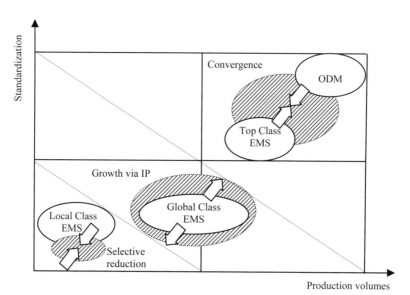

Figure 10.5   Strategic evolution of the electronics outsourcing industry

STRATEGIC GROWTH PATHS

On the subject of the positioning of electronics outsourcing companies within the life cycle, some strategic paths of growth seem to emerge.

- Selection of sectors and focus
- Higher added value and intellectual property
- Intellectual property sharing
- Aggregation of Global Class EMSs

SELECTION OF SECTORS AND FOCUS

OEMs' decision to outsource electronic activities to ODMs or to Top Class EMSs depends on the level of standardization of the technology underlying the product segment, on production volume, and on the competition dynamics between OEMs and the two types of suppliers. Top Class EMSs have implemented a growth strategy in high production volumes industries where the OEMs normally achieve very limited profits and are exposed to strong price competition. Thus EMS segments will clearly be increasingly pressured by their clients, who are also under intense competitive stress, to reduce their sales prices. In the same markets, the competitive pressure in electronics outsourcing is affected by the presence of ODMs who, compared to EMSs, bring the competitive strength of Porter's 'substitute business' in terms of price competitiveness and capability to meet the increasingly demanding clauses in contracts with OEMs.

Competitive pressure induces EMSs to commit constant attention to the process with the aim of controlling costs using a strategy that characterizes the ODMs as a strong point and that therefore obliges the EMSs to compete on an unfavorable ground. For example, if, in the past, the construction of personal computer power subsystems was left to the EMSs' assembly, today these products are supplied by ODMs specialized in power supply systems, autonomously designed and manufactured, potentially, for all personal computer manufacturers. Also the migration of IP from systems to components is such that it helps the ODMs over the EMSs in the segments characterized by high production volumes. Yet, addressing sectors with low production volumes, often characterized by a high level of customization, might not be the right strategy for the growth of Top Class EMSs, because their characteristic high fixed costs require economies of scale to fully pay back those costs.

Among two possible directions, respectively typical of Top Class EMSs and of Global Class EMSs, the orientation towards products that meet market segments characterized by product specificity and medium volumes implies the definition of a strategy that maximizes company flexibility, especially for design competence, and that uses product customization as a competitive advantage to differentiate with respect to mass production. Due to the heterogeneity of their target sectors, the focus of EMSs on the production of specific goods with similar features is strategic. Because of the variety of products requested with respect to performance, planning, volume and delivery times, EMSs have differentiated over the years, focusing on the demand suited to their structural and dimensional characteristics.

It should be considered that Top Class EMSs are moving towards large production volumes to distribute their high fixed costs. Therefore, the medium-volume segment of products specialized in specific clients seems to be of great interest for medium-size EMSs (Global Class), whose business organization is closer to specialization in the production of medium volumes, with a high level of loyalty of customers who buy regularly and repeatedly.

Table 10.2 lists the industries that, for production volumes, standardization level, complexity of manufacturing and typology of clients appear to be more suitable for Top Class EMSs and ODMs or for Global Class EMSs. The focus on the sectors that are more appropriate for each segment seems to be a crucial strategic condition for company growth.

Table 10.2   Target industries for Top Class EMSs/ODMs and Global Class EMSs

Top Class EMSs/ODMs (high volumes, standardization)	Global Class EMSs (medium volumes, specialization)
PCs and notebooks	Industrial automation
IT peripherals (printers, routers, etc.)	Traffic control
Mobile phones	Railways and transportation
Digital cameras	Machines and equipment
MP3 players	Aero-space systems
Automotive	Safety system
LCD TV screens	Medical and life support systems
Building & Home automation	Electronic instruments
	Vending

HIGHER ADDED VALUE AND MORE INTELLECTUAL PROPERTY

A source of competitive advantage is emerging for EMSs, both Top Class, who find themselves in competition with ODMs, and Global Class. They can improve their margins through the extension of their offerings by adding services adjacent to their core business, such as product engineering, management of the supply chain, component purchase activities, installation, management of products returned by the clients, maintenance, external service, integration with existing hardware, and creation of specific solutions for individual customers.

Actually, there is a growing interest in the development of business models that aim at offering high-added-value services. Companies along the electronic sector chain are primarily focusing on design services, pursuing the profits associated with differentiation strategies, aware that the basis of the future competitiveness of their product is created at this stage of the value chain.

High-added-value and IP services generate higher profit margins with respect to mere production activity, because they require specific technological competences that are better rewarded by the market. Furthermore, a more stable and in depth relationship with clients increases loyalty to OEMs, not only because of the reputation factor, but also due to the exit barriers associated with the unavoidable costs of switching; these are due to the mutual adaptation of the technologies and of the players involved in the partnership. This kind of relationship allows EMSs to maintain higher margins on services added to production that can be offered to the OEM or, in agreement with the OEM, directly to consumers, both during and after the sale of the product.

SHARING OF INTELLECTUAL PROPERTY

EMSs should start planning partnerships with OEMs; in this way EMSs could develop their own technological competence and supply design services in cooperation with the OEMs. At present, many EMSs are already supplying this kind of service and in most cases the OEMs are financing the R&D expenses, later claiming their rights to the intellectual property they develop. Alternatively, the EMSs could autonomously develop innovations on the products so that they can capture higher margins on each manufactured unit.

A crucial factor for this strategy is the opportunity that the EMSs have to supply design services that allow the transfer of cost reductions due to ownership of the plants (design for manufacturability) and the competence involved in maintenance operations to the OEM client. At the same time, the knowledge developed in the design phase should also improve their competence in production and maintenance activities, thus generating a positive synergy between the various company departments.

The partnership underlying such a product co-design model can be regulated by cost-plus contracts where a higher margin is granted to the suppliers or, better, by the sharing of technological innovation. The implementation of relationships in the generation of intellectual property will ensure the EMSs an increase in their profits provided that in the process a higher value is generated for their OEM clients.

Different cooperation levels can be implemented depending on the complexity of the products, the demand variability coming from the market, the degree of innovation embedded in the engineering, the requests in order processing, and support throughout the product's life cycle. There is a noticeable difference between the mere outsourcing of printed circuits and a model that involves the primary and complete management of the processing of an order.

CONVERGENCE TOWARDS THE ODM MODEL

EMSs can choose to make investments themselves in R&D and create products that can be sold to their OEM clients. The IP developed during the entire life cycle of the product would remain with the EMSs, by then having become similar to ODMs, and their client base could expand to include more OEMs and some end clients, as in the case of the mobile phone industry.

This expansion of the client base would certainly increase volumes, and the R&D costs could be paid back through a high number of products. This strategy is recommended if the EMS's dimensions increase; this implies some important adjustments involving the entire organization of the company.

As the focus changes from a service-oriented to a product-oriented organization, a gradual change takes place towards a greater attention to the product and the consequent need to develop R&D skills. The ODM model involves a higher investment risk. ODMs assume the risks related to the purchase of materials and the possibility that their intellectual property investments may not bring positive returns, at least in the short term. ODMs also assume risk related to the maintenance of a stock of products that might soon become obsolete.

Finally, the possibility of conflicts along the supply chain should not be ignored. This strategy might not be adequately shared by the OEMs, thus placing existing contracts at serious risk and thereby creating problems with clients.

Despite these considerations, the well-planned acquisition of ODM products with the aim of creating a supplement to the business of Top Class EMSs is considered to be a profitable strategy. EMSs should start negotiations with OEM clients to demonstrate the mutual benefits coming from the use of such business models. Additionally, EMSs can identify new market segments that are undergoing a commodization trend and will soon be the object of strong interest from the ODMs who would certainly be able to overcome the competition of traditional EMSs.

AGGREGATIONS BETWEEN GLOBAL CLASS EMSs

M&A activities have supported the consolidation of various sectors, especially in the periods characterized by economic expansion and, since the early 2000s, by the available financial resources of institutional investors, such as private equities and hedge funds.

The electronics outsourcing industry had a similar path, especially the Top Class EMS segment, particularly in the periods 2000–2001 and 2004–2007. The competitive dynamics also put pressure on the achievement of strategic alternatives by intermediate-size EMSs (Global Class EMS). In fact, only the main players in the Top Class EMS sector seem to have reached a satisfactory competitive positioning in terms of product mix, production capacity and low-cost labor. M&A operations have supported the expansion of a few Top Class companies, cost leaders in a segment that was previously very fragmented. Once they had achieved consolidation, the market leaders have dominated the competitive scenario through economies of scale, presence in all of the world's geographical areas and a wide range of products/services. Often, the success of these companies was reached to the disadvantage of smaller businesses, unable to re-position themselves and to compete effectively.

The hundreds of M&A operations that have occurred over the last ten years have generated a group of Top Class EMSs who dominate in the manufacturing realm and are characterized by very high volumes and a limited mix.

On the other hand, for many medium-capitalization companies, there are still dimensional problems that make it difficult to implement, with the required speed, programs that need economies of scale, such as for example investment in production in low-labor-cost countries. This has encouraged some EMSs to use a different strategy, concentrating on niche sectors with a lower competition level and a higher profit performance.

Today's positioning of a Global Class or Local Class player requires the definition of strategies that create value in a sector that has entered its maturity phase and that is characterized by a high concentration level. Two distinct strategies can be outlined in electronics outsourcing: (1) to be an EMS characterized by high volumes and a low mix, the strategy implemented by Top Class companies; and (2) to focus on businesses characterized by low volumes and a high mix, such as Global Class EMSs, who supply, among others, OEMs in the military/aerospace, medical, industrial and instruments sectors, encouraging the capacity to supply complex products and services for particular clients.

Although many Top Class EMSs could also supply production services in lower volumes, the acceptance of these kinds of orders is sometimes carried out unwillingly, without the necessary commitment and, above all, without a structure that can handle production orders that are too small for companies with annual revenues exceeding one billion US dollars. This situation often persuades OEMs to prefer Global Class or niche suppliers, because the production could represent an important portion of their revenues and profitability, and thus gives considerable interest to the client.

While the 'high volumes/low mix' strategy has inspired the consolidation processes of Top Class EMSs companies, the 'medium volume/medium mix' strategy is creating a consolidation opportunity for the Global Class companies' shareholders through acquisitions of medium or small EMS companies. The opportunity is growing through the acquisition of companies of the same size or smaller in different regions, while remaining focused on customer service. M&A operations should target small or medium–small businesses with a strong orientation to the domestic market that operate in niche business sectors and that are growing, using acquisitions as a starting point for further development in the region.

This approach should guarantee the possibility of acquiring new clients, improving economies of scale, and allowing access to markets characterized by wider growth opportunities with respect to established segments. These objectives should contribute to the achievement of a client base with low volumes and a high mix, in sectors characterized by high capital return, and low market penetration rates relatively protected from the global outsourcing trend.

The companies should develop specific engineering skills, stable collaborations with a diversified client base, and be able to generate a significant added value in terms of IP. The industrial objectives can be reached through the defense of niche areas, characterized by high growth and profitability rates, with lower probabilities of competition by companies based in low-labor-cost countries; this could happen due to a number of reasons including the need for geographic proximity to the client and the high degree of complexity in the production process.

The merger of Global Class EMSs on a regional basis is promoted by several considerations. First of all, the company being acquired remains close to the client, both physically and for the customized service it can provide. Secondly, the integration of two companies can guarantee economies of scale and a stronger purchasing power towards component suppliers. Finally, a higher degree of diversification achieved in the client base and the capacity to take advantage of these new business relationships allows the company to present a lower risk profile and to increase its revenues. All these advantages could lead to a relatively higher evaluation of EMS businesses and should provide a solid base for the generation of value for shareholders.

The exogenous growth approach has already been widely adopted by Top Class EMSs and has allowed them to rapidly increase their production capacity to meet the increase in demand on one side and to expand their business in new sectors on the other. The same policy appears to be interesting to Global Class EMSs as well for different purposes, summarized as follows:

- Acquisition of skills in other industrial sectors, that are different with respect to the company business but attractive in terms of profitability (for example, medical, aerospace and defense).
- Acquisition of capability that can expand client services through vertical integration both upstream, with more experienced EMSs in the design and engineering process of electronic subsystems, and downstream, in

order to widen the range of services offered to OEMs, especially for maintenance and after sales activities.

- Creation of new business opportunities, by taking advantage of the geographic position of the acquired company or, more simply, by reaching important clients with whom the acquired company had established consolidated relationships of partnership and supplies.
- Increase in production capacity through the acquisition of production facilities located in low-labor-cost countries, mainly in Eastern Europe or Asia (China, India and Taiwan).

The EMS industry has been and still is characterized by merger processes, because increases in electronic applications and growing demand have led companies in this sector to develop a preference for this policy which, although more risky, has allowed them to respond more promptly to market needs. Yet, in the historical context that followed the 2000–2002 turmoil, the results of the acquisition processes generated an excessive overload of fixed costs that prevented them from promptly reacting to a unexpected fall in demand.

LESSONS FROM THE CRISES

We have commented on the negative trend for revenues and profits of the EMS industry at the beginning of the new millennium (Figure 5.4). All the companies within the EMS industry were affected. It is commonly agreed that excessive production capacity was the main cause of the dire performance of EMSs in that period.

Due to the rapid growth in the 1990s of the overall electronics industry, especially in telecommunications and the Internet, EMS companies significantly increased their production capacity. Indeed, the total assets of Top Class EMSs quadrupled in only two years (1998–2000) and investment in new production facilities had generated a high level of potential supply.

New investments were also those deriving from the purchase of production sites that were previously used by OEMs who, through the outsourcing of an increasing quantity of products and services, have led the EMSs to purchase excess assets. As a consequence of the rapid increase in demand, this action has allowed the OEMs to support the rapid growth strategy implemented by the EMSs. This has also allowed the EMSs to achieve a logistic positioning close to their OEM clients, with whom they have entered supply contracts.

In the latter half of the 1990s, production capacity was fully exploited, reaching 80 per cent in 2000. The following year, though, due to the downsizing of the demand associated with the development of Internet technologies and with the world recession that followed September 11, 2001, volumes were reduced by approximately 17 per cent. Furthermore, the indicators of production capacity utilization in 2002 decreased to an average value of 50 per cent. It was only in 2003 that the same indicators began to grow again, reaching average values of 60 per cent. North American companies started to use their plants again with indexes ranging between 40 and 50 per cent, while Asian companies exceeded 80 per cent.

The entire world economy experienced a significant slowdown. In fact, as shown in Figure 10.6, the world economy growth trend, in terms of GDP (gross domestic product), highlights how the EMS sector is widely correlated. These data confirm the consideration that the main contribution to the negative conjuncture data in the 2000–2002 period was external to the sector itself, as is clearly shown by the successive trend characterized by a significant increase.

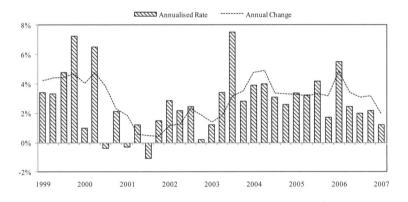

Source: Department of Commerce USA.

Figure 10.6   Trend of the world gross domestic product

Production over-capacity, generated by excessive investments and over-estimation of the sector's growth, has seriously affected the production system and the whole EMSs' value chain, although with different intensity for worldwide EMSs (Top Class EMS), specialized in very high volumes of mass production, than for smaller EMSs, whose position depends on their specific industrial know-how.

Several causes and events provide an explanation of the significant drop of profits that occurred in the 2000–2002 time period.

- *Limited bargaining power of EMSs*
  Aware of the problems associated with excessive production capacity, OEMs were able to negotiate excellent prices. EMS companies had to operate with lower profit margins in order to take advantage of excess capacity.
- *High costs of fixed assets*
  EMSs were forced to face high fixed costs, including the costs of plants, equipment and management, together with the financial charges due to debts incurred in the acquisition of other EMS companies. Decrease of production volume caused an increase in the impact of costs per product unit because of the plant depreciation.
- *Excessive and obsolete stocks*
  EMS companies provided stock levels based on OEM forecasts and purchased electronic components to be able to face the forthcoming expected demand. Due to the sudden narrowing in demand, they were forced to negotiate with OEMs on their responsibilities for excess and obsolete materials. In most cases, EMSs had to bear the costs of the surplus stock.
- *Aggressive acquisition policy*
  EMS companies also acquired the production lines of OEM clients in the period immediately after the 2001 market decline. In order to obtain new contracts and to increase their geographic presence, EMSs implemented an aggressive strategy of acquisitions and expansion of production capacity, although most of the acquired plants turned out to be low quality. These acquisitions, that seemed to appear strategically advantageous, did not always yield the expected results, due to difficulties in integrating with the other activities carried out by the EMSs.
- *Closure of some production plants*
  In response to the strong decline in the demand, the majority of EMS companies dramatically cut the number of plants, especially where the labor cost was higher. Approximately 80 per cent of the factory closures occurred in the USA.
- *Problems in supply chain management*
  Management of the EMS industry supply chain involves a large number of activities, including demand forecasting, stock organization, production planning, logistics, and the management of products and relationships with suppliers. Demand forecasts were used to predict the quantities of end products requested by OEMs and to ensure the availability of the necessary components to feed the production process. Many problems associated with this activity arose during the growth of the 1990s. EMS businesses were not, in fact, able to plan their

production, since they had no opportunity to know the trend of their OEM clients' demand. For this reason, EMSs made plans based on incomplete information that caused errors in stock management. At the same time, since the actual capacity used by the EMSs was quite high, OEMs' clients often overstated their forecasts in order to preserve part of the EMSs' production capacity. When the demand decline started, EMSs had an unnecessary stock of end products and raw materials that the OEMs did not want, and therefore did not request, generating important excesses of stock.

- *Operational inefficiency*
  Due to the rapid and continuous expansion that characterized the sector until 2000, many EMS companies focused mostly on expanding their market shares and on maximizing their turnover level, neglecting optimization of their production and management efficiency. This led the companies not so much to compete on factors like product quality or differentiation, but to increase their volume and implicitly generate a price war.

The above considerations highlight the sector's weakness in unfavorable economic periods and teach lessons regarding the need to keep a high degree of efficiency and flexibility in electronics outsourcing operations. EMS and ODM companies deserve major attention in operational and organizational efficiency.

As a matter of fact, the successive global crisis that began in 2008, although having a very strong impact on global outsourcing activities, has not found the most virtuous EMS/ODM companies unprepared, because they had long before changed their cost structures. For these companies, the 2008–2009 downturn might even be positive in the long term. In fact, many OEM companies have revived the trend of structural change within the organization, aiming towards a higher degree of flexibility and are encouraging the outsourcing of some additional activities. It is not known what the overall effects of this crisis on electronics outsourcing will be, but only that the previous growth forecast for EMSs and ODMs have been revised; substantial stability is expected in the years to come.

It should be remembered, however, that crises do not always evolve in the same way. In particular, the largest OEMs had already closed most of their production plants during the previous crisis and for some of them the quota of outsourced manufacturing has been, for a long time, as high as 100 per cent. Therefore, a growth strategy for EMS/ODM companies could follow the switch toward outsourcing of sectors which until now had either not resorted to it, or had done so in a limited way; these could be, for example, the medical and aerospace industries, that are still characterized by a low level of production volume and high mix. This situation might be particularly positive for Global Class EMSs, which are more flexible and organized to face complex and medium quantity industrial production demands.

Bibliography

Abernathy, W.J. and K.B. Clark (1985), 'Innovation: Mapping the Winds of Creative Destruction', *Research Policy*, **14** (1), 3–22.

Abernathy, W.J. and J.M. Utterback (1978), 'Patterns of Industrial Innovation', *Technology Review*, **80** (7), 40–47.

Adizes, I. (1979), 'Organizational Passages: Diagnosing and Treating Life Cycle Problems of Organizations', *Organizational Dynamics*, **8** (1), 3–25.

Adizes, I. (1989), *Corporate Lifecycles: How and Why Corporations Grow and Die*, Englewood Cliffs, NJ: Prentice Hall.

Amit, R. and P.J.H. Schoemaker (1993), 'Strategic Assets and Organizational Rent', *Strategic Management Journal*, **14** (1), 33–46.

Andrews, Philip W.S. and T. Wilson (eds) (1951), *Oxford Studies in the Price Mechanism*, Oxford: Clarendon Press.

Andrews, K.R. (1971), *The Concept of Corporate Strategy*, Irwin: Homewood.

Ansoff, H.I. (1965), *An Aanalytic Approach to Business Policy for Growth and Expansion*, New York: McGraw-Hill.

Barnes, E., J. Dai, S. Deng, D. Down, M. Goh, H.C. Lau and M. Sharafali (2000), 'Electronics manufacturing service industry', White Paper, School of Industrial and Systems Engineering Georgia, National University of Singapore.

Baumol, W.J. (1959), *Business Behavior, Value and Growth*, New York: Macmillan.

Berle, A.A. and G.C. Means (1933), *The Modern Corporation and Private Property*, New York: Macmillan.

Black, B. (1989), *Bidder Overpayment in Takeovers*, Stanford Law Review.

Bralla, J.G. (1998), *Design for Manufacturability Handbook*, New York: McGraw Hill.

Carlsson, B. (1989), 'Flexibility and the Theory of the Firm', *International Journal of Industrial Organization*, **7** (2), 179–203.

Carbone, J. (2007), 'Targeting Design', *Purchasing*, 30–36.

Cassia, L., M. Fattore and S. Paleari (2006), *Entrepreneurial Strategy: Emerging Businesses in Declining Industries*, Cheltenham, UK and Northampton, MA, USA: Edward Elgar.

Chatterjee, S. (1986), 'Types of Synergy and Economic Values: The Impact of Acquisitions on Merging and Rival Firms', *Strategic Management Journal*, **7**, 119–139.

Chatterjee, S. (1992), 'Sources of Value in Takeovers: Synergy or Restructuring – Implications for Target and Bidder Firms', *Strategic Management Journal*, **13**, 267–286.

Coase, R.H. (1937), 'The Nature of the Firm', *Economica*, **4** (16), 386–405.

Danbolt, J. (2004), 'Target Company Cross-border Effects in Acquisitions into the UK', *European Financial Management*, **10**, 83–108.

Datta, D. (1991), 'Organisational Fit and Acquisition Performance: Effect of Post-Acquisition Integration', *Strategic Management Journal*, **12**, 281–297.

Datta, D., G.E. Pnches and V.K. Narayanan (1992), 'Factors Influencing Wealth Creation from Mergers and Acquisitions: A Meta-Analysis', *Strategic Management Journal*, **13**, 67–84.

Dean, T.J., R.L. Brown and C.E. Bamford (1998), 'Differences in Large and Small Firm Responses to Environmental Context: Strategic Implications from a Comparative Analysis of Business Formations', *Strategic Management Journal*, **19** (8), 709–728.

Delattre A., T. Hess and K. Chiech (2003), *Strategic Outsourcing: Electronics Manufacturing Transformation in Changing Business Climates*, Internal Report, Bermuda: Accenture.

Dennis, D. and J. McConnell (1986) 'Corporate Mergers and Security Returns', *Journal of Financial Economics*, **16**, 143–187.

DeJong, H.W. (1989), 'The Takeover Market in Europe: Control Structures and the Performance of Large Companies Compared', *Review of Industrial Organization*, **6**, 1–18.

Domberger, S. (1998), *The Contracting Organization: A Strategic Guide to Outsourcing*, Oxford: Oxford University Press.

Drazin, R. and R.K. Kazanjian (1990), 'A Reanalysis of Miller and Friesen's Life Cycle Data', *Strategic Management Journal*, **11** (4), 319–325.

Fine, C.H. and D.E. Whitney (1996), '*Is the Make-Buy Decision Process a Core Competence?*', Working Paper, Cambridge, MA, USA: MIT Center for Technology, Policy and Industrial Development.

Foster, R. (1986), 'Working the S-curve – Assessing Technological Threats', *Research Management Journal*, **4**, 153–173.

Fuller, K., J. Netter and M. Stegemoller (2002), 'What do Returns to Acquiring Firms Tell Us? Evidence from Firms that make Many Acquisitions', *Journal of Finance*, **67**, 1763–1793.

Gaughan, P.A. (2001), *Mergers, Acquisitions, and Corporate Restructuring*, New York: John Wiley & Sons.

Goold, M. (1996), 'Parenting Strategies for the Mature Business', *Long*

Range Planning, **29** (3), 358–369.

Goold, M. and K. Luchs (1993), 'Why Diversify? Four Decades of Management Thinking', *Academy of Management Executive*, **7** (3), 7–25.

Grant R.M. (2008), *Contemporary Strategy Analysis*, Oxford: Blackwell Publishing.

Greiner, L.E. (1972), 'Evolution and Revolution as Organizations Grow', *Harvard Business Review,* **50**, 37–46.

Grossman, G. and E. Helpman (2005), 'Outsourcing in a Global Economy', *Review of Economic Studies*, **72**, 135–159.

Hamel G. and C. Prahald (1990), 'The Core Competencies of the Corporation', *Harvard Business Review*, May–June, 79–91.

Hamermesh, R.G. and S.B. Silk (1979), 'How to Compete in Stagnant Industries', *Harvard Business Review*, September–October, 161–168.

Hanks, S.H. (1990), 'The Organization Life-Cycle: Integrating Content and Process', *Journal of Small Business Strategy*, **1**, 1–13.

Harrigan, K. (1980), *Strategies for Declining Businesses*, Lexington, MA: Lexington Books

Healy, P., K. Palepu and R. Ruback (1992), 'Does Corporate Performance Improve After Mergers?' *Journal of Financial Economics*, **31**, 135–175.

Healy, P., K. Palepu and R. Ruback (1997), 'Which Takeovers are Profitable: Strategic or Financial?', *Sloan Management Review*, **38**, 45–57.

Heshmati, A. (2001), 'On the Growth of Micro and Small Firms: Evidence from Sweden', *Small Business Economics*, **17** (3), 213–228.

Huang, G.Q. (2001), *Design for Quality – Principles and Techniques*, Taunton, Somerset, UK: Research Studies Press Ltd.

Hunt, S.D. and R.M. Morgan (1995), 'The Comparative Advantage Theory of Competition', *Journal of Marketing*, **59** (2), 1–15.

Jemison, D.B. and S.B. Sitkin (1986), 'Corporate Acquisitions: A Process Perspective', *Academy of Management Review*, **11** (1), 145–163.

Jensen, M.C. and W.H. Meckling (1976), 'Theory of the Firm: Managerial Behavior, Agency Costs, and Ownership Structure', *Journal of Financial Economics*, **3**, 305–360.

Jovanovic, B. (1982), 'Selection and the Evolution of Industry', *Econometrica*, **50** (3), 649–670.

Jovanovic, B. and G.M. MacDonald (1994), 'The Life Cycle of a Competitive Industry', *The Journal of Political Economy*, **102** (2), 322–347.

Kamath, R.R. and J.K. Liker (1994), 'A Second Look at Japanese Product Development', *Harvard Business Review*, November–December, 154–170.

Kaplan, S. and M. Weisbach (1992), 'The Success of Acquisitions: Evidence From Divestitures', *Journal of Finance*, **47**, 107–138.

Kazanjian R.K. and R. Drazin (1989), 'An Empirical Test of a Stage of Growth Progression Model', *Management Science*, **35** (12), 1489–1503.

Kishimoto, C. (2005), 'Profitability in Taiwan's Electronics Manufacturing Services' Firms: A Comparison with American Firms', *The International Centre for the Study of East Asian Development*, Working Paper Series, **11**.

Kitching, J. (1967), 'Why do Mergers Miscarry?', *Harvard Business Review*, November–December, 84–101.

Kotabe, M. and M.J. Mol (2004), 'A New Perspective on Outsourcing and the Performance of Firm', in M. Trick (ed.), *Global Corporate Evolution: Looking Inward or Looking Outward*, Pittsburgh: Carnegie Mellon University Press.

Lavagno L., G. Martin and L. Scheffer (2006), *Electronic Design Automation for Integrated Circuits Handbook*, London, UK: Taylor & Francis.

Lei, D. and M.A. Hitt (1995), 'Strategic Restructuring and Outsourcing: The Effect of Mergers and Acquisitions and LBOs on Building Firm Skills and Capabilities', *Journal of Management*, **21** (5), 835–859.

Levin, R.C., A.K. Klevorick, R. Nelson and S.G. Winter (1987), 'Appropriating the Return from Industrial Research and Development', *Brookings Papers on Economic Activity*, **3**, 783–831.

Levitt, T. (1965), 'Exploit the Product Life Cycle', *Harvard Business Review*, November–December, 81–94.

Lewellen, W., C. Loderer and A. Rosenfeld (1985), 'Merger Decisions and Executive Incentive Problems: an Empirical Analysis', *Journal of Accounting and Economics*, **7**, 209–231.

Lin, Y.J. and Y. Tsai (2005), 'What's New about Outsourcing', in S. La Croix and P.A. Petri (eds), *Challenges to the Global Trading System: Adjustment to Globalization in the Asia-Pacific Region*, New York: Routledge.

Linder, J.C. (2004), 'Transformational Outsourcing', *Sloan Management Review*, **40**, 52–58.

Linder, J.C., S.L. Jarvenpaa and T.H. Davenport (2002), *Innovation Sourcing Strategy Matters*, Cambridge, UK: Accenture Institute for Strategic Change.

Livermore, S. (1935), 'The Success of Industrial Mergers', *Quarterly Journal of Economics*, **50**, 68–96.

Loh, L. and N. Venkatraman (1992), 'Determinants of Information Technology Outsourcing: A Cross-sectional Analysis', *Journal of Management Information Systems*, **9** (1), 7–24.

Lundvall, B. and S. Borras (1997), *The Globalizing Learning Economy: Implication for Innovation Policy*, Targeted Socio-Economic Studies, DG XII, Commission of the European Union, Luxemburg.

Marris, R. (1964), *The Economic Theory of Managerial Capitalism*, New York: Free Press.

Matsusaka, J.G. (1993), 'Takeovers Motives During the Conglomerate Merger Wave', *Rand Journal of Economics*, **24**, 357–379.

McGahan, A.M. and B.S. Silverman (2001), 'How does Innovative Activity Change as Industries Mature?', *International Journal of Industrial Organization*, **19** (7), 1141–1160.

Miles, Raymond E. and C. Snow (1978), *Organizational Strategy, Structure and Process*, New York: McGraw-Hill.

Miller, D. and P.H. Friesen (1984), 'A Longitudinal Study of the Corporate LifeCycle', *Management Science*, **30** (10), 1161–1183.

Moeller, S.B., F.P. Schlingemannb and R.M. Stulz (2004), 'Firm Size and the Gains from Acquisitions', *Journal of Financial Economics*, **73**, 201–228.

Mol, M.J. (2007), *Outsourcing: Design, Process and Performance*, Cambridge: Cambridge University Press.

Montgomery, C.A. and H. Singh (1984), 'Diversification Strategy and Systematic Risk', *Strategic Management Journal*, **5**, 181–191.

Morck, R., A. Shleifer and R.W. Vishny (1988), 'Management Ownership and Market Valuation: An Empirical Analysis', *Journal of Financial Economics*, **20**, 293–315.

Mulherin, J.H. and A.L. Boone (2000), 'Comparing Acquisitions and Divestures', *Journal of Corporate Finance*, **6**, 117–139.

Mullin, R. (1996), 'Managing the Outsourced Enterprise', *Journal of Business Strategy*, **17**, 28–36.

Nellore, R. and K. Soderquist (2000), 'Strategic Outsourcing through Specifications', *Omega*, **28** (5), 525–540.

Normile, D. (2004), 'These Slim Margins are Not by Design', *Electronic Business*, **9**, 47–54.

Olsen R.F. and L.M. Ellram (1997) 'A Portfolio Approach to Supplier Relationships', *Industrial Marketing Management,* **26**, 101–113.

Peng M.W. and J. Tan (2004) 'Organizational Slack and Firm Performance During Economic Transitions', *Strategic Management Journal*, **24** (13), 1249–1263.

Porter, M.E. (1980), *Competitive Strategy: Techniques for Analyzing Industries*, New York: Free Press.

Porter, M.E. (1983), 'The Technological Dimension of Competitive Strategy', in Robert Burgelman and Richard S. Rosenbloom (eds), *Research on Technological Innovation, Management and Policy*, Greenwich, CT: JAI Press, 1–33.

Porter, M.E. (1985), *Competitive Advantage*, New York: Free Press.

Porter, M.E. (1987), 'From Competitive Advantage to Corporate Strategy', *Harvard Business Review*, May–June, 53–59.

PriceWaterhouseCoopers (2004), *Electronics Manufacturing at a Crossroads*.

Quinn, J.B. and F.G. Hilmer (1994), 'Strategic Outsourcing', *Sloan Management Review*, **35**, 43–55

Quinn, J.B. (2000), 'Outsourcing Innovation: The New Engine of Growth', *Sloan Management Review*, **41**, 9–21.

Ragatz G.L., R.B. Handfield and T.V. Scannell (2003) 'Success Factors for Integrating Suppliers into New Product Development', *Journal of Product Innovation Management*, **14** (3), 190–202.

Random House Unabridged Dictionary (2006), Westminster: Random House.

Ravenscraft, D. and F.M. Scherer (1991), 'The Role of Acquisitions on Foreign Direct Investment: Evidence from the US Stock Market', *Journal of Finance*, **46**, 825–844.

Rossi, S. and P.F. Volpin (2004), 'Cross-country Determinants of Mergers and Acquisitions', *Journal of Financial Economics*, **74**, 277–304.

Rumelt, R.P. (1982), 'Diversification Strategy and Profitability', *Strategic Management Journal*, **3**, 359–369.

Salter, M. and W. Weinhold (1979), *Diversification through Acquisition*, New York: Free Press.

Sanchez, R. (1995), 'Strategic Flexibility in Product Competition', *Strategic Management Journal*, **16** (5), 135–159.

Schwert, G.W. (1996), 'Markup Pricing in Mergers and Acquisitions', *Journal of Financial Economics*, **41**, 153–162.

Shleifer, A. and R.W. Vishny (1991), 'Takeovers in the 1960s and the 1980s: Evidence and Implications', in *Fundamental Issues in Strategy*, Harvard, Boston: Harvard Business School Press.

Sikora, M. (1995), 'The Winding Trail: A 30-Year Profile of M&A Dynamism', *Mergers & Acquisitions*, 45–50.

Singh, H. and C.A. Montgomery (1987), 'Corporate Acquisitions and Economic Performance', *Strategic Management Journal*, **8**, 377–386.

Smith, K.W. and S.E. Hershman (1997), 'How M&A Fits into a Real Growth Strategy', *Mergers & Acquisitions*, 38–42.

Stanworth, M. and J. Curran (1976), 'Growth and the Small Firm', *Journal of Management Studies*, **13** (2), May, 95–110.

Steiner, P.O. (1975), *Mergers: Motives, Effects, Policies*, Ann Arbor: University of Michigan Press.

Sutton, Johon (1998), *Technology and Market Structure*, Cambridge, MA: MIT Press.

Van Mieghem, J.A. (1999), 'Coordinating Investment, Production and Subcontracting', *Management Science*, **45** (7), 954–971.

Venkatesan R. (1992), 'Strategic Sourcing: to Make or Not to Make', *Harvard Business Review*, November–December, 98–107.

Williams, P.F., D.E. D'Souza, M.E. Rosenfeldt and M. Kassaee (1994), 'Manufacturing Strategy, Business Strategy and Firm Performance in a Mature Industry', *Journal of Operation Management*, **13** (1), 19–33.

Williamson, O.E. (1964), *The Economics of Discretionary Behavior*, Prentice Hall: Englewood Cliffs.

Williamson, O.E. (1975), *Markets and Hierarchies: Analysis and Antitrust Implications*, New York: Free Press.

Wright, P., M. Kroll, A. Lado and B. Van Ness (2002), 'The Structure of Ownership and Corporate Acquisition Strategies', *Strategic Management Journal*, **23**, 41–53.

Zhai, E., Y.J. Shi and M. Gregory (2007), 'The Growth and Capability Development of Electronics Manufacturing Service (EMS) Companies', *International Journal of Production Economics*, 107 (**1**), 1–19.

Index